THE INSIDE STORY OF
VATICAN II

THE TITLE OF THIS BOOK

[*Editor's note:* The original title of this book was *The Rhine Flows Into the Tiber: A History of Vatican II.* On this page and in the "Author's Preface," the author's references to the book by its original title have been retained.]

The title of this book captures a key insight which emerges from its pages. The largest and most influential group at the Council was made up of Council Fathers and *periti* (experts) from countries along the Rhine River—Germany, Austria, Switzerland, France, The Netherlands—and from nearby Belgium. This "European Alliance" is represented in the title by "The Rhine," while "The Tiber" stands for Vatican Council II itself, which was held in St. Peter's Basilica in the immediate vicinity of the Tiber. Thus, the title neatly sums up the fact that the Fathers from the Rhine countries exercised a predominating influence on the Second Vatican Council.

THE INSIDE STORY OF
VATICAN II

A Firsthand Account of the
Council's Inner Workings

Rev. Ralph M. Wiltgen, S.V.D.

TAN Books
Charlotte, North Carolina

Nihil Obstat: Gall Higgins, O.F.M. Cap.
                 Censor Librorum

Imprimatur: ✠ Terence J. Cooke, D.D., V.G.
                 New York, N.Y.
                 December 15, 1966

The Nihil Obstat and Imprimatur are official declarations that a book or pamphlet is free of doctrinal or moral error. No implication is contained therein that those who have granted the Nihil Obstat and Imprimatur agree with the contents, opinions or statements expressed.

This book was first published in 1967 by Hawthorne Books in New York, New York, under the title *The Rhine Flows Into the Tiber: A History of Vatican II*. The "Author's Preface" was added in a 1978 edition by Augustine Publishing Company in Devon, England. The 1978 edition was reprinted in 1985 by TAN Books. This new TAN revised edition has been re-typeset with minor updates and corrections and a new "Publisher's Note."

Cover design by Caroline Kiser

Cover image: *Old Key* ©iStockphoto.com/earnang

ISBN: 978-0-89555-186-3

Cataloging-in-Publication data on file with the Library of Congress

Printed and bound in the United States of America.

TAN Books
Charlotte, North Carolina
www.TANBooks.com
2014

DEDICATION

In gratitude
to
Michael and Martha Wiltgen of Chicago
my father and mother

It is clear that the history of this Council will have to be written according to the best approved norms laid down for historians by the ancient writers. The first of these is: "Do not dare to say anything false, and at the same time do not dare to keep back the truth. Let there be nothing in what you write that arouses suspicions of favoritism or animosity" (Cicero, Or. 11, 15).

Pope Paul VI
January 31, 1966

Publisher's Note

The time is right for *The Inside Story of Vatican II*, a new edition of the book formerly titled *The Rhine Flows into the Tiber*, by Rev. Ralph M. Wiltgen. Although some who wish to discredit the Council have pointed to its words in support of what they believe went wrong with Vatican II, the author had no such intention. Much like the Council itself, this book has been misinterpreted far too often. It is time to set the record straight.

The Inside Story of Vatican II is Catholic at its core, and it should be reclaimed as such. The author, Rev. Ralph M. Wiltgen, was a supporter of Vatican II and of the Holy Fathers seated in Rome in his lifetime. The imprimatur was given to the book by none other than Cardinal Terence J. Cooke, known for his enthusiastic support of the Council.

Wiltgen's eyewitness account does provide details of the strategies, plots, divisions, rumors, secret conversations, and dramas that occurred among the Council Fathers. Nevertheless, Wiltgen believed that his book demonstrates how the Holy Spirit mysteriously worked within the Council to bring about what God desired from His Church.

This valuable inside look at the Council is solidly journalistic. Praised for its frankness and objectivity, *The Inside Story of Vatican II* offers an intriguing account of what happened during the Council, with minimal interpretation by the author. It is a resource like no other, allowing the reader to feel like an eyewitness himself.

We hope our readers will use this new edition to deepen their understanding of the Church and her history. As the beauty of the Council is regaining notice, and as old misunderstandings are overcome, much of the folly we have endured is fading away, and the dissenters are being exposed for their lack of faith. We trust you will discover for yourself the inside story of Vatican II, and the working of the Holy Spirit within it.

One overlooked victory of the Council was the official recognition that Mary is the Mother of the Church, *Mater Ecclesiae*. In becoming the Mother of the Head, she became the Mother of the whole Body of Christ. Our prayer is that the Mother of the Church will lead all souls, especially those who have fallen away, back into the true fold of her Divine Son.

— *The Publisher*

Author's Preface

Reviewers have summarized *The Rhine Flows into the Tiber* as follows: It tells the story of Vatican II from beginning to end, reducing four years of conciliar debate to a few hundred pages and correlating it to outside meetings and actions . . . it describes how each of the 16 conciliar documents was painstakingly hammered out . . . it leaves the reader with an overwhelming impression of the tangible operation of the Holy Spirit in the Council . . . and it brings to light how the Council's activity, contrary to what other books have said, was guided constantly by groups rather than by individuals.

This last point explains why my book repeatedly has been cited publicly by those who charge that the Council's 16 documents have been vitiated, even invalidated, by pressure groups. Apparently not everyone is aware that the formation of thought groups in Vatican II was as natural a process as it is in any other legislative assembly. With 2,150 Council Fathers from all parts of the world in attendance, it was inconceivable that all should propose identical amendments for every item on the agenda. It was likewise inconceivable that each of the 2,150 Council Fathers would propose amendments completely different from everybody else's.

The natural outcome was the formation of thought groups, and even the smallest of these had an impact on the formulation of texts about which it showed particular concern. These groups gave life and fire to the Council, and one wonders whether anything could have been accomplished at all without them. They were like so many separate committees busily engaged in formulating and amending Council texts in a way which they judged best for the overall interests of the Church. And because one group did not always accept the ideas of the other, conflict arose. Except for a few instances of papal intervention, however, harmony was eventually restored through the use of normal legislative processes.

The largest and most influential group of all was made up of Council Fathers and *periti* (or experts) from countries along the Rhine river—Germany, Austria, Switzerland, France, the Netherlands—and from nearby Belgium. Because this group exerted a predominant influence over the Second Vatican Council, I have titled my book *The Rhine Flows into the Tiber*. The "Tiber" stands for the Vatican Council, which was held in St. Peter's Basilica in the immediate vicinity of the Tiber. This title was suggested by correspondent George Weller after my manuscript had been completed. He took the idea from Juvenal (A.D. 60–140), a Roman poet who said that the Orontes river of Syria had flowed into the Tiber (cf. Satire III, lines 58ff.). By this Juvenal meant that Greek influence from Antioch—the Orontes flowed through Antioch—was having an impact on Rome.

The internationally renowned theologian Father Yves Congar, O.P., discussed this thesis in 1977 in *Revue des Sciences Philosophiques et Théologiques* (Paris). He said: "Father Wiltgen . . . was remarkably well informed and his report, which shows the unfolding of the entire Council, is full of precise details. . . . In short, the Rhine was in reality that broad current of vigorous Catholic theology and pastoral science which had got under way in the early 1950s and, with regard to liturgical matters and biblical sources, even earlier than that." In 1967, *Cross and Crown* (Chicago) had said in its review of my book: "To point to such influence is not to claim conspiracy against Rome; it is to recognize influences which readers familiar with recent theology can find in the conciliar documents."

For writing this history I have had access to a complete set of all official correspondence, documents and working papers received by the Council Fathers from the Council's secretariat. I had access to all correspondence and documentation sent by the Rhine group to its members as well as additional documentation from other groups and episcopal conferences, the minutes of meetings, private correspondence, etc. I also met and interviewed numberless Council Fathers and *periti* as director of an independent and multilingual Council news service with over 3,000 subscribers in 108 countries. Being based in Rome, I could see the entire Council unfold before my eyes. What I saw and what I heard, and the facts that I ferreted out, I now pass on to you.

Let me assure you that *The Rhine Flows into the Tiber* is completely different from any other history of Vatican II. I sincerely hope that you enjoy it and that it makes the Second Vatican Council come alive for you.

Rev. Dr. R. M. Wiltgen, S.V.D.
December 8, 1977

Contents

Reviews of the First USA Edition

Published as *The Rhine Flows Into The Tiber*

"A faithful and revealing account of Vatican II."
The Evangelical Presbyterian (Northern Ireland)

"To its credit, a reliable, restrained, unspectacular, balanced and sober report." *The Tablet* (Brooklyn, USA)

"An extremely handy, factual, concise book . . . his chronicle is the best kind of journalism: he states the facts about Who, What, When and Where, with a minimum of Why . . . no knife is slipped between any episcopal ribs . . . Rev. Wiltgen has done a fine job . . . in describing the 'politicking' that went on during the entire Council. What is more, he has done it charitably, factually, giving a fine example of how to speak the truth in love." *The Anglican* (Sydney, Australia)

"No one up to now has presented such a clear and forceful picture of the influence which they [the German Bishops] exerted."
The Canadian Register (Kingston)

"The Council Fathers granted him exclusive interviews and spoke more openly with him than they could have and would have with journalists who were interested in sensational news rather than in what was really happening."
Het Missiewerk (Nijmegen, Netherlands)

"Masterly coverage of what went on behind the scenes."
The Catholic Weekly (Sydney, Australia)

"Rynne and Kaiser . . . were biased towards the liberal progressive . . . but Rev. Wiltgen [is] . . . simply concerned with capturing the ebb and flow of the Council, the actual situations, the varying fortunes, successes and failures of the various parties or alliances that sprung up in the course of the Council." *New Zealand Tablet* (Dunedin)

"The distinctiveness of this book is due to nothing less than its thorough and honest reporting . . . its entire objectivity."

The Register (Denver, USA)

"A work in which, as opposed to many others, the action of the Council appears as constantly guided not only by individuals but also by groups."

IDO-C International Documentation on the Conciliar Church (Rome)

"Few books about the Second Vatican Council can match *The Rhine Flows into the Tiber* for thorough, objective reporting done in a style the layman can enjoy and comprehend . . . Father Wiltgen doesn't cloud his subject material with personalities or exaggeration . . . Church history you can't afford to miss."

Catholic Digest Book Club (New York)

"Calmly, factually, without taking sides, Father Wiltgen unfolds the true story of the Council . . . perhaps the most overwhelming impression left with the reader is the tangible operation of the Holy Spirit in the Council."

The Catholic Journalist Newsletter (New York City)

"This is the work of a particularly authoritative witness, who drew his information directly from the sources themselves. If you add to this his perfect objectivity and his total impartiality . . . you can easily see that here we have a document of the highest value on the Council . . . the thesis was more than delicate; it was dangerous . . . and it required all the skill of an experienced journalist to treat it correctly . . . his service on behalf of truth consisted in making known the facts, which he has done with full competence."   *Ephemerides Carmeliticae* (Rome)

"A careful reading of *The Rhine Flows into the Tiber* establishes beyond doubt that the Bishops of the Rhine countries did assume and maintain leadership during conciliar theological discussions. In recording the history of this coalition, Father Wiltgen deserves credit for a remarkably lucid presentation."   *Clarion Herald* (USA)

"Abstains from praising or condemning . . . the role of Pope Paul VI stands out more truthfully."   *The Clergy Monthly* (India)

"The tremendous number of direct quotations will fascinate any reader and they give a definite air of authority to the work . . . the theme of the German influence in the Council . . . was known to all who attended . . . from discussion and debate the light of truth evolved . . . Father Wiltgen's book shows that Vatican II was not and can never be judged a stereotype . . . the overall reduction of four years of conciliar debate and its correlation to outside meetings and actions is truly remarkable."

The Homiletic and Pastoral Review (New York City)

"Well and clearly written . . . a good deal more balanced than some earlier books on the story of Vatican II . . . an essential guide for the historian."

Zealandia (New Zealand)

"The author, aware of the drama inherent in his subject matter, has for the most part adopted a restrained, almost laconic style, allowing the Council, as it were, to tell its own story . . . characterized by a candor, an incisiveness, an objectivity and a comprehensiveness which make it a 'must' for all those who take an interest in the forces which are shaping tomorrow's world." *The Christian Minister* (South Africa)

"Father Wiltgen does not attempt to interpret the Council to his readers; he simply recounts what happened. His writing is detailed, factual, and unemotional . . . unquestionably the best account of the Council that has appeared." *Social Justice Review* (USA)

"Excellently documented report."

Eglise Vivante (Louvain, Belgium)

"As a study in Church politics this is a very enlightening work . . . those who feel that the Council was too much in the hands of the innovators, as well as those who feel that it did not innovate enough, would learn from this book to respect the balance that the Council finally achieved. The tone of the book is temperate and balanced."

Sursum Corda (Australia)

"An indispensable working tool."

La Pensée Catholique (Paris)

"We are given much information, hitherto unrevealed or unknown, of the behind-the-scenes operations that notably influenced the progress and conclusions of the Council . . . Father Wiltgen had access to much that escaped others or was deliberately omitted from their books."
Zeitschrift fuer Missionswissenschaft und Religionswissenschaft
(Münster, West Germany)

REVIEWS OF THE FIRST BRITISH EDITION

"This is an extremely lucid book . . . a very fair and complete account of the Council . . . one is constantly struck throughout the book by the calm and deliberative tone the author maintains . . . it is amazing how well this book reads now almost thirteen years after the Council ended . . . a contemporary history that will be often referred to in future times as the best account by a witness of this momentous event."
Richard Mullen in *Christian World* (Oxford)

"Thoroughly recommended as one of the most interesting and objective works on Vatican II ever published." *The Times* (of Malta)

"Balanced and factual . . . should prove of great value to future historians of the Council." Rev. M. Nassan, SJ in *Catholic Herald* (London)

"A popular history of Vatican II."
L'Osservatore Romano, English Edition (Vatican City)

"An accurate, unbiased, yet at the same time fascinating account of the four sessions of Vatican II. This will be found a useful and enjoyable book by anyone who desires a clear and concise, overall view of the Council's history." Rev. E. Doyle, OFM in *The Universe* (London)

"This history of Vatican II by the director of the Council News Service is treated in light enough fashion to hold the interest of the average reader. It is also profound enough to stimulate scholars and others who should know more about the debates which produced the documents of Vatican II." *The Word* (Roscommon, Ireland)

"His account of the proceedings bears the stamp of authority . . . for the general reader there is scarcely a page which does not repay study."
Catena (London)

"Among all the contemporary accounts of the Council one alone stands out for its objectivity . . . Rev. Wiltgen has put the entire Church into his debt by writing an account of the *true* Council . . . He is a talented writer. His account is as absorbing and exciting as any thriller . . . everyone must agree upon his instinct for selecting the issues which proved to be truly significant."

Christian Order (London)

"A classic study of Vatican II."　　　*Mowbrays Journal* (London)

"Remains the best contemporary account of the proceedings [of Vatican II] . . . does no more than show the influence on the Council of the 'Rhine theologians' . . . this influence is incontestable. Whether it was good or bad, Rev. Wiltgen leaves for the reader or the historian to say . . . *The Rhine Flows into the Tiber* is an historical testimony of great value."

P. H. Hallet in *National Catholic Register* (Los Angeles)

THE INSIDE STORY OF
VATICAN II

THE FIRST SESSION

October 11 – December 8, 1962

A Leap Forward

The long white procession of bishops in miters and flowing copes seemed never to end. It came down the Royal Staircase, through the Bronze Door and halfway across the square. Then it turned abruptly to the right, mounted the steps and disappeared through the main entrance of St. Peter's. It was Thursday, October 11, 1962, the feast of the Divine Maternity of the Blessed Virgin Mary, and the opening day of the Second Vatican Council.

The cobblestones underfoot were wet and shiny from the rain that had fallen all night long, but they quickly dried in the bright morning sun.

I stood on the front steps watching all 2,400 Council Fathers pass by. These men for the most part were unknown outside their own dioceses. But some of them, because of what they would say, or do, were destined to live forever in the histories of this Council. Names like Frings, Ottaviani, Liénart, Meyer, Bea, Suenens, Léger, Maximos IV Saigh, and Sigaud were just a few of the many that would never be forgotten.

Not all of the bishops were smiling as they passed. Many believed that the Council had been convoked simply to rubber-stamp previously prepared documents. Some United States bishops had intimated that they would put in a token appearance for two or three weeks, and then go home. And all the bishops of Paraguay had been informed by a high ecclesiastical dignitary that everything had been so well prepared in Rome that the Council would soon be over.

Pope John finally appeared at the end of the procession,

his face radiant with joy. Repeatedly he bowed to the crowd, giving his blessing, and gladly accepting their greetings in return. For, so to speak, this Council was his creation, the twenty-first ecumenical council in the history of the Catholic Church, and the second to be held in the Vatican. (He had been Pope for scarcely three months when he told seventeen astonished cardinals of his intention to call an ecumenical council, on January 25, 1959, in the Benedictine monastery adjoining the basilica of St. Paul Outside-the-Walls.)

At the main entrance to St. Peter's, his portable throne was lowered, and he proceeded down the long aisle on foot. The Council Fathers, now in their places in the huge Council hall (it was 75 feet wide and 624 feet long), applauded and cheered him as he passed. They represented every part of the world: North America (14 percent), South America (18 percent), Central America (3 percent), Europe (39 percent), Asia (12 percent), Africa (12 percent), and Oceania (2 percent).

When Pope John reached the altar at the front of the hall, he knelt down to pray. Then followed the first official prayer of the Second Vatican Council, the *Veni, Creator Spiritus* ("Come, Creator Spirit"), in which the Pope and the Council Fathers together called upon the Holy Spirit for light and guidance in the task ahead. Mass was then celebrated, after which the Book of the Gospels was solemnly enthroned upon the altar, a custom dating back to the earliest councils.

Finally, Pope John made his opening address. He was confident, he said, that the Church would draw new energy and new strength from the Council, and "look to the future without fear." His contagious optimism burst forth as he said: "We feel we must disagree with those prophets of doom who are always forecasting disaster, as though the end of the world were at hand. . . . They say that our era in comparison with past eras is getting worse, and behave as though they had learned nothing from history, the real teacher of life." For history, said the Pope, showed that things had not in fact been any better in the olden days.

Pope John wished to leave no doubt about his orthodoxy. "The greatest concern of the Ecumenical Council," he asserted, "is this, that the sacred deposit of Christian doctrine should be guarded and taught more efficaciously." The Church, moreover, must never depart "from the sacred patrimony of truth received from the Fathers." At the same time, it "must ever look to the present, to the new conditions and forms of life introduced into the modern world, which have opened new avenues to the Catholic apostolate."

The Council, he said, was not to concern itself with a point-by-point exposition of basic doctrines of the Church as taught by ancient and modern theologians, as these were already "well known and familiar to all." For this, he added, a Council was not necessary. He stressed that there should be a "renewed, serene and tranquil adherence to all the teachings of the Church in their entirety and preciseness, as they still shine forth in the acts of the Council of Trent and the First Vatican Council."

The Pope now came to the most important section of his address: "The Christian, Catholic and apostolic spirit of the whole world expects a leap forward toward a doctrinal penetration and a formation of consciences in most faithful and perfect conformity to authentic doctrine." This doctrine, he said, was to be studied and expounded "by using modern methods of research and the literary forms of modern thought. The substance of the ancient doctrine of the Deposit of Faith is one thing, and the way in which it is presented is another." Great patience and careful consideration were necessary, he stressed, so that the teachings to be drawn up by the Council would be "predominantly pastoral in character."

Although Pope John called attention to "fallacious and dangerous teachings, opinions and concepts," he elaborated on this theme with characteristic optimism. Men's views, he pointed out, change from age to age, and the errors of a particular generation often vanish as quickly as they arise, "like fog before the sun." The Church has always opposed errors, he recalled, and "frequently it has condemned them with the greatest severity." Nowadays, however, the Church "prefers to make use of the medicine of mercy. . . . It considers that it meets the needs of the present day by demonstrating the validity of its teachings rather than by condemnations."

He firmly believed, he said, that man had become "ever more deeply convinced of the paramount dignity" of the human person, of the perfection which was his goal, and of the duties which this implied. "Even more important, experience has taught men that violence inflicted on others, the might of arms and political domination, are of no help at all in finding a happy solution to the grave problems which afflict them."

In conclusion, he reminded the Council Fathers of

their obligation to respond to the inspirations of the Holy Spirit, so that their work might fulfill the expectations of the hour and the needs of the peoples of the world. That, he said, "requires of you serenity of mind, brotherly concord, moderation in proposals, dignity in discussion and wise deliberation."

The stage was set. The business of the Second Vatican Council could begin. It was announced that the first General Congregation (meeting) would open on Saturday, October 13, at 9 A.M.

THE EUROPEAN ALLIANCE

The crucial question before the Council Fathers was the membership of the ten Council commissions. The German bishops discussed possible candidates at the residence of seventy-five-year-old Joseph Cardinal Frings, Archbishop of Cologne, whose dynamic qualities of leadership were unimpaired by frailness, age and partial blindness. Considerable agitation was caused when someone reported that the Roman Curia had prepared a list of candidates for distribution at election time. To counteract this move, it was proposed that each national episcopal conference should be permitted to nominate candidates from its own ranks for each commission. Cardinal Frings, president of the episcopal conference of Germany, later learned that seventy-eight-year-old Achille Cardinal Lienart of Lille, president of the episcopal conference of France, had the same idea. The two cardinals then agreed upon a plan of procedure.

After the Mass which opened the first General

Congregation on October 13, the Council Fathers received three booklets prepared by the General Secretariat. The first contained a complete listing of Council Fathers, all of whom were eligible for office unless they already held some position. The second listed the Council Fathers who had taken part in the various preparatory commissions of the Council. This was the so-called "Curial" list which had caused so much agitation among the German bishops. As the General Secretariat later explained, the list was prepared simply as an aid to Council Fathers so that they could see who already had had experience in particular fields. But since all preparatory commission members originally had been appointed to office by the Holy See, some Council Fathers resented this list. The third booklet contained ten pages with sixteen consecutively numbered blanks on each page, on which the Council Fathers were to enter the candidates of their choice.

Each of the ten Council commissions was to be presided over by a cardinal appointed by the Pope, and to consist of twenty-four members, two thirds elected by the Council Fathers and one third appointed by the Pope. The papal appointments would be made after the announcement of the election results.

Archbishop Pericle Felici, Secretary General of the Council, was explaining the election procedures to the assembled Fathers in his fluent Latin when Cardinal Liénart, who served as one of the ten Council Presidents, seated at a long table at the front of the Council hall, rose in his place and asked to speak. He expressed his conviction that the Council Fathers needed more time to study the qualifications of the various candidates. After consultations among the national episcopal conferences, he explained, everyone would know who were the most qualified candidates, and it would be possible to vote intelligently. He requested a few days' delay in the balloting.

The suggestion was greeted with applause, and, after a moment's silence, Cardinal Frings rose to second the motion. He, too, was applauded.

After hurried consultation with Eugène Cardinal Tisserant, who as first of the Council Presidents was conducting the meeting, Archbishop Felici announced that the Council Presidency had acceded to the request of the two cardinals. The meeting was adjourned until 9 A.M. on Tuesday, October 16.

The first business meeting, including Mass, had lasted only fifty minutes. A Dutch bishop on his way out of the Council hall called to a priest friend some distance away, "That was our first victory!"

The different national episcopal conferences immediately set to work drawing up their lists. The German and Austrian bishops, because of linguistic bonds, decided to establish a combined list. The two German cardinals were not eligible, Cardinal Frings being a member of the Council Presidency, and Julius Cardinal Döpfner of Munich, a member of the Secretariat for Extraordinary Council Affairs. Franziskus Cardinal König of Vienna, however, who held no conciliar office, was immediately placed at the head of the list of candidates for the most important commission of all, the Theological Commission. At the close of the discussions, the German-Austrian group had a list of twenty-seven candidates: three Austrians, twenty-three Germans and one

Dutch-born bishop from Indonesia who had received his liturgical training in Germany and Austria.

Other episcopal conferences were similarly preparing their lists. Canada had twelve candidates; the United States, twenty-one; Argentina, ten; Italy, fifty. The superiors general presented six of their number for the Commission on Religious, and one of their number for each of the other commissions.

Nevertheless, as these lists began to form, it became frighteningly apparent to the liberal element in the Council that their proposal for individual lists by episcopal conferences was no real safeguard against ultraconservative domination of the commissions. For it was expected in those early days of the Council that countries like Italy, Spain, the United States, Britain and Australia and all of Latin America would side with the conservatives. Italy alone was believed to have some 400 Council Fathers, the United States about 230, Spain close to 80, and Latin America nearly 650. Europe had over 1,100, including those of Italy and Spain. Africa, with its nearly 300 votes, was in the balance, and might be won for either side. Such considerations prompted the bishops of Germany, Austria and France to propose a combined list with the bishops of Holland, Belgium and Switzerland. At the same time, Bishop Joseph Blomjous, a Dutch-born bishop in charge of Mwanza diocese in Tanzania, together with African-born Archbishop Jéan Zoa of Yaoundé, in Cameroun, had been busy organizing the bishops of English- and French-speaking Africa. They offered their list of candidates to the group headed by Cardinal Frings, thus assuring numerous African votes.

The six European countries, which now formed an alliance in fact, if not in name, found additional liberal-minded candidates among cardinals, archbishops and bishops of other countries. Thus they incorporated in their list eight candidates from Italy, eight from Spain, four from the United States, three from Britain, three from Australia, and two each from Canada, India, China, Japan, Chile and Bolivia. Five other countries were represented by one candidate each, and Africa by sixteen. This list of Cardinal Frings came to be called the "international" list and contained 109 carefully picked candidates so placed as to guarantee broad representation of the European alliance on the ten commissions.

By the evening of Monday, October 15, at least thirty-four separate lists of candidates had been prepared and handed in to the Secretary General of the Council, who arranged for them to be printed in a twenty-eight-page booklet entitled *Lists of Council Fathers as Proposed by Episcopal Conferences for Use in Electing Council Commissions.*

Tuesday, October 16, was spent entering the names of 160 candidates on the ballot sheets. The student body of the Pontifical Urban College was enlisted to count the ballots—a tedious job, there being approximately 380,000 entries in longhand. At the third General Congregation, on Saturday, October 20, the Secretary General announced that Pope John, acting on the suggestion of the Council Presidency, had dispensed with Article 39 of the Council Rules of Procedure, which required an absolute majority (50 percent plus one) in all elections. A plurality would now suffice, and the sixteen Council Fathers who received

11

the largest number of votes for each commission would be considered as elected to that commission.

The results of these elections were eminently satisfying to the European alliance. Of the 109 candidates presented by the alliance, 79 were elected, representing 49 percent of all elective seats. When the papal appointments were announced, they included eight more candidates put forward by the European alliance. Alliance candidates constituted 50 percent of all elected members of the most important Theological Commission. In the Liturgical Commission, the alliance had a majority of 12 to 4 among elected members and 14 to 11 after the papal appointments had been made.

Eight out of every ten candidates put forward by the European alliance received a commission seat. Germany and France were both represented on all but one of the commissions. Germany had eleven representatives; France, ten. The Netherlands and Belgium each won four seats; Austria, three; and Switzerland, one.

But the election returns did not satisfy everyone. One of the African bishops said it had been understood that, in exchange for African support for all alliance candidates to the Theological Commission, the alliance would support all African candidates to the Commission on the Missions; yet only three of the nine candidates from Africa had been voted into office. Again, not one of the fifteen superiors general proposed as candidates by the conference of superiors general was elected, although they represented communities which were exceptionally competent in liturgy, education, missions, and the religious life.

At the last moment, it was announced that Pope John

would appoint nine members to each commission instead of the eight provided for in the rules of procedure. Of the ninety appointed by him, eight were superiors general. Of the 250 Council Fathers elected or appointed to the ten Council Commissions, 154, or 62 percent, had served on a preparatory commission, and so had previous experience.

After this election, it was not too hard to foresee which group was well enough organized to take over leadership at the Second Vatican Council. The Rhine had begun to flow into the Tiber.

THIRD VICTORY

The work of the Council, briefly, was to examine schemas (preliminary drafts) of constitutions and decrees, and then amend them, accept them or reject them. To understand what was implied by the rejection of a schema, something which happened repeatedly during the first session, we must look into the background of the schemas, which were prepared over a period of three years and five months of intense work prior to the opening of the Council.

The first phase of the work began on Pentecost (May 17) 1959, when Pope John created an Ante-Preparatory Commission, presided over by his able Secretary of State, Domenico Cardinal Tardini, to assist him in determining the subject matter of the Council. (Canon law stipulates that it is the Pope's responsibility to determine the subject matter and the procedures to be followed at an ecumenical council.) The Pope chose one representative from each of ten Sacred Congregations of the Roman Curia to be members of the commission, and as Secretary he appointed another very able Curial official, Monsignor Felici.

Twelve days after his appointment to the presidency of the Ante-Preparatory Commission, Cardinal Tardini invited the Sacred Congregations of the Roman Curia to make a comprehensive study of all matters under their authority, and to offer specific proposals on matters which they felt could usefully be presented to the future preparatory commissions. Three weeks later, he sent out 2,593 copies of a letter to as many prelates around the world, informing them that Pope John XXIII desired their assistance in drawing up topics for discussion at the Council. Originally, Cardinal Tardini had planned to send a questionnaire indicating suitable topics. But since this might have been regarded as a form of pressure, limiting discussion to certain questions, and since he knew how eager the Pope was to create an atmosphere of free and open discussion, he had decided against it. He added in his letter that the prelates were at liberty to consult "prudent and expert clerics" in formulating their replies. The letter was sent not only to those entitled to attend the Council by virtue of canon law, but also to titular bishops, vicars and prefects apostolic, and superiors general of nonexempt religious congregations.

In July 1959, Cardinal Tardini invited the rectors of Catholic universities and the deans of the theological faculties in Rome and around the world (sixty-two in all) to prepare a series of studies on issues which they regarded as especially timely and important. He told the rectors and deans in Rome: "From what we can foresee today, it is more than probable that the Council will have a character that is practical, rather than dogmatic; pastoral, rather than ideological; and that it will provide norms, rather than definitions. This does not remove the possibility or necessity of recalling and reaffirming those points of doctrine which are more important today, and which are more attacked today. Nor does it remove the possibility or necessity of first giving rapid and tranquil summaries and reminders of the doctrinal principles before stating the practical norms."

A second letter was mailed by Monsignor Felici to the prelates who had not replied by March 21, 1960. "The Supreme Pontiff," he wrote, "who is directly and personally concerned with the guidance and preparation of Council activities, will be most grateful to you for a reply." He enclosed a copy of the letter sent by Cardinal Tardini nine months previously.

A total of 1,998 replies (77 percent) was received to the two letters. Some of the highest returns came from Mexico (92 percent), Spain (93 percent), Ireland (94 percent), Congo (95 percent) and Indonesia (100 percent). The United States made a 70-percent return (151 out of 216), and Canada a 69-percent return (62 out of 90). These percentages were low due to the poor response from titular bishops and archbishops in the two countries. The response from heads of dioceses and archdioceses in the United States was 89 percent, in Canada, 90 percent. In Germany, it was 100 percent.

Monsignor Felici worked quietly with nine assistants in a ten-room office in the shadow of St. Peter's. Their job was to classify and summarize the recommendations which came in through the mails. The letters were first photostatted and then the originals were filed. The photostats were cut into sections and classified according to subject matter. Pope John said later that he had personally followed these labors, which had been conducted "with accuracy and care," and that he had most attentively examined the suggestions made by the bishops, the proposals of the Sacred Congregations of the Roman Curia, and the wishes and special studies presented by the Catholic universities.

The replies of the prelates filled eight huge volumes; those of the universities and theological faculties, three; and those of the Sacred Congregations of the Roman Curia, one. In addition to these twelve volumes, there were one containing all Pope John's statements on the Council, two containing an analysis of the proposals made by the prelates, and a final one containing an index. These sixteen volumes of nearly ten thousand pages were to serve as a basis for the work of the future preparatory commissions. Monsignor Felici and his staff completed all this work in the space of one year.

The Ante-Preparatory Commission was now in a position to indicate what subjects should be given thorough study in the Council. It was also able to suggest—and this was another of its tasks—what structural organization would be required to carry out the second phase of the preparatory work for the Council.

On Pentecost (June 5) 1960, Pope John launched the second phase of the preparatory work. Twelve preparatory commissions were established, and three secretariats. Over these was a Central Preparatory Commission, with three subcommissions. The Pope himself was president of the Central Preparatory Commission, which had 108 members and twenty-seven consultants from fifty-seven countries (its counterpart at Vatican I had had nine members—all cardinals—and eight consultants from four countries). This central body was the coordinating agency for the other groups, supervised their work, amended their texts, declaring them suitable or unsuitable for treatment by the Council, and reported to the Pope the conclusions reached by individual commissions and secretariats, so that he might be able to make the final decisions as to what subjects should be dealt with at the Council.

When Pope John founded the Central Preparatory Commission, he made forty-eight-year-old Monsignor Felici its Secretary General, elevating him to the rank of archbishop three months later. Although jurisprudence was the Italian archbishop's specialty, Latin was his hobby, and he had published several books of Latin verse. He was born in Segni, where his maternal uncle, the rector of the local seminary, instilled in him a love for Latin. Ordained a priest at the age of twenty-two, and installed as a judge on the Roman Rota, the supreme court of the Catholic Church, at the age of thirty-six, he went on to become director of the Roman Rota's college of jurisprudence, before being chosen by Pope John for Council work.

The topics to be studied, as chosen or approved by the Pope, were mailed to the members of preparatory commissions and secretariats by Archbishop Felici on July 9, 1960. Four months later, the activity of these bodies officially began when Pope John received the 871 men involved—among them 67 cardinals, 5 patriarchs, 116 archbishops, 135 bishops, 220 secular priests, 282 religious priests and 8 laymen—in St. Peter's basilica.

After two years' work, ending on the eve of the Council with the dissolution of most of these bodies, a total of seventy-five schemas had been prepared. Some were merely chapters of full schemas, some were later combined with others by the Central Preparatory Commission, and still others were considered too specialized for treatment by the Council, and were referred to the Pontifical Commission for the Revision of the Code of Canon Law. In this way, the seventy-five schemas were ultimately reduced to twenty. These, as Monsignor Vincenzo Carbone, an official of the General Secretariat, subsequently pointed out, were only "preliminary drafts, capable of further improvement." As at other councils, they would be perfected "only through discussion in the Council, with the help of the Holy Spirit." It was certain, however, that no other council had had a preparation "so vast, so diligently carried out, and so profound."

On July 13, 1962, three months before the opening of the Council, Pope John decreed that the first seven schemas, officially called the "First Series of Schemas of Constitutions and Decrees," should be sent to the Council Fathers around the world. Since they were consecutively numbered, most bishops assumed that it was intended to treat them in their numerical sequence.

Shortly thereafter, seventeen Dutch bishops met at 's-Hertogenbosch, at the invitation of Bishop Willem Bekkers, to discuss the schemas. There was general dissatisfaction with the first four dogmatic constitutions, entitled "Sources of Revelation," "Preserving Pure the

Deposit of Faith," "Christian Moral Order," and "Chastity, Matrimony, the Family and Virginity," and general agreement that the fifth, on the liturgy, was the best. The proposal was then discussed and approved that a commentary should be prepared, and be widely distributed among the Council Fathers, pointing out the weaknesses of the dogmatic constitutions, and suggesting that the schema on the liturgy be placed first on the Council agenda.

In effect, the only author of the resulting commentary, published anonymously, was Father Edward Schillebeeckx, O.P., a Belgian-born professor of dogmatics at the Catholic University of Nijmegen, who served as the leading theologian for the Dutch hierarchy. It contained a devastating criticism of the four dogmatic constitutions, which were charged with representing only one school of theological thought. Only the fifth schema, on the liturgy, was described as "an admirable piece of work."

It should be noted that the liturgical movement had been active in Europe for several decades, and that quite a large number of bishops and *periti* from the Rhine countries had been appointed by Pope John to the preparatory commission on liturgy. As a result, they had succeeded in inserting their ideas in the schema and gaining approval for what they considered a very acceptable document.

On the opening page of his lengthy commentary, Father Schillebeeckx wrote: "If you are of the opinion that the following commentary requires more time for study and reflection, it might be well to request of the Council Presidency that schemas V, VI and VII should be treated first, and only afterwards the first four." In a second remark, he went even further: "One might well raise the question whether it would not be better to rewrite the first four schemas completely." Such complete revision was, in fact, the real aim in view. A third remark suggested that Vatican II should follow the example of the Council of Trent, and refrain from settling questions which were still controverted among the theologians. Father Schillebeeckx also suggested that a classroom style should be avoided, both in language and in treatment, and that "the good news should be proclaimed with good will and in a positive way."

Latin, English and French versions of the commentary were prepared. Close to 1,500 copies were printed in Rome by seventy-two-year-old Bishop Tarcisio van Valenberg, a Dutch Capuchin, and were distributed to bishops from all countries as they arrived for the Council.

Prior to the distribution of this commentary, individual episcopal conferences had not been aware of what bishops from other countries thought of the first four dogmatic constitutions. As one prelate put it, "It was only after seeing the commentary that the Council Fathers dared speak out their secret thoughts about the schemas."

In consequence of this Dutch initiative, numerous petitions were submitted to the Council Presidency, by episcopal conferences and individual bishops, asking for a delay in the treatment of the four dogmatic constitutions, and requesting that the schema on the liturgy should be treated first. Actually, no decision had been made as to the sequence in which the schemas were to be debated; this was a matter within the jurisdiction of the Council Presidency, as determined by the Rules of Procedure of the Council.

The proposal was strongly supported by Cardinals Frings, Liénart, and Bernard Alfrink of Utrecht, the Netherlands, at a meeting of the ten Council Presidents, following the brief first General Congregation on October 13. On the following Monday, Pope John received the ten Presidents in private audience. The next morning, it was announced in the Council hall that the first schema to be presented for discussion would be the constitution on the liturgy.

With this announcement on Tuesday, October 16, during the second General Congregation, the European alliance had scored another victory. Although the first two victories—the postponement of elections and the placing of hand-picked candidates on the Council commissions—were given extensive press coverage, this third victory passed unnoticed.

SACRED LITURGY

The official news bulletin of the Council Press Office on October 22, 1962, carried only two sentences on the first debate on the liturgy, one giving the names of the prelates who had spoken that morning, the other stating, "There were twenty interventions [speeches], and all of them referred to the schema as a whole, some defending it and others attacking it." The hundreds of journalists who had made the trip to Rome in order to inform their readers of what was being said at the Council ran their fingers through their hair in desperation as they read this scanty report.

The first speaker on that day was Cardinal Frings. He

informed the Council that the Central Preparatory Commission had in fact examined a longer text than the one which was now before the Council Fathers. Some important passages had been deleted, including the important "Declarations" which explained seeming innovations, and each Council Father should therefore receive an additional copy of the schema in the complete form in which it had been drawn up by the Preparatory Commission.

Cardinal Frings' request was a sequel to the publication on Saturday, October 20, of a six-page report by Bishop Franz Zauner of Linz, Austria. Bishop Zauner, a candidate of the European alliance, had been elected to the Liturgical Commission by over two thousand votes, the highest number received by any Council Father for any commission. He had also been a member of the Preparatory Commission on the Liturgy, and therefore knew the details of the text which that body had presented to the Central Preparatory Commission.

Bishop Zauner gave his general approval, but drew attention to eleven specific passages in the schema which he and "some other Council Fathers from various nations" wanted to have changed.

One concerned the section headed "The Language of the Liturgy." Here the bishop asked for the restoration of the provision in the original text authorizing episcopal conferences to "set the limits and determine the manner in which a vernacular language might be allowed in the liturgy, provided these decisions were acceptable to the Holy See." The text now before the Council read that bishops might simply "propose" such suggestions to the Holy See.

Another concerned the matter of concelebration, that

is, the simultaneous celebration of the same Mass by two or more priests. The present schema allowed concelebration in only two cases: the Mass for the blessing of the sacred chrism on Holy Thursday, and large gatherings of priests. In the light of these restrictions, Bishop Zauner asserted, "concelebration seems to be something exceptional, . . . although the practice is actually legitimate and greatly esteemed by the Oriental brethren of our own day, as it was in the Roman Church in the Middle Ages."

Another of the bishop's major objections was to the flat statement in the schema that Latin should be retained for the recitation of the Divine Office, in accordance with the time-honored tradition of the Western Church. He asked for the restoration of the following proviso, which had been deleted from the original text: "But when knowledge of the Latin language is very insufficient, and when there is no legitimate hope of altering the situation, episcopal conferences will be allowed to establish norms regarding the use of another language for their regions." The proviso had originally been included by the Preparatory Commission because some of tomorrow's priests are studying in public schools, where they receive insufficient Latin or none at all; if, therefore, they have to read the Divine Office in Latin, they will derive little spiritual benefit from it.

As Bishop Zauner's report became more widely known, increasing numbers of Council Fathers demanded from the floor that the text as drawn up by the Preparatory Commission on the Liturgy should be printed and distributed among them. But no official action was taken in the matter at the time.

On the day that Cardinal Frings spoke, an address was also made by Giovanni Battista Cardinal Montini, Archbishop of Milan, who a year later would be presiding over the second session of the Council as Pope Paul VI. He expressed general satisfaction with the schema, particularly since it stressed the pastoral aspect of the liturgy. It was apparent from the tone of his address that he wished to mediate between liberals and conservatives, pointing out that the schema provided a balance between two extreme points of view. On the one hand, he said, it gave no authorization to those who would introduce changes in venerable practices on a whim, thereby prejudicing important elements in the liturgy both of human and of divine origin; on the other hand, it did not endorse the view that a rite was absolutely unalterable, or that ceremonies which had arisen as a result of historical circumstances must at all costs be retained. Provided that the basic elements were safeguarded, he said, then the form in which liturgy had been handed down, and which was like a garment clothing the divine mysteries, could be changed and made more applicable to present needs. "Such changes, of course, must be carried out prudently and wisely."

Cardinal Montini went on to say that the schema in no sense constituted a break with divine and Catholic worship inherited from the past. On the contrary, it recommended that commissions be formed after the Council "to make this inheritance more evident, more understandable and more useful to men of our day." And he supported the statement in the schema that "bishops active in the care of souls would also have to be represented" on such post-conciliar commissions. Unknowingly, Cardinal Montini was laying down norms which he himself would later have to follow as Pope Paul VI.

As to the language of the liturgy, he said that traditional languages "such as Latin within the realm of the Latin Church" should be retained intact "in those parts of the rite which are sacramental and, in the true sense of the word, priestly." Any difficulty experienced by the laity in understanding the instructional parts of the sacred liturgy should be promptly removed.

Cardinal Montini also declared his wholehearted support of the principle that "ceremonies must once again be reduced to a more simple form." This did not mean casting off the beauty of divine service and its symbolic power, but merely shortening ceremonies and removing from them whatever was repetitious and overcomplicated. This principle, he felt, should guide the announced reform of the liturgy, since it corresponded so well to the temper of modern man.

On the following day, the Council was addressed in French—although Latin was the prescribed language of the debate—by Maximos IV Saigh, a venerable bearded old man of eighty-four years, the Melchite Patriarch of Antioch, who soon became known for his blunt and forceful speeches. He explained that, while he did not belong to the Latin Rite, he wished to add to the discussion the testimony of a patriarch from the East "who follows with great interest the progress of the liturgical movement in the Latin Church."

He called the schema as a whole an outstanding accomplishment; "all honor is due," he said, "to the commission which prepared it and likewise to the liturgical movement itself, which was responsible for the schema's coming into existence."

The patriarch then turned to the matter of language in the liturgy. Christ himself had spoken the language of his contemporaries, he said, "and he offered the first Eucharistic Sacrifice in a language which could be understood by all who heard him, namely, Aramaic." The Apostles had maintained this practice. "Never could the idea have come to them that in a Christian gathering the celebrant should read the texts of Holy Scripture, sing psalms, preach or break bread, and at the same time use a language different from that of the community gathered there." The use of Latin in the liturgy of the Latin Church, he said, "seems altogether abnormal to the Eastern Church." And even the Roman Church itself, at least in the middle of the third century, had used Greek in its liturgy, "because this language was spoken by the faithful of that time." Greek had been abandoned in favor of Latin precisely because Latin had meantime become the language of the faithful. "Why, then, should the Roman Church cease to apply the same principle today?"

In the East, the patriarch pointed out, there had never been a problem of liturgical language. "For actually every language is liturgical, since the Psalmist says, 'Let all peoples praise the Lord.' Therefore man must praise God, announce the Gospel, and offer sacrifice in every language, no matter what it is. We Orientals cannot understand how the faithful can be gathered together and made to pray in a language which they do not understand. The Latin language is dead, but the Church is alive. Language is a medium of grace . . . The language used must be a living language, since it is meant for men and not for angels."

The patriarch suggested in conclusion that episcopal conferences be authorized by the schema to decide whether and in what manner the vernacular should be introduced into the liturgy. The text as it stood gave such conferences "no other right than merely to propose to the Holy See in Rome the introduction of the vernacular. But no conference of bishops is even needed for that; every single Catholic can make a suggestion."

Archbishop Enrico Dante, Secretary of the Sacred Congregation of Rites, spoke out strongly against the schema on liturgy. Legislation on the subject, he said, must remain the exclusive prerogative of the Holy See. Latin should continue to be the language of the liturgy, and the vernacular should be used only for instructions and certain prayers. This position was supported by three other members of the Curia: Antonio Cardinal Bacci, a member of the Sacred Congregation of Rites, who was regarded as the outstanding Latinist in the Vatican; Archbishop Pietro Parente, a consultant to the Sacred Congregation of Rites, who was also first assistant to Alfredo Cardinal Ottaviani in the Sacred Congregation of the Holy Office; and Archbishop Dino Staffa, Secretary of the Sacred Congregation of Seminaries and Universities. Giuseppe Cardinal Siri, Archbishop of Genoa, and a leading conservative, suggested that a joint commission of members from the Theological and Liturgical Commissions be appointed to revise the entire schema.

On October 30, the day after his seventy-second birthday, Cardinal Ottaviani addressed the Council to protest against the drastic changes which were being suggested in the Mass. "Are we seeking to stir up wonder, or perhaps scandal, among the Christian people, by introducing changes in so venerable a rite, that has been approved for so many centuries and is now so familiar? The rite of Holy Mass should not be treated as if it were a piece of cloth to be refashioned according to the whim of each generation." Speaking without a text, because of his partial blindness, he exceeded the ten-minute time limit which all had been requested to observe. Cardinal Tisserant, Dean of the Council Presidents, showed his watch to Cardinal Alfrink, who was presiding that morning. When Cardinal Ottaviani reached fifteen minutes, Cardinal Alfrink rang the warning bell. But the speaker was so engrossed in his topic that he did not notice the bell, or purposely ignored it. At a signal from Cardinal Alfrink, a technician switched off the microphone. After confirming the fact by tapping the instrument, Cardinal Ottaviani stumbled back to his seat in humiliation. The most powerful cardinal in the Roman Curia had been silenced, and the Council Fathers clapped with glee.

Again and again the request was made from the floor that the schema on the liturgy should be given to the Council Fathers in its entirety, as Cardinal Frings had suggested. The feeling was widespread that some high-handed, behind-the-scenes action had been responsible for cutting down the original text to its present form. The position was finally clarified by Carlo Cardinal Confalonieri, a member of the Curia and chairman of the sub-commission on amendments, a division of the Central Preparatory Commission to which all draft texts had had to be submitted. He told the assembled Council Fathers on November 5 that his subcommission alone had been responsible for the changes made.

This admission in the Council hall was regarded as another triumph for the liberals. And it was followed by an even more impressive triumph: the eventual restoration of most of the passages—including the "Declarations"—which had been deleted from the Preparatory Commission's original draft.

THE PRESS AND SECRECY

Everyone connected in any way with the First Vatican Council (1869-70) was ordered by Pope Pius IX to observe strict secrecy on every conceivable aspect of Council business. The Pope explained that secrecy had also been imposed upon those partaking in earlier Councils, whenever the occasion had warranted it. "But now more than ever such caution appears necessary," he said, "since every opportunity is quickly seized by the powerful and destructive forces of wickedness to inspire hateful attacks against the Catholic Church and its doctrine." This rigid secrecy obligation, and the lack of a Council Press Office, forced journalists assigned to cover Vatican I to obtain their information in devious ways. The resultant coverage was considered by Church authorities to be lacking in objectivity and balance, however good the intentions of the journalists concerned might have been.

To avoid any repetition of this situation at Vatican II, it was early decided to make special efforts to provide journalists with authentic information. At a press conference held by Cardinal Tardini on October 30, 1959, and attended by over a hundred journalists, it was announced that a Council Press Office would be established to give journalists an opportunity to obtain "precise and topical information on the various phases of the Council." This Press Office opened its doors on April 18, 1961, operating first as an information service for the Central Preparatory Commission. In this capacity, it issued a total of 112 news releases during the preparatory phase of the Council.

In June 1961, Pope John told those engaged in the preparatory work that he did not wish to "forget the journalists," whose desire for news on the Council he appreciated. "Nevertheless," he added, "we invite them courteously to reflect that an ecumenical council is neither an academy of science nor a parliament, but rather a solemn meeting of the entire hierarchy of the Church to discuss questions regarding the ordinary life of the Church and the good of souls. It is clear that all of this interests the journalists, but it also requires special respect and reserve."

In October of the same year, Pope John received the press in audience and said that everything would be done to provide them with detailed information on the preparation and development of the Council. "In fact, we are fully conscious of the precious service that the press will be able to perform in making the Council known in its true light, and in making it understood and appreciated by the public at large as it deserves to be. Indeed, it would be most unfortunate if, for lack of sufficient information, or for lack of discretion and objectivity, a religious event of this importance should be presented so inexactly as to distort its character and the very goals which it has set for itself."

A month later, the Pope told the Central Preparatory Commission that not everything could be made known to the press. "There are some deliberations which necessarily . . . must remain veiled in silence."

Six days before the opening of the Council, Amleto Cardinal Cicognani, the Secretary of State, blessed and inaugurated the newly expanded Council Press Office, facing St. Peter's. The office was equipped with all modern facilities, and in the course of the four sessions issued 176 news bulletins and 141 special studies in English, French, Italian, German, Spanish, Portuguese, Polish, Arabic and Chinese. Even before the Council opened, over a thousand journalists from around the world had been accredited.

Monsignor Fausto Vallainc, the Director of the Council Press Office, was immediately responsible to the Secretary General during the first session, an arrangement which proved most unsatisfactory and was changed before the second session. On the opening day of the Council, he issued a bulletin to the effect that the Council Press Office would do "all in its power to fulfill the requests of journalists and facilitate their work. . . . Naturally this office has certain necessary limitations, since the information to be given out must always first be approved, and may never violate the laws of necessary reserve, discretion and secrecy required for the good of the Council."

The matter of secrecy was specifically treated in three different articles of the Rules of Procedure of the Council, endorsed by Pope John two months before the Council opened. In its mildest form it was imposed upon observer-delegates from non-Catholic Christian Churches invited to attend the Council. Article 18 provided: "The observers may inform their own communities of those things that take place in the Council. They are bound to observe secrecy, however, with regard to all other persons, in the same way as the Council Fathers, as indicated in Article 26." The wording of the obligation as it related to the Council Fathers was very brief: "The Fathers are obliged to keep secret the Council discussions and the opinions of individuals." The secrecy obligation imposed by Article 27 was even more stringent: "Procurators, Council *periti*, ministers, officials and all others who have anything to do with Council affairs are obliged before the Council opens to take an oath in the presence of the President or his delegate, stating that they will faithfully fulfill their office and observe secrecy regarding documents, discussions, opinions of individual Fathers, and votes."

Although Monsignor Vallainc made heroic efforts to supply information, it was so anonymous that the press could quote no one. He was in a dilemma. He knew what the reporters wanted, and realized the validity of their requests, but he could not oblige. And this angered the journalists with whom he was in daily contact. If he ventured to give more detailed information than usual, those Council Fathers who believed this to indicate partiality toward conservatives or liberals, or to be injurious to the Council, complained to the authorities, and Monsignor Vallainc would receive new instructions from Archbishop Felici. His job was to remain as neutral as possible.

Throughout the first session, representations were made through a variety of channels urging improvements in the press arrangements. Notably, the Spanish Information Center drafted a memorandum on the subject for presentation to the Council Secretariat; more or less formal representations were also made by the press committee of the United States hierarchy, by many individual bishops of various countries, and by individual journalists. Although there was some improvement in the bulletins issued to the press, they never became quite satisfactory. There continued to be emphasis on basic agreement among the Council Fathers, with disagreement being evident only on minor points, even in cases where it later became apparent that the disagreements were much more than minor. And the presentation of arguments on both sides of an issue tended to give the impression that there was about equal division, when this was not at all the case in fact.

There was an attempt among some Council Fathers, especially those from Canada, to do away with the secrecy obligation altogether and to allow the press to attend all meetings inside St. Peter's. This proposal, however, met with strong opposition not only from Council authorities, but also from many Council Fathers. The secrecy obligation was never formally revoked or even mitigated during the first session.

It is not surprising, therefore, that Manuel Cardinal Gonçalves Cerejeira of Lisbon should have risen in the Council hall on November 16, to say that he was obliged to make "a sad observation," namely, that the secrecy obligation regarding Council matters was very poorly observed, since everything said at the previous meeting two days earlier was already public knowledge. Actually, much of what Council Fathers regarded as leakage of Council information was news that had been issued by the

Council Press Office itself. Each day, shortly after a meeting, there was an oral briefing for the press in the Council Press Office, and two or three hours later the same information was available to the press in bulletin form. Many Council Fathers found themselves in the embarrassing position of withholding information from persons outside the Council, only to find the selfsame news in the next morning's paper.

The French *La Croix*, a daily published in Paris by the Augustinians of the Assumption, enjoyed the special confidence of the French hierarchy. These bishops knew that *La Croix* would faithfully print what they said, and would not sensationalize the news. As a result, numerous and lengthy direct quotations of statements by French bishops in the Council hall appeared in *La Croix*. Archbishop René Stourm of Sens, press representative for the French hierarchy, later said that the French bishops regarded themselves as responsible to their people, and wanted to keep them informed; hence they had used the press.

Many Council Fathers from Italy, France and Canada sent weekly newsletters on the Council to their diocesan newspapers. Some of these newsletters, such as that of Cardinal Montini, were widely reproduced in the press. Coadjutor Archbishop John Patrick Cody made a weekly broadcast from Rome to New Orleans via telephone to keep the people of his archdiocese informed, but only during the second session.

Simultaneously with the opening of the Council, several national information centers were established. These grew rapidly in importance, because of the general need of the press for information about the Council, and they also began to exert an altogether unexpected influence on the Council's deliberations.

The most elaborate, most influential and most regular service was the one provided by the United States hierarchy; it might well be regarded as one of that hierarchy's greatest contributions to the Council. Officially it was known as the U. S. Bishops' Press Panel. It operated within the limits of the rules governing the Council, and its principal purpose was to provide more information on Council proceedings and throw light on the highly complex questions treated in the debates. The panel during the first session regularly numbered eleven members, all experts on subjects related to the Council's work—dogmatic theology, moral theology, sacred Scripture, ecumenism, council history, canon law, liturgy, seminaries, etc. These experts would clarify definitions and positions, and provide the press with background material on matters under discussion in the Council hall on any one day. As the Council progressed, these briefings were increasingly well attended.

The German hierarchy established an information center at which a bishop or theologian read a weekly background paper. The Spanish hierarchy opened an information office which was concerned chiefly with supplying information to the Spanish bishops themselves. The Dutch hierarchy opened a documentation center which during the first session issued a series of forty research papers in Dutch. The French and Argentine hierarchies also established information offices.

In a pre-Council survey that I made of press attitudes in regard to Council coverage, the chief of the Rome bureau of *Newsweek*, Mr. Curtis Pepper, told me, "Nothing can substitute for interviews with important people." He cited the meeting of the World Council of Churches in New Delhi, where he and other representatives of the press had been given every opportunity to interview churchmen. "This," he said, "cleared up ambiguities and led to more accurate reporting on the part of the press." These views were confirmed by Mr. Robert Kaiser of the Rome bureau of *Time*, who said, "What the press needs is access to bishops and theologians who have the freedom to speak frankly about something which is a human event involving intelligent men in dialogue."

Most of the Council Fathers who came to Rome distrusted the press. They believed they would be misquoted, and therefore refused to meet and cooperate with journalists they did not know. And such a vast assortment of tongues were spoken by the Council Fathers that most journalists would be automatically restricted to their own linguistic groups. Because I was a priest and a member of an international and multilingual missionary order, I was in a more advantageous position to make contact with Council Fathers from many different parts of the world.

Like all other journalists, I had to overcome the obstacle of secrecy. Convinced by Mr. Pepper and Mr. Kaiser of the importance of press conferences, I felt it imperative to find a way for a Council Father to speak before the press without fear of breaking the obligation of Council secrecy. At the same time, his words must obviously have some direct bearing on the Council; background talks were not enough. The solution reached was actually very simple. Instead of asking a Council Father to speak about what was going on in the Council hall, I would merely ask him to state in practical terms the needs and wishes of his own diocese in regard to the matter currently under discussion. This did not violate secrecy, and was still topical information for the press. For it was clear that what a bishop might say in this connection would echo views that he, or someone else, was voicing in the Council hall.

To overcome a bishop's fear of being misquoted, I suggested that he first give me a private interview, which I would then write up and submit to him for his approval. After the transcript was cleared, translations of it would be made. At the subsequent press conference, each journalist would receive this bulletin in his own language. It contained numerous direct quotations, which the press was free to use. This procedure guaranteed the accuracy of the substance of any story which the press might carry, and it allayed the fears of the Council Father concerned. The press conference itself was conducted in two, and sometimes three, languages; the bulletins were available in six languages. In this way, the Divine Word News Service was able to organize fifteen widely quoted press conferences for seven bishops and eight archbishops from twelve countries during the first session. This practice was widely adopted in subsequent sessions.

THE MISSION VIEWPOINT ON THE LITURGY

The choice of the schema on the liturgy as the first topic of debate was to have a number of unexpected side effects. The very practical considerations in the schema affecting the Church's life of worship were of paramount concern to missionary and Asian- and African-born bishops. Had the debate begun with any other topic, these bishops might not have become actively and totally engaged in it until much later. They knew better than anyone else the importance of liturgical reform, particularly in respect to language. At the same time, they knew that they could not effect the desired changes singlehanded. And since the European alliance was altogether sympathetic to their views, they rallied to its support, causing it to grow in size and power. Still another consequence of the priority given to the debate on the liturgy was that Father Schillebeeckx and other opponents of the four dogmatic constitutions were given ample time to pinpoint the inadequacies of those texts and to demand their complete revision. A number of lectures were organized on the topics concerned and were widely attended by Council Fathers.

The only representative from Asia on the Liturgical Commission was Dutch-born Bishop Willem van Bekkum of Ruteng, Indonesia, who had gained international repute by the paper he had read on liturgical reform and the missions at the Pastoral Liturgical Congress held in Assisi in 1956. His candidacy had been favored by the European alliance, partly because he had received his formal training in liturgy from the two leaders of the liturgical movement in Germany and Austria. On October 23, the day after the discussion on the schema began, I persuaded him to let me arrange a press conference for him. The announced topic was the adaptation of the liturgy to Indonesian culture.

As was anticipated, the press turned out in large numbers. The Bishop said that he had been able, with the help of his Indonesian flock, to "Christianize clan feasts in which original socioreligious structures were preserved." Before the Council opened, he said, he had felt that proposals such as he wished to make would have no chance of a hearing, but now he was "highly optimistic." "At private meetings in the past few days with missionary bishops from other parts of the world," he said, "I have learned that our experience in Ruteng has been multiplied hundreds of times throughout Asia and Africa. And I have found warm sympathy for these ideas among liturgical experts from the West." Traditional Indonesian practices such as harvest thanksgiving feasts, feasts honoring the dead, and agricultural new year feasts could "safely be transformed in Christ" and sanctioned by the Church. On the subject of language, Bishop van Bekkum stressed the importance of spontaneity in worship and pointed out that spontaneity disappeared when the faithful were confronted with a foreign tongue. He hoped that languages other than Latin—those of Asia and Africa, for instance—might become "sacramental languages" through their introduction into the liturgy, and especially into the Mass. The result, he said, would be "a much richer and more vital liturgy."

As Bishop van Bekkum walked out of the press conference, he met Archbishop Bernardin Gantin, the African-born head of Cotonou archdiocese in Dahomey. Upon learning of the conference, the Archbishop told the Bishop, "You are our spokesman." An hour later, news programs throughout Italy and international news agencies were spreading Bishop van Bekkum's ideas far and wide. *L'Osservatore Romano* surprised its readers with an exclusive interview. The Bishop's own comment on his press conference, which had lasted an hour and a half, was: "I could never have explained so much in the ten minutes allotted to speakers on the Council floor."

The press conference had turned out so well that I was eager to try the experiment again. On Sunday, October 28, I approached Archbishop Eugene D'Souza of Nagpur, India, with the suggestion that he might wish to pass on to reporters his thoughts regarding the use of Indian languages and local customs in the liturgy. Realizing that the cause of liturgical reform had been advanced by the published statements of Bishop van Bekkum, the Archbishop agreed, and the conference was held the next day. He had reason to believe that there was serious opposition, because Cardinal Döpfner had told him, "We are standing before a thick stone wall, and it does not look as though we shall get through."

Archbishop D'Souza told a roomful of reporters, "The marriage rite as it now stands is unintelligible to many of our Catholic people living in rural areas." To make it more understandable, some local customs had been incorporated in certain regions of India. "For example, since a ring means nothing at all to some of our people, a dish called a *thalee* is handed by the husband to the wife." In other places, he said, the "marriage knot" was used as the external sign or symbol of the marriage contract. "The whole rite of most of our sacraments and sacramentals ought to have local color." And on the subject of language, he added: "The use of the vernacular in the administration of the sacraments is a must, for the simple reason that the beautiful rites are completely lost on our people if they are in Latin." If local languages and customs were not introduced into the liturgy, the Church would "never make the impact it should on our country. . . ."

Similar considerations were voiced at a press conference given by Bishop Lawrence Nagae of Urawa, Japan, who maintained that Catholicism had made such slow progress in his country (with 300,000 Catholics) because its presentation had been too Western. "If Catholicism is to be recognized and accepted by the working class, which makes up the bulk of the Japanese population, it is necessary for the Catholic Church to appear as a very modern and dynamic spiritual and social force." The Catholic Church must have something special to say to modern man and something special to give him, he went on. "Modern Japan, seeing only ceremonies and institutional practices in the Catholic Church, considers the Catholic religion on a par with its own traditional religions, outdated and defunct, incapable of making any serious and worthwhile contribution to modern Japanese life."

He therefore called for a simpler liturgy and a more direct approach, so that the people might be able "to participate more immediately with the priest." He also called for the elimination from the liturgy of elements such as genuflections, which, he said, stemmed from Western culture and were meaningless to the Japanese. "In our country, where we make a profound bow to show reverence, we would prefer to use that motion in place of the genuflection." Other ceremonies and symbols, too, were unintelligible to the Japanese—for instance, the kissing of objects during liturgical services. This practice should be made more infrequent, he said, since "the kiss in the

Orient is out of place." He also said that the Sign of the Cross should not have to be made so frequently.

The schema on the liturgy went into its ninth day of discussion on November 5. Twenty-four Council Fathers spoke at this meeting, emphasizing many of the same topics, preoccupations, and differences as had been voiced at earlier meetings. Some called for the shortening of the Mass prayers at the foot of the altar, ending the Mass with the *Ite, missa est* and the blessing, using the pulpit for the Mass of the Word and the altar for the Mass of the Sacrifice, and pronouncing only the words *"Corpus Christi"* ("Body of Christ") when distributing Holy Communion. One of the speakers that morning was German-born Bishop William Duschak of Calapan vicariate in the Philippines, who stressed the need for what he called an ecumenical Mass, modeled closely upon the Last Supper, over and above the existing form of the Latin Rite Mass.

The communiqué issued by the Council Press Office that day made no mention of Bishop Duschak's proposal. In fact, it stressed the "necessity of preserving the present structure of the Mass in its substance," and indicated that "only minor changes may be allowed." A press conference, however, had been arranged for him in the afternoon, and when newsmen heard that the Bishop had spoken in the Council hall that morning, they turned up at his conference in exceptionally large numbers. To inform newsmen of these press conferences, I had to distribute my notices on the front steps of the Council Press Office, since it was not allowed during the first session to post a notice on the bulletin board inside. Authorities maintained that reporters would then consider the press conference to be official.

Bishop Duschak told the press that he had devoted a lifetime of study to pastoral liturgy, and that his present suggestion was the product of over thirty years of priestly work in the Philippines. "My idea," he said, "is to introduce an ecumenical Mass, stripped wherever possible of historical accretions, one that is based on the essence of the Holy Sacrifice, one that is deeply rooted in Holy Scripture. By this I mean that it should contain all the essential elements of the Last Supper, using language and gestures that are understandable, adopting the method and spirit of the prayers and words that were used then. It should be a kind of celebration of the Mass which all members of a community, even if they happen to be attending Mass for the first time in their lives, can readily understand without involved explanations and without special historical commentaries." Man-made prayers, he said, should be used very sparingly; the emphasis should instead be placed on the words of promise in Holy Scripture, the words Christ spoke at the Last Supper in instituting the Holy Sacrifice, and in his priestly prayer for unity, and St. Paul's admonitions regarding the Eucharist as contained in the first Epistle to the Corinthians.

Bishop Duschak did not accept the conventional reasons for keeping the Canon of the Mass intact. "If men in centuries gone by," he said, "were able to choose and create Mass rites, why should not the greatest of all ecumenical Councils be able to do so? Why should it not be possible to ordain that a new Mass formula be drawn up with all due reverence, one that is suited to, desired and understood by modern man, who lives in a world which is daily becoming smaller and more uniform?" The substance of the Holy Sacrifice would remain, he said, but the rite, form, language, and gestures would be accommodated to our modern age, thus making it possible for modern man to derive greater spiritual benefit from it. The entire Mass, moreover, should be said aloud, in the vernacular, and facing the people. "I believe it is also likely that if the world receives such an ecumenical form of Eucharistic celebration, the faith of non-Catholic Christian communities in the sacramental presence of Christ might be renewed or even rectified."

Bishop Duschak emphasized that he was not proposing the abolition of the existing form of the Latin Mass. He was merely proposing that an additional form or structure of the Mass be introduced. Asked whether his proposal originated with the people whom he served, he answered, "No, I think they would oppose it, just as many bishops oppose it. But if it could be put into practice, I think they would accept it."

When a high-ranking conservative official of the Council Press Office saw the bulletin that I had prepared for reporters attending this press conference, he seriously asked me to examine my conscience and decide once and for all to discontinue publishing bulletins, since this was the task of the Council Press Office. But when I sought advice from some progressive Council Fathers, they said, "Carry on! If you run into trouble, we'll get rid of the roadblocks for you."

Before the Council ended, the Commission for the

Implementation of the Constitution on the Sacred Liturgy had already approved of three distinct Mass formulas on a limited experimental basis, in which the entire Mass, including the Canon, was to be said aloud, in the vernacular, with the priest facing the people. A part of Bishop Duschak's proposal was already being put into practice.

"The Christian Life Is Not a Collection of Ancient Customs"

In the early days of November, I was approached by Archbishop Geraldo Sigaud of Diamantina, Brazil, who was known to me as a conservative—that is, a Council Father who used more than average caution in advocating change. In disappointed tones, he remarked that I seemed to be arranging press conferences only for speakers who were in favor of the vernacular. Whereupon I assured him that if a Council Father in favor of Latin were willing to speak to the press, I would just as readily arrange a press conference for him. The Archbishop told me that he knew just such a man, and within twenty-four hours had introduced me to a friend of his, Bishop António de Castro Mayer of Campos, Brazil. The press conference took place on November 7, and was very well attended.

"Can we be sure," the Bishop asked, "that the translation of the Mass into the vernacular will convey to the faithful all the nuances of the Latin text? . . . Here we are dealing with a most serious question, one that cannot be decided without profound thought."

The use of a language not readily understood by all "lends a certain dignity to the divine service, giving it a mysterious tone which, in a certain degree, is natural for things pertaining to God." The wisdom of the centuries, Bishop Mayer said, had dictated the use of an archaic language in the liturgical services of certain non-Latin rites of the Catholic Church, and also in the best-known non-Catholic religions. And since a variety of missals were available with the Mass text translated into living languages, it was not necessary for the priest to say the Mass in the vernacular. Bishop Mayer doubted that a spiritual revival among peoples and nations would necessarily follow upon the introduction of the vernacular in the Mass, as some had claimed.

At the same time, the Bishop conceded that "in certain cultural areas, where the language is far removed from Latin, a gradual changeover could be made. The changeover would be from Latin to a language more in keeping with the local culture, provided that a universal basic element were retained." He explained here that he did not necessarily mean that the language to be substituted should be the vernacular. Moreover, the changeover would have to be achieved gradually and organically, "always inspired and directed by the Holy See, which enjoys the special assistance of the Holy Spirit in all that pertains to divine worship and the salvation of souls." As for the peoples of Western lands that possessed the Latin Rite, there seemed to be no reason, as far as Bishop Mayer could see, for abandoning any of the Latin in the Mass, even for a long time to come.

Bishop Mayer's remarks contrasted greatly with remarks made on the same day by Pope John at a public audience granted after he had watched the morning meeting of the Council on closed-circuit television. Explaining the activities of the Council Fathers, the Pope said: "The business at hand is not to make a careful study of some old museum or of some school of thought from the past. No doubt this can be helpful—just as a visit to ancient monuments can be helpful—but it is not enough. We live to advance, appreciating at the same time whatever the past has to offer us in the line of experience. But we must move ever further onward along the road which Our Lord has opened up before us." And, to make sure that there should be no misunderstanding as to his meaning, he added, "The Christian life is not a collection of ancient customs."

On the previous Sunday, both by action and by word, he had expressed himself in favor of the vernacular. It was the fourth anniversary of his coronation, and the faithful of Rome as well as the Council Fathers were present at a celebration in St. Peter's. Speaking in Latin to the Council Fathers, the Pope said: "This should be the common language used by prelates of the Universal Church when communicating with . . . the Apostolic See, and it should be regularly used at Council meetings." After greeting them in Latin, he said, he would switch to Italian, "especially since it can be more easily understood by very many of those present, that is, by the people, who have come together here in great numbers to honor the anniversary in the pontificate of their Pastor and Father." This was the very same argument that the missionary bishops had been using for the introduction of the vernacular in the Mass.

Pope John spoke at length in Italian on the merits of the Ambrosian Rite, in which Cardinal Montini of Milan was celebrating the anniversary Mass in honor of the Pope that day. He pointed out that, in externals, the Ambrosian Rite Mass appeared different from the Latin Rite Mass, but that this external difference was no obstacle whatsoever to the "sincere fidelity to Rome" of the Catholics of Milan. These words provided encouragement to bishops from Africa and Asia who had been advocating in the Council not only the introduction of the vernacular in the Mass, but also the adaptation of the Mass and other religious functions to the local culture.

As Pope John put it, "It is only natural that new times and circumstances should suggest different forms and approaches in the external transmission and presentation of doctrine. But the living substance is always the pure, evangelical, and apostolic truths with which the teachings of our Holy Church perfectly conform." Missionary bishops took this to mean that the Pope supported their stand.

Because the Rules of Procedure contained no provision for limiting the number of speakers who might address the assembly on a given chapter, the Council moved along very slowly during its first month. Numerous complaints and suggestions were lodged with Council officials, causing Pope John to authorize the Council Presidency to call for a vote of cloture when a topic appeared exhausted. On November 6, the day on which this new faculty was announced, it was immediately put to use, since by this time as many as seventy-nine speakers had addressed the assembly on the second chapter of the first schema. Two other methods of speeding up the Council were also adopted about this time: less important schema chapters were discussed as a unit, and groups of Council Fathers had representatives speak for them.

For their own instruction and guidance, the Council Fathers began to form groups, on either linguistic or nationalistic lines, and many of them met at a specified time and place each week. One of these groups was the Conference of German-language Council Fathers, which met each Monday evening in the residence of Cardinal Frings to determine policy for the coming week. It counted among its nearly one hundred members all the bishops of Germany, Austria, Switzerland, Luxembourg, Scandinavia, Iceland, and Finland, as well as many missionary bishops and superiors general of German, Austrian and Swiss ancestry. And its forte was that it not only united for the sake of discussion, but also nearly always acted as a bloc.

UPDATING LITURGICAL PRACTICES—SOME UNDERLYING ISSUES

Throughout the discussion of the first four chapters of the schema on the liturgy, the question of the vernacular came up again and again. It appeared prominently in Chapter I, in which general principles were stated. It came up again in Chapter II, in connection with the Mass; in Chapter III, on the sacraments; and in Chapter IV, on the Divine Office. This endless preoccupation with the introduction of the vernacular into the liturgy often appeared to outsiders as so much unnecessary and repetitious talk. A simple solution, one might have thought, would be to let those countries have the liturgy in the vernacular whose bishops favored this, and let those whose bishops pre-ferred Latin retain that language. But, like most simple solutions, this one did not go deep enough.

As long as Latin texts and Latin rites were universally used in the Church, the Roman Curia would be compe-tent to check and control them. But if hundreds and even thousands of local languages and customs were introduced into the liturgy, the Curia would automatically lose this prerogative. Episcopal conferences with knowledge of the local languages and understanding of local custom would then become the more competent judges in the matter. And this was precisely what the evolving majority was insisting upon. It wanted episcopal conferences to be authorized to make certain important decisions in regard to liturgical practices. The Curia, on the other hand, cor-rectly surmised that, if it agreed to the principle of local jurisdiction in liturgical matters, a precedent would be established enabling episcopal conferences to gain still wider powers of decision in other areas as well. This was one of the reasons for its opposition to the introduction of the vernacular and of local customs into the liturgy.

During Vatican I (1869-70) the Curia had led the majority, and the German-speaking bishops and the bish-ops of France had led the minority. But now the tables were turned, and—in the space of one short month—the German-speaking and the French bishops had found themselves at the helm of Vatican II. The sides taken in this first great encounter on the liturgy proved a severe blow for the Curia, because the positions taken crystal-lized and profoundly influenced the overall voting pattern that was to characterize the Council.

Historians concede that the early Christian Church successfully adapted itself to the prevailing Roman culture of the time. And they ask whether the same process could not be achieved in India, Japan, Africa, the South Sea Islands, and elsewhere. At the beginning of Vatican II, the Church in all those countries was identical in appearance with the Church in Rome. Will this still be the case fifty years hence? The discussions and decisions of the Council leave no room for doubt that, in external appearance, the Church in those countries may well be very different.

Changes were also proposed in the matter of the Divine Office, or breviary. Paul Cardinal Léger of Montreal, for instance, made a very radical proposal, which was warmly applauded, for the thorough reorganization of the Divine Office. One form, he suggested, should be prescribed for clergy engaged in the active apostolate, and another for monks. For the first, the breviary should be made up of three sections, one to be said in the morning, one in the evening—both in Latin—and a third consisting of special passages to be freely selected and read in any language. Other speakers proposed that the whole of the Divine Office should be in the vernacular. A French bishop proposed that a priest be automatically dispensed from certain parts of the Divine Office if he celebrated two Masses or preached twice on the same day.

Other speakers, on the contrary, stressed the importance of the breviary for the spiritual life of priests engaged in the active ministry, as well as for monks, and rejected the suggestion that it should be shortened. Some wished more space to be given to New Testament texts, while omitting certain psalms of a historic character relating specifically to incidents in the history of the Hebrew people.

The official news bulletin of the Council Press Office stated that the reason given by Council Fathers for shortening the Divine Office was "to give priests the possibility of dedicating themselves more to apostolic activities." It went on to say, with regard to such proposals, that it had been emphasized "that every type of pastoral activity, no matter how generous, is made sterile if it is not nourished by the priest's prayer." Some Council Fathers maintained that the report was tendentious, since it did not present the manifold reasons given for shortening the breviary. Since the Canadian hierarchy was most immediately concerned, it lodged an official protest.

Numerous reasons had in fact been given by Council Fathers for reducing the length of the Divine Office, over and above the consideration of apostolic activities. For instance, a reduction in the time spent on the formal prayers of the breviary might leave more time for meditation, spiritual reading, examination of conscience, and other practices of personal piety. The reason underlying the proposal for the recitation of the breviary in the vernacular was that this would facilitate a greater understanding of the text and would therefore produce greater spiritual benefits.

To speed up the proceedings, the last four chapters were discussed as a unit. The result was a veritable kaleidoscope of proposals. For instance, there were proposals in favor of a fixed liturgical calendar throughout the world. And although arguments were voiced to the contrary, there seemed to be a consensus in favor of a fixed date for Easter, such as the first Sunday in April, for example. It was stressed that an understanding would have to be reached in the matter with the Eastern and Protestant Churches, and with the civil authorities.

Ways and means were also suggested whereby the faithful would be enabled to observe Sundays and holy days of obligation with more regularity. One proposal, in this connection, was that the obligation to attend Mass on Sunday should be transferred to a weekday in the case of persons prevented from attendance on Sunday.

Again, Bishop Johannes Pohlschneider of Aachen, Germany, suggested that the Lenten fast be restricted to Ash Wednesday, Good Friday, and the morning of Holy Saturday. He gave two reasons: one, that modern men generally did not observe the law "because of the speed of modern life and widespread nervous tensions," the other that many bishops and priests dispensed themselves from fasting on the grounds that it deprived them of the strength they needed to perform their extensive pastoral duties. If bishops and priests did not fast, Bishop Pohlschneider observed, the faithful could hardly be expected to do so. At the same time, since "the Christian life cannot exist for long without a spirit of penance and self-denial," the faithful should constantly be admonished to make "specific sacrifices."

The last speaker on October 30 was Auxiliary Bishop Ildefonso Sansierra of San Juan de Cuyo, Argentina, who expressed the hope that "the wish of very many bishops and priests" for the inclusion of the name of St. Joseph in the Canon of the Mass would not be forgotten. On November 5, the same request was made at great length by Bishop Albert Cousineau of Cap Haïtien, Haiti, a former superior of the St. Joseph Oratory in Montreal, who asked that "the name of Blessed Joseph, Spouse of the Blessed Virgin Mary, be introduced into the Mass wherever the name of the Blessed Virgin Mary is mentioned."

At the end of the eighteenth General Congregation, on November 13, the Cardinal Secretary of State made a special announcement on the subject. He said that the Holy Father, wishing to conform to the desire "expressed by many Council Fathers," had decided to insert the name of St. Joseph in the Canon of the Mass, immediately after the name of the Most Holy Virgin. This action was to serve for all time as a reminder that St. Joseph had been the Patron of the Second Vatican Council. "This decision of the Holy Father," added the Cardinal, "will go into effect next December 8, and in the meanwhile the Sacred Congregation of Rites will prepare the necessary documents."

Cardinal Montini later described this unexpected move as "a surprise for the Council from the Pope."

In some quarters Pope John was severely criticized for taking what was termed independent action while the Ecumenical Council was in session. Actually, his decree was only the culmination of sporadic but intensive campaigns, dating back to 1815, through which hundreds of thousands of signatures of the hierarchy and the laity had been gathered and sent to the Vatican. The campaigns had become particularly intensive at the announcements of Vatican I by Pope Pius IX, and of Vatican II by Pope John. Immediately after Pope John's announcement, Monsignor Joseph Phelan of St. Joseph's Church in Capitola, California, launched a drive together with his parishioners and netted some 150,000 signatures.

Chiefly responsible for the action taken by Pope John, however, were Fathers Roland Gauthier and Guy Bertrand, directors of the Center of Research and Documentation at the St. Joseph Oratory in Montreal, who in 1961 composed a seventy-five-page booklet giving the history of these campaigns. They explained that the placement of St. Joseph's name after that of the Virgin Mary in the Canon of the Mass would, doctrinally and liturgically, give official recognition to St. Joseph's eminence in sanctity, after Mary, over all other saints. These two Holy Cross Fathers, through collaboration with the Discalced Carmelites of the Sociedad Ibero-Americana de Josefología in Valladolid, Spain, and the St. Joseph Fathers of Blessed Leonard Murialdo of the St. Joseph Research Center in Viterbo, Italy, were able to have their booklet appear in English, French, Spanish, Portuguese and Italian, and sent copies of it with a petition to the Council Fathers around the world, long before the Council began.

In mid-March 1962, Pope John was presented with six volumes containing the signed petitions of 30 cardinals, 436 patriarchs, archbishops and bishops, and 60 superiors general. While examining the signatures, Pope John said, "Something will be done for St. Joseph." These signatures confirmed him in his personal desire to do something special for St. Joseph, whom he had venerated from childhood with a very special devotion.

On October 19, three days before the liturgy came up for discussion in the Council hall, Father Edward Heston of the Holy Cross Fathers—who had submitted the petitions in the name of the three centers—was officially informed that Pope John had decided to take action on the proposal, and was going to include the name of St. Joseph in the Canon of the Mass.

November 13, the day on which Pope John's decision was made public in the Council hall, also marked the end of the long discussion on the liturgy, which had taken up fifteen meetings, with an average of twenty-two speeches a day. It was announced at the end of the morning that discussion would begin on the following day on the schema on the sources of revelation.

DEADLOCK AND SOLUTION

It was not hard to predict that the schema on the sources of revelation would run into serious trouble on the Council floor. Its opponents, led by Father Schillebeeckx and the Dutch bishops, had been agitating against it outside the Council hall for over a month. Although the Preparatory Commission which had drawn up the document had included liberals like Bishop John Wright of Pittsburgh, Bishop Joseph Schröffer of Eichstätt, and Monsignor Gerard Philips of Louvain, the schema was regarded as bearing the stamp of Cardinal Ottaviani and Father Sebastian Tromp. The latter, though Dutch and a Jesuit, was placed second only to Cardinal Ottaviani as a champion of conservatism. Cardinal Ottaviani had chosen him to be secretary of the Preparatory Theological Commission, and had appointed him to the same post in the Theological Commission of the Council.

A number of lectures had been organized during the

first month of the Council, featuring eminent liberal theologians, and these had been well attended by Council Fathers. The lecturers pointed to the weaknesses in the schema, charging that it was too negative, too aggressive, too intolerant, too one-sided, and altogether outmoded. It lacked a pastoral tone, they said, condemned good Catholic authors by quoting them out of context, and was marked by a number of theological errors. One of the main objections was that it recognized two sources of revelation instead of one.

The schema on the sources of revelation was presented by Cardinal Ottaviani on November 14. It was his first appearance in the Council hall since he had been silenced by Cardinal Alfrink two weeks earlier. He spoke of the pastoral value of the schema, and said that it was the first duty of every shepherd of souls to teach the truth, which always and everywhere remained the same. He then introduced Monsignor Salvatore Garofalo, another well-known conservative, and had him read the introductory report on the schema. Monsignor Garofalo had been a member of the Theological Preparatory Commission, and had been retained by Cardinal Ottaviani as a consultant to the Theological Commission of the Council.

Monsignor Garofalo, who was not a Council Father, said that the primary task of the Council was to defend and promote Catholic doctrine in its most precise form. There was no question of a renewal of doctrine, he said, but only of a closer study and knowledge of existing doctrine. He described the thorough work which had gone into the preparation of the schema, and pointed out that learned men from many nations and various universities had contributed to it. He then explained briefly the contents of the five chapters.

The reaction from the Council floor was swift and deadly. Cardinal Alfrink of Holland, Cardinal Frings of Germany, Cardinal Bea of the Curia, Cardinal König of Austria, Cardinal Liénart of France, Leo Cardinal Suenens of Belgium, Cardinal Léger of Canada, Joseph Cardinal Ritter of the United States, and Patriarch Maximos IV all categorically expressed their dissatisfaction with the schema. They were supported by Archbishop Adrianus Soegijapranata of Semarang, president of the episcopal conference of Indonesia, who said that he was speaking on behalf of all the bishops of his country. He attacked not only the schema on the sources of revelation, but the other three dogmatic constitutions as well, saying that none of them corresponded to the pastoral preoccupations of the Council. Since the vast majority of the bishops of Indonesia were Dutch, and since their chosen theological adviser was the Dutch Jesuit, Father Peter Smulders, who vehemently opposed the four dogmatic constitutions, the position of the Indonesian hierarchy was not unexpected.

Cardinal Siri of Genoa and Fernando Cardinal Quiroga y Palacios of Santiago de Compostela, Spain, expressed general satisfaction with the schema, saying only that it required certain amendments. The only speaker to express complete satisfaction with the text as it stood was Ernesto Cardinal Ruffini of Palermo, Italy. He then called attention to an alternative text which was being circulated among Council Fathers, and asked, "By what authority?"

A rival schema was in fact circulating. It was in mimeographed form, headed by the following statement: "Since it appears impossible for the Council to discuss all the schemas and vote on them, it would seem necessary to omit some and to shorten others and combine them. Therefore the presidents of the episcopal conferences of Austria, Belgium, France, Germany, and Holland make bold to propose as a basis for discussion the following compendium of material from the first two schemas. These are here presented in a more positive and pastoral tone."

A group of Council Fathers from Latin America—that was how they identified themselves—put out a two-page statement attacking the first two dogmatic constitutions. "These two schemas," it stated, "as they stand, contradict the purpose of this Council. They lag behind the present stage of progress in theology and the study of Sacred Scripture, they do not correspond to the present stage of ecumenism, they fall short of the expectations of the modern world, and they are lacking in clarity of doctrine." Each of these five points was elaborated, and the following conclusion stated: "It is clear that these two schemas are no answer to modern theological and pastoral needs. Therefore, let them be completely rewritten along the lines of these observations."

At the twentieth General Congregation, on November 16, the tempest continued in full force. Nine of the twenty-one speakers sought to defend the schema by suggesting amendments to it. Two dared speak out in praise of the schema. Realizing the drama of the situation, one of them said that he felt like Daniel in the lions' den. Nine other speakers revived previously stated objections or brought up new ones. They demanded that the schema in its present form be rejected and replaced by another.

Some of them proposed the appointment of a special committee to draw up a new schema, such a committee not to be restricted to one school of thought.

At the twenty-first General Congregation, Cardinal Döpfner, who had been one of the sixty-seven cardinals on the Central Preparatory Commission, remarked that some of the Council Fathers had begun to wonder how it was that members of the Theological Preparatory Commission and the Central Preparatory Commission were so vehemently attacking a schema which they had previously approved. He explained that things had not been so very peaceful at the meetings of the preparatory commissions. "The same objections that are being made now on the Council floor were made then," he said, "but they were simply set aside."

Cardinal Ottaviani rose, unannounced, to protest against this statement. He reminded the Council Fathers, further, that canon law prohibited the rejection of schemas which had been approved by the Pope. Whereupon Norman Cardinal Gilroy of Sydney, Australia, who was presiding, pointed out that under Article 33, Section 1, of the Rules of Procedure governing the Council, schemas could in fact be rejected. The section read: "Every Council Father is permitted to speak on every schema proposed, and may accept it, or reject it, or amend it." Once again, Cardinal Ottaviani sat down in defeat.

Of the eighteen speakers at the stormy twenty-second General Congregation, two defended the schema, seven called for major changes in the text, and nine rejected it completely.

Great concern was expressed over the apparent deadlock. It was suggested that discussion of the schema be postponed to the second session. Auxiliary Bishop Alfred Ancel of Lyons thought that the Pope might wish to assign some additional experts from the opposing school of thought to prepare a completely new schema.

At this point Bishop Emile De Smedt of Bruges, Belgium, took the floor on behalf of the Secretariat for Promoting Christian Unity. "Numerous Council Fathers," he said, "have shown a truly ecumenical preoccupation in their examination of the schema on the sources of revelation. All sincerely and positively desire that the schema should foster unity. Views differ, however, some saying that it meets the requirements of ecumenism, and others saying that it does not. In order that you may better judge the matter, perhaps you would be pleased to hear from our Secretariat what precisely is required before a proposal can be designated ecumenical. Our Secretariat, as you know, was established by the Supreme Pontiff in order to assist the Council Fathers in examining the various texts from the viewpoint of ecumenism."

Bishop De Smedt recalled that although his Secretariat had offered its assistance to the Theological Preparatory Commission, that body, "for reasons which I have no right to judge," had not accepted the proffered assistance. "We proposed the formation of a joint commission, but the Theological Preparatory Commission answered that this was not opportune. Thus it was the Theological Preparatory Commission alone that took upon itself the most difficult task of giving an ecumenical character to our schema. With what success?"

He concluded with a dramatic plea: "We who have

received from the Holy Father the task of working in this Council toward the happy establishment of dialogue with our non-Catholic brethren beg all of you, Venerable Fathers, to hear what the Secretariat for Promoting Christian Unity thinks of the proposed schema. As we see it, the schema is lacking notably in the ecumenical spirit. It does not constitute an advance in dialogue with non-Catholics, but an obstacle. I would go even further and say that it causes harm. . . . If the schemas prepared by the Theological Preparatory Commission are not drafted in a different manner, we shall be responsible for having crushed, through the Second Vatican Council, a great and immense hope. That hope is shared by all those who, with Pope John XXIII, in prayer and fasting expect that now finally some serious and notable steps will be taken in the direction of fraternal unity among all those for whom Christ our Lord prayed 'that all may be one.'"

As he stepped away from the microphone, the assembly broke out in thunderous applause.

At the twenty-third General Congregation, on the following day, seven speakers voiced approval of the schema, four approved but suggested amendments, and two insisted on its rejection.

By this time, eighty-five Council Fathers had spoken on the schema as a whole, and the Secretary General intervened to point out that the time had come to examine the individual chapters. However, he said, since a number of Council Fathers had expressed objections to the form of the schema, the Council Presidency considered it advisable to request a vote whereby each Council Father might in conscience make known his opinion in the matter. The question to be voted on was: Should the discussion of the schema on the sources of revelation be interrupted?

A total of 2,209 Council Fathers voted. Of this number, 1,368, or 62 percent, voted in favor of interrupting the discussion; 822, or 37 percent, against; and 19, or 1 percent, submitted invalid ballots. Since the Rules of Procedure required a two-thirds majority for the adoption of a proposal, the Council Fathers who wished to interrupt the discussion were technically defeated, and the discussion on the schema as it stood would have to continue.

Efforts were now made to bypass the Rules of Procedure, which, in the words of Giacomo Cardinal Lercaro of Bologna, Italy, had led to "the absurd position of making the vote of a rather small minority prevail over that of a strong majority." He called this "an evident weakness" in the Rules of Procedure.

On the following day, Archbishop Felici read a communication from the Secretary of State, which said that the Pope had taken into consideration the various views manifested in the interventions of the preceding days. These had led him to foresee a laborious and prolonged discussion of the schema. It therefore seemed to him useful to have the schema revised by a special commission before the discussion was resumed. This special commission on revision should include all Council Fathers on the Theological Commission and the Secretariat for Promoting Christian Unity. The task of the commission would be to revise the schema, shorten it, and bring out in greater relief the principles of Catholic teaching already treated at Trent and Vatican I. The commission was to present the revised schema to the Council Fathers once more for their study. In place of the present schema, the next General Congregation would take up the discussion of the schema on communications media.

The victory of the conservatives had been short-lived. The liberals had won the election encounter; they had won the debate on liturgy; and now they had won the debate on revelation. They became increasingly conscious of the strength of their numbers. And the conservatives became gradually less sure of their position.

Four days later, *L'Osservatore Romano* announced the composition of the new commission on revision on its front page. The reference was no longer to the schema on the sources of revelation, but to the schema on divine revelation. This seemed to confirm that the liberal camp, which opposed the notion of two sources of revelation, had prevailed. The new commission on revision had two presidents, Cardinals Ottaviani and Bea. Six cardinals had also been added, among them Cardinals Frings and Liénart.

IN SEARCH OF UNITY

Pope John XXIII celebrated his eighty-first birthday on Sunday, November 25, 1962, at the Pontifical Urban University, by saying Mass for the 320 major seminarians gathered there from all parts of the world.

In his address, the Pope expressed his conviction that God was guiding the Council. "You have proof of this in what has happened during the past few weeks. These weeks may be regarded as a sort of novitiate for the Second Vatican Council." It was only natural, he said, when many persons were examining this or that point, that opinions and proposals should vary about the best way of putting fundamental principles into practice. "This is a sacred kind of liberty for which the Church, especially in these circumstances, has proved its respect. Through this, it has won profound and universal admiration."

Before leaving, the Pope thanked the student body for their prayers and added that, with the help of those prayers, he would prepare himself "for the new period of life—however long it may be—which the Lord will grant us." Did he have a premonition of his death? He reminded the seminarians to pray for "the continued progress and happy outcome of the Ecumenical Council."

The next morning, November 26, it was announced for the third time that the solemn closing of the first session of the Council would take place on December 8 in St. Peter's, and that Pope John would preside.

November had been a very strenuous month for the Pope. In addition to his other duties, he had made it a point to receive in audience thirty-seven episcopal conferences, or nearly two a day, excluding Sundays. Few of the bishops were aware that the Pope had for some time been under close medical observation because he was hemorrhaging. The night after his eighty-first birthday, he suffered an exceptionally severe hemorrhage, and was forced to cancel further audiences. He was confined to his bed for eight days, but he stubbornly forced himself to conduct the closing ceremonies on December 8. A similar siege of the same malady was to cost him his life early in the following June.

Pope John may well have feared that he would not live

to see the second session if it began as late as October 1963. This may have influenced his decision to open the second session on May 12 and close it on June 29, the feast of SS. Peter and Paul. But although these dates had been decided upon in consultation with episcopal conferences, their announcement resulted in immediate protests from many of the Council Fathers, on both pastoral and economic grounds. Some of the Council Fathers thought that, after a seven-week spring session, they might have to return for another session in the fall of the same year. For bishops with extensive dioceses to cover, especially in Africa, Asia, and Latin America, the intervals between Council sessions would then be too short to permit them to carry out their pastoral obligations. In addition, heavy traveling expenses were entailed, and missionary bishops in New Guinea and many other distant countries had had to furnish their own fares for the first session. If bishops from wealthier countries, they suggested, would help pay the traveling expenses of those who came from great distances, their attendance would be facilitated.

It was widely suggested that the second session should begin on September 1, 1963, and close on December 15. The Pope's severe hemorrhage on the night of November 26 may have influenced his decision, for the following morning Archbishop Felici announced that he had changed the opening date to September 8, 1963. No closing date was announced.

Had the second session begun on May 12, 1963, as originally planned, its first three weeks would have coincided with the last three weeks of Pope John's life.

On the first day of the discussion of the schema on communications media, November 23, the Secretary General announced that the next subject for discussion would be the schema on Church unity, drawn up by the Preparatory Commission for the Oriental Churches. This would be immediately followed by the schema on the Blessed Virgin Mary.

This announcement caused a considerable stir in the Council hall. For on the very same day, another schema, entitled "On the Church," had been distributed, containing a chapter headed "On Ecumenism." The Council Fathers were thus faced with three different documents treating of the same general topic, namely, the promotion of Christian unity. There was, first of all, the schema on Church unity; then the chapter on ecumenism in the schema on the Church drawn up by the Theological Preparatory Commission under the chairmanship of Cardinal Ottaviani; and finally, as some of the Council Fathers were aware, a schema entitled "On Catholic Ecumenism," prepared by the Secretariat for Promoting Christian Unity, under the chairmanship of Cardinal Bea.

Council Fathers active in the ecumenical movement were thoroughly dissatisfied with the chapter on ecumenism prepared by Cardinal Ottaviani's Theological Preparatory Commission. They believed that their best hope of altering this chapter was to have it treated together with the other two schemas on Christian unity. The strategy was to discuss them one after the other, and eventually to have them combined. If a revised common text were issued by a group including the President of the Theological Commission (Cardinal Ottaviani), the President of the Secretariat for Promoting Christian Unity (Cardinal

Bea), and the President of the Commission for the Oriental Churches (Cardinal Cicognani), then the conservative influence on the final text would be greatly diminished.

An even more important target of the liberals was the schema on the Church as a whole. If it could be discussed immediately after the schema on Church unity, then the barrage of criticism which would be directed against it would make it possible to refer it back to the new Theological Commission for revision. And although that Commission was still headed by Cardinal Ottaviani, it also included eight carefully chosen representatives of the European alliance, who would be able to carry great weight.

The liberal element was thus more confident than ever. Not only was it well represented on the Theological Commission, but it had also gained strong support from both African and Latin American Council Fathers, the latter spearheaded by Raul Cardinal Silva Henríquez of Santiago, Chile. At first, the African-born bishops from former French African territories had been somewhat cool toward the French hierarchy, being anxious to avoid any semblance of colonial subservience, but that attitude rapidly wore off in the heat of debate, and their strong cultural ties with France prompted many bishops from French-speaking African and Asian countries to support the European alliance. In addition, superiors general and missionary bishops born in the countries which made up the European alliance gave it their support almost without exception. And the alliance also received the support of numerous other missionary bishops and bishops of Latin American countries who were grateful for the very generous financial assistance which they had received from

Cardinal Frings during the preceding years through his two fund-raising agencies, *Misereor* and *Adveniat*. Many of those who used the occasion of the Council to visit Cardinal Frings and thank him personally found themselves joining the alliance.

The success of the alliance strategy became apparent on November 26, at the twenty-seventh General Congregation, only three days after the original order of business had been announced. On that day, the Secretary General announced that, after the schema on Church unity, and before the schema on the Blessed Virgin Mary, the Council would discuss the chapter on ecumenism prepared by the Theological Commission, the schema on Catholic ecumenism prepared by the Secretariat for Promoting Christian Unity, and the schema on the Church prepared by the Theological Commission.

Cardinal Cicognani introduced the schema on Church unity at the same meeting. "We wish," said the Cardinal, "once again to profess solemnly the fraternal ties by which we are united with the separated Orientals in Christ," and he asked them to "reflect that once we were united, we were one." The purpose of the present document, he explained, was "to prepare the way for unity in the truth and charity of Christ." He also pointed out that the schema stressed the religious and historical importance of the Oriental rites, and made no reference to past dissensions. "Never in the annals of the Church has so much been said about the unity of the Church as in modern times," he said, "and never since the time of Pope Leo XIII has so much been done to bring it about."

The separated Orthodox Churches today have some

157 million members around the world. The Oriental Churches, as distinct from the Orthodox, belong to the Catholic Church. "Oriental Churches" is a term endorsed by long usage to designate those members of the Catholic hierarchy and laity who follow Eastern Rites.

In drawing up the schema, Cardinal Cicognani said, the Commission had sought to bear in mind not only the theological differences between the Churches, but also the manner in which the Orthodox Churches were accustomed to express their theology. Representatives of all six of the principal Eastern Rites in the Oriental Churches had therefore assisted in drawing up the text. The Preparatory Commission for the Oriental Churches had in fact represented twenty-four countries and sixteen religious communities, and also the main subdivisions of the five principal Eastern Rites—the Alexandrian, Antiochian, Byzantine, Chaldaean, and Armenian rites.

The first speaker to take the floor was Cardinal Liénart. He asserted that the schema contained grave defects in both content and form, and should be rejected. Cardinal Ruffini of Palermo and Michael Cardinal Browne, Vice-President of the Theological Commission, felt that the schema should be included in the larger schema on the Church. Cardinal Bacci of the Roman Curia expressed his support of the schema as it stood and proposed only slight corrections.

On the following day, a number of speakers asked that the three documents dealing with Christian unity should be combined by the three bodies that had drafted them, and that the new schema should be submitted for discussion at the second session. The schema was criticized for not referring to mistakes and faults of the Catholic Church which had contributed to the original separation. It was pointed out, moreover, that the wording was so harsh and arrogant, and manifested so little of the true ecumenical spirit, that the very form of the schema might offend the separated brethren at whom it was aimed. Three speakers called for its outright rejection.

At the next meeting, several speakers proposed a complete revision of the schema. Some said that it made far too many concessions; others maintained that it was much too authoritarian. One speaker said that the schema should not include an admission of fault on the part of the Western Church. Auxiliary Bishop Ancel of Lyons retorted that the admission of mistakes was not a renunciation of the truth, for which he was loudly applauded. Another speaker said that the tone of the decree should reflect the respect due to the Orthodox Churches by reason of their large numbers, ancient traditions, the evangelization which they had fostered, and the frequent martyrdom that they had suffered. The same speaker wanted the schema to emphasize that the religious, historical and liturgical heritage of the East was a heritage of the Church as a whole, without distinction of East and West.

Speaker after speaker asked that the three documents be combined in a single schema.

On November 30, the fourth day of debate, the Council Fathers were still divided. The meeting ended with a near-unanimous decision in favor of cloture of the debate. On the following day, by a vote of 2,068 to 36, the Council decided that the three documents should be combined in one schema.

71

What the First Session Achieved

The Council took up the discussion of the all-important schema on the Church at its thirty-first General Congregation, on December 1, exactly one week before the closing of the first session. The first speaker was Cardinal Ottaviani, who, as President of the Theological Commission, wished to make some introductory remarks.

Only three days before, he had pointed out that it would be impossible to complete the discussion of the thirty-six-page schema on the Church in the few days left, and he had therefore asked the Council Fathers to discuss the shorter six-page schema on the Blessed Virgin Mary, as had originally been announced. There would have been no trouble in completing the discussion of that schema, he said, and the happy result would have been that the Council Fathers, "with the assistance of Our Lady," would then have concluded the first session "in union and harmony." But his plea had been ignored.

The Cardinal proceeded to stress the caliber of the membership of the Theological Preparatory Commission, which had prepared the schema on the Church. It had consisted of thirty-one members, with thirty-six consultants from fifteen countries. Most of these men were university professors or professors in major ecclesiastical institutions of learning in different parts of the world. Each had several publications of outstanding importance to his credit, and some of these were used as textbooks in seminaries and universities. As a result, the Theological Preparatory Commission had considered itself intellectually equipped to carry out the weighty task of drawing up a schema on the Church. It had, moreover, borne in mind the pastoral aspect of the Council.

That morning, fourteen Council Fathers came to the microphone. Six of them called for revisions so complete as to be tantamount to outright rejection of the text as it stood. The schema was criticized for being too theoretical, for being too legalistic, for identifying the Mystical Body purely and simply with the Catholic Church, for referring only condescendingly to the laity, for insisting excessively on the rights and authority of the hierarchy, and for lacking a charitable, missionary, and ecumenical approach.

One of the speakers, Bishop De Smedt, summed up his criticism in three epithets: the schema, he said, was guilty of triumphalism, clericalism, and legalism.

The last speaker that day was Bishop Luigi Carli of Segni, Italy. He maintained that certain Council Fathers had carried their ecumenical preoccupations to excess. It was no longer possible, he charged, to speak about Our Lady; no one might be called heretical; no one might use the expression "Church militant"; and it was no longer proper to call attention to the inherent powers of the Catholic Church.

The days that followed witnessed much disagreement among the Council Fathers. Some speakers affirmed the pastoral character of the schema; others denied it. Some said that sufficient importance was given to the laity; others said that the treatment of the subject was too superficial. Valerian Cardinal Gracias of Bombay called for more delicacy in the treatment of Church-state relations. "The text as it stands," he said, "is an open invitation to governments to martyr us." Cardinal Bea objected to the manner in which Sacred Scripture was quoted, and he wanted pastoral preoccupations to be apparent from the text itself, and not only from some parenthetical exhortation added to the text.

Cardinal Bacci of the Roman Curia expressed belief that the Council Fathers were in accord on the doctrinal substance of the document, and that the schema would prove satisfactory after some corrections had been made in the style. Bishop Giulio Barbetta of the Roman Curia took issue with Bishop De Smedt, insisting that the text was neither triumphal nor clerical in tone, nor legalistic.

Maronite Bishop Michael Doumith of Sarba, Lebanon, a member of the Theological Commission, severely criticized the chapter on bishops. He said that, just as a mother gives her child a toy with a thousand warnings not to break it, so, too, "they give us, with a thousand cautions, a concept of the episcopacy." He could not erase from his mind, he said, the painful impression that bishops, according to the schema, were no more than functionaries of the Pope. Bestowal of episcopal consecration on those who were not in charge of a diocese, he maintained, resulted in functionalism and secularization in the episcopacy. Cardinal Alfrink pointed out, in that connection, that some one third of the bishops in the Church were titular, and that no reference was made to them in the schema. (Titular bishops have no diocese of their own.)

On the first day of the debate on the schema, Cardinal Alfrink had called for a careful coordination of texts in order to avoid useless repetition in the Council agenda. This proposal, whose adoption was to alter profoundly the organizational structure of the Council, as well as the future form and content of the schemas, was supported in the following three meetings by Cardinals Léger, Suenens, and Montini.

On December 1, the Secretary General had opened the meeting by saying that the health of the Holy Father was showing improvement—an announcement greeted with loud and prolonged applause. At noon on December 5, Pope John appeared at his window to recite the *Angelus*, and many Council Fathers left the basilica early in order to see him. He spoke briefly, gave his blessing, and later said that their red robes had made them appear like a gigantic flame in the sun.

On the same day, December 5, carrying out the suggestions of the four cardinals, Pope John founded a new Coordinating Commission "to coordinate and direct the work of the Council." It was to be composed exclusively of cardinals, with Cardinal Cicognani as President, and Cardinals Liénart, Döpfner, Suenens, Confalonieri, Spellman, and Urbani as members. The European alliance was represented by three members on this powerful six-member Commission, and therefore had control of 50 percent of the seats. It was growing in influence and prestige, because it had had control of only 30 percent of the seats in the Council Presidency since the beginning of the Council.

In addition to founding the Coordinating Commission, Pope John under the same date approved the norms which were to govern the Council in the interval between the first and second sessions. The first of these norms stipulated that, during that period, all the schemas should "be subjected once more to examination and improvement" by the Council commissions. This implied, of course, that not only the schema on the Church would have to be revised, but the dogmatic constitutions as well which had been attacked by Father Schillebeeckx and the Dutch bishops.

All the norms were read to the Council Fathers at the morning meeting of December 6, and they were recognized by the liberals as yet another victory over the Curia.

The Council Fathers were surprised to see Pope John walk into the Council hall at midday on Friday, December 7, the last business meeting of the session. He recited the *Angelus* with them and addressed them at length. He was back again the following day to take part in the solemn ceremonies which marked the close of the first session. He congratulated the Council Fathers on what they had accomplished, and urged them to be diligent in the work that lay ahead. "The first session," he told them, "was like a slow and solemn introduction to the great work of the Council." It was also understandable, he said, that in such a vast gathering "a few days" should have been needed to arrive at agreement on topics about which "in all charity and with good reason there existed sharply diverging views." But even this manifestation of differences had had a providential place in the triumph of truth, "for it has shown to all the world the holy liberty that the sons of God enjoy in the Church."

The Pope pointed out that modern communications made it possible for the intensive work on the preparation and revision of schemas to continue in the interval before the second session. He asked each bishop, "though preoccupied with pastoral administration, to continue to study and investigate the schemas that have been distributed, and also whatever else may yet be sent. In this way, the session which will begin in the month of September of next year . . . will proceed more surely, more steadily and with greater speed." If preparations went forward seriously, there were grounds for hope that the Ecumenical Council might end at Christmas, 1963, which would be four hundred years after the conclusion of the Council of Trent.

The German theologian Father Joseph Ratzinger called the absence of any approved Council text at the end of the first session "the great, astonishing, and genuinely positive result of the first session." The fact that no text had gained approval was evidence, he said, of "the strong reaction against the spirit behind the preparatory work." This he called "the truly epoch-making character of the Council's first session."

Several days before the end of the first session, Father Hans Küng, a Swiss theologian on the Catholic Theological Faculty of the University of Tübingen, Germany, was invited to speak at the U.S. Bishops' Press Panel. In his address, he mentioned the fact that Pope John, when asked in a private conversation why he had convoked the Council, had gone to his window, opened it, and said, "To let some fresh air into the Church." Father Küng asserted jubilantly that what had once been the dream of an *avant-garde* group in the Church had "spread and permeated the entire atmosphere of the Church, due to the Council." If for some reason the Council itself were to come to an end, the movement in the Church would not end, he said, and another Council would soon have to be called.

Father Küng was asked to enumerate some of the

achievements of the first session. In reply, he said that "many of us" had feared that unfortunate statements might be officially issued by the Council on matters of dogma and ecumenism. So far, however, "all such attempts have been rejected." This spirit in the Council had brought about a change of atmosphere throughout the Church. "No one who was here for the Council will go back home as he came. I myself never expected so many bold and explicit statements from the bishops on the Council floor."

Father Küng called the rejection of the schema on the sources of revelation "a great step in the right direction. It was something all of us in Germany had hoped for. But being a very small minority, we did not dream it possible." In conclusion, he said that "perhaps the most decisive outcome of the first session is the realization on the part of the bishops that they, and not merely the Roman Curia, make up the Church."

Bishop Sergio Méndez Arceo of Cuernavaca, Mexico, said at the end of the session, "It has been a most successful Council." He noted that some Council Fathers had complained that there was too much talking and even too much repetition on the Council floor. "But I feel," he explained, "that this was necessary, if we were all to find out what the others' thoughts were. St. Peter's basilica, where our meetings were held, was like a giant pressure cooker which rapidly and profoundly transformed the outlook of the bishops of the entire world."

Rejection of schemas and rapid transformations of outlook were the earmarks of the first session of Vatican II.

THE SECOND SESSION

September 29 – December 4, 1963

Preparing for the Second Session

If the words of Father Küng were true—that "no one who was here for the Council will go back as he came"—they were no more true for anyone than for the German-speaking bishops and their theologians. They had come to the first session of the Council, hoping that they might win some concessions. They returned home, conscious that they had achieved complete victory. And they were confident that numberless other victories were yet to come.

When early in the first session the Council Fathers elected to office seventeen of the twenty-one candidates for Council Commissions proposed by the more than two hundred United States bishops, it almost seemed as though the Council was looking to them for leadership. But as the weeks of the first session passed, the American bishops gave the impression of being too retiring and too disunited to take over leadership. Was it because their *periti* had prepared no program for them? There had been nothing retiring or disunited, however, about the bishops from the Rhine countries. They had shown at the first session how important it was to have a specific text to fight for. The schema on the liturgy had been such a text, and the alliance was able to operate effectively because it knew beforehand what it wanted, and what it did not want.

The deadline for amendments to the schema on the Church was February 28, 1963, and the German-speaking bishops and theologians, for their part, set to work immediately. They decided to hold a meeting of all German-speaking Council fathers at Munich on February 5 and 6 to prepare a detailed analysis of the schema and draw up practical suggestions for its revision. Representatives from other European alliance countries were invited to attend the meeting: among others, Bishop Jan van Dodewaard of Haarlem, Holland; Coadjutor Bishop Leon Elchinger of Strasbourg, France; and Father John Schütte, Superior General of the Divine Word Missionaries, who would be well placed to communicate the views of the alliance to the conference of superiors general in Rome. All this organizational activity centered around Cardinal Döpfner, who was also a member of the Coordinating Commission of the Council, and who communicated to that meeting the decisions arrived at by that Commission at its first session in the Vatican, from January 21 to 27. Two significant decisions made at that session had been to treat the schema on the Blessed Virgin Mary independently of the schema on the Church, and to reduce the latter to four chapters.

The Munich meeting produced a detailed criticism of the schema on the Church, as well as a substitute schema of forty-six articles. It was divided into five chapters, as Cardinal Suenens had suggested, rather than into four chapters, as the Coordinating Commission had decreed. The analysis and substitute schema were sent to Pope John XXIII and Cardinal Ottaviani, President of the Theological Commission, together with a special introduction. This stated that the analysis listed reasons "why it seems that the existing schema must undergo a thorough revision." It stated further that, in drawing up the substitute schema, the German-speaking Fathers had continually borne in mind the general norms laid down by the Pope on December 5, 1962, at the end of the first session. Those norms had insisted "especially upon the pastoral aspect" of Council decrees. The introduction likewise stated that the German-speaking Council Fathers had also borne in mind the directives of the Coordinating Commission, in particular, "that a connection be shown with the First Vatican Council, that the role of the Supreme Pontiff and his primacy should be recalled and should be presented at the same time from an ecumenical point of view, and that the significance of episcopal collegiality and of the episcopacy itself should be placed in a clear light."

Each of the Council Fathers in Austria and Germany received copies of these documents from Cardinal Döpfner under date of February 16. In addition, they received a commentary on the substitute schema, together with a bibliography of some thirty-five titles of theological works in German and French. The introductory sentence of the commentary explained that the purpose of the schema was to avoid certain shortcomings of the schema on the Church drawn up by the Theological Preparatory Commission. The substitute schema was much shorter, and sought to be more pastoral in tone and to correspond to the spirit of ecumenism. "In no way does it intend to keep silent about or to conceal Catholic truths, not even those which Protestants either doubt or deny. However, it always tries to give consideration to Protestant objections, but without, of course, treating those objections explicitly."

The German-speaking Council Fathers were now well prepared for the opening debate of the second session, the schema on the Church. Still further preparations were to be made at a second conference held in August of the same year, at Fulda.

It is worth noting that the opening words of the substitute schema, "*Lumen gentium*" ("Light of nations"), taken from Pope John's address of September 11, 1962, were subsequently adopted as the opening words and official title of the Council's dogmatic constitution on the Church.

THE MECHANICS OF THE LITURGICAL COMMISSION

In the latter half of November and early December 1962, toward the end of the first session, the Liturgical Commission presented a revised introduction and lengthy first chapter of its schema to the plenary Council assembly for twenty-eight separate votes. Contrary to general expectations, there was very little opposition. The largest number of negative votes on a single ballot was 150. The average number of negative votes was forty. And when a vote was taken on the chapter as a whole, on December 7, only eleven of the 2,018 Council Fathers cast negative votes.

Some credited this near-unanimous acceptance to the close attention that the Liturgical Commission had given to the observations made by Council Fathers during the debate. Moreover, before submitting the drafts to a vote, the Liturgical Commission had presented an exhaustive printed report filling five booklets to each of the Council Fathers explaining in detail what it had done, and why.

Elated at this reaction, the Liturgical Commission revised the text of the remaining chapters of the schema, and gathered in Rome for a working session starting April

23, 1963. Each subcommission had to report to the full Commission on the work it had done, and the full Commission then examined the proposed changes line by line and word by word.

I asked one of the members of the Liturgical Commission, Archbishop Paul Hallinan of Atlanta, Georgia, who was in Rome for the meeting, if he would give a press conference on the procedure used by the Commission in conducting its business. He agreed readily, and met the press on May 7 in the Columbus Hotel.

"What I should like especially to point out," he said, "is the careful consideration given by the Liturgical Commission to each statement made by the Council Fathers last fall. We examined each of the statements, and divided them roughly into four categories." The first category included "proposals already covered by the schema itself, or by previous amendments to the schema." The second covered "proposals which our Liturgical Commission has passed on to other commissions where the matter in question is treated more directly." The third covered proposals which the Commission considered too detailed, "and these have been referred to a post-conciliar commission to be set up after the Council ends." The fourth and final category included "all real amendments to the liturgy schema, and these are what we have processed in our subcommission and Commission meetings."

Archbishop Hallinan then explained the functioning of the Liturgical Commission and its subcommissions. The discussion on the liturgy in the Council hall had extended from October 22 to November 13, 1962, and during that time each Council Father had been free to present whatever proposals or observations he wished. He could do so either orally or in writing. "This material filled some ten mimeographed volumes, and ran to nearly a thousand pages," the Archbishop said. "The proposals on the Sacrifice of the Mass alone filled nearly 250 pages."

Throughout the session, the Commission had met daily. As soon as a Council Father had spoken in the Council hall, the General Secretariat would forward the text of his address to the Liturgical Commission. "Basically, the processing of proposals was the same last fall as during this current session of the Liturgical Commission," the Archbishop said.

Each of the thirteen subcommissions included both Council Fathers and *periti*. After a particular subcommission had examined the Council proposals for which it was responsible, it would formulate the corresponding amendments and draw up a report explaining why they had been so formulated. "This report was then read before a full session of the Liturgical Commission, and all Commission members, as well as the *periti*, took part in the discussion that followed." Archbishop Hallinan was chairman of the Subcommission on the Sacraments, and said that his first report and the accompanying discussion had lasted two and a half days. But after the Subcommission had revised the text once again, the next report and discussion took only a half hour.

At the time of the press conference, the Liturgical Commission had already been in session for two full weeks. "All discussions regarding the amendments proposed by Council Fathers on the Mass, the Sacraments,

86

and the Divine Office have now been completed," said Archbishop Hallinan. "This week we are voting on the final form of the amendments which are to be presented to the Council Fathers for their vote in September." Once the Council Fathers accepted the amendments, as well as the individual chapters, by the required two-thirds majority, "all that remains is a final, formal vote taken in the presence of the Holy Father in a public meeting. Then, with the assent of the Holy Father, the constitution on the Sacred Liturgy will be promulgated and will become law for the entire Catholic Church. At this point, the Liturgical Commission of the Second Vatican Council will have completed its work."

The Archbishop maintained that there was "very good reason for the optimism and the confidence that has accompanied this three-week period on the part of all the members of the Commission. . . . In the first place, we have been assured by Cardinal Larraona that the Holy Father himself is very pleased with the work of the Liturgical Commission. In an audience about three weeks ago, he expressed his confidence that the work done by the Liturgical Commission and the Council Fathers was a real step toward the *aggiornamento*. This naturally is a cause of confidence and satisfaction to us all."

He then referred to the "very democratic style" in which Arcadio Cardinal Larraona, President of the Liturgical Commission, conducted its meetings. His policy of giving everyone at all times full opportunity to speak freely and develop his own thinking had had its effect. The Commission members had instructed one another. "You cannot help but learn from men who are in totally different environments—in Africa, behind the Iron Curtain, in Latin America, and elsewhere. It is certainly true to conclude," he went on, "that this Commission has worked in a truly conciliar way. It has been international, it has been open, it has been free, and it has certainly consisted of a group of dedicated men."

Archbishop Hallinan said that the optimism of the members of the Liturgical Commission had also been caused in large part by the enthusiasm that the Council Fathers themselves had shown in the closing days of the Council, when they voted "with almost unanimity on behalf of the renewal—the *aggiornamento*. And now this has carried over. You could feel it in the working of the Commission."

Some thirty to forty *periti* had been assigned to the Commission. "These men," said the Archbishop, "represent probably the finest minds in the liturgical world today in terms of research, in terms of hard work, in terms of zeal, in terms of experimentation and everything else. They come from all different continents. And to have this group here was just like having a library shelf with the best liturgical books in the world. Only these were not the books; these were the authors. It was a very remarkable privilege to have these men here."

Father Frederick McManus, a professor of canon law at the Catholic University of America, and long associated with the liturgical movement in the United States, sat beside the Archbishop during the press conference. The Archbishop introduced him to the press as "our American *peritus* in this field, one of the outstanding liturgists in the United States, a man who has the confidence of the bishops and of the laity in the very fast growing movement within the United States toward the liturgical revival."

THE LAST MONTHS OF POPE JOHN'S LIFE

After the first session, in order to prove to the world that he was in good health again, Pope John XXIII paid a visit to Bambino Gesú Hospital on the Janiculum Hill, where he spoke with the sick children and addressed the nurses, Sisters, and other hospital personnel: "As you can see, I am in perfect health, although I am not in shape to run a race or take part in some other competitive sport. But I have, thanks be to God, the excellent use of every sense and of my entire body, and so am able to admire here this imposing spectacle of charity and innocence."

On the feast of the Epiphany, January 6, 1963, Pope John XXIII issued a lengthy letter to all Council Fathers throughout the world. He told them that the picture of them all in St. Peter's basilica, gathered in Council, was constantly before his eyes. And nothing was dearer to him than to be occupied "in thought and word with the serious and sacred subject of the Council." He reminded them that the period between January 6 and September 8, 1963, when the Council was to resume its labors, "must be considered as a true continuation of the work to be accomplished by the Council."

It also was their sacred duty, he told them, "not only for each one of them to be present at the coming meetings in the Vatican basilica, but also to be most closely united in spirit for those eight months with all their brothers in the episcopate. They must show themselves prompt in replying to letters whenever the Commission headed by our Cardinal Secretary of State should ask anything of them. Each and every one must give close study to what has been sent to him, and must fulfill his obligations regarding correspondence. As a result of such alacrity, the labors of the Council will without doubt progress wisely, and this great task, toward which the eyes of all are turned, will hasten to its desired conclusion."

Pope John insisted that for the bishops "every matter connected with the Council must be regarded as the apple of their eye." They should do everything "quickly" and "properly." In studying the Council documents, they should use the services of priests "outstanding in knowledge and virtue."

The Coordinating Commission met in the Vatican under the presidency of the Secretary of State from January 21 to January 27. On January 28, the Pope received all the members of this Commission in audience, and also some other Council officials. He told them how eager he was to keep his finger on the pulse of the Council at every stage of its development. He was satisfied with what had been done so far, and with the decisions adopted by the Coordinating Commission. As a result of these, he said, there was hope "that the Council, already off to such a good start, will very quickly be able to reach all its goals." He stressed the importance of organic unity in the Council agenda, and said that the work of preparation "must go forward swiftly."

There was intense activity among the commissions and subcommissions during the early part of 1963. Commissions had all been divided into subcommissions, and the subcommission members, through correspondence, were able to settle upon texts which they then presented at plenary sessions of the commissions concerned when they convened in Rome. Seven commissions and the Secretariat of Cardinal Bea held meetings in Rome in the period between February 20 and April 1.

The Coordinating Commission, which supervised and coordinated the activity of these commissions, held a number of meetings in the Vatican starting on March 25. On March 28, it examined the first two chapters of the schema on the Church, and also the revised schema on ecumenism. The latter had been prepared by a special joint commission composed of members from the Theological Commission, the Commission for Oriental Churches, and the Secretariat for Promoting Christian Unity. The presidents, vice-presidents, and secretaries of these two Commissions and of the Secretariat had therefore been invited to attend the meeting.

Pope John decided to attend the meeting, too, and walked in at 6 P.M., accompanied by Cardinal Cicognani and Archbishop Felici. He had been receiving daily reports on the work of the Coordinating Commission, and he expressed great pleasure at all that had been accomplished. He then informed those present that on that day, March 28, he had founded a Pontifical Commission for the Revision of the Code of Canon Law. As far back as January 25, 1959, when Pope John first announced that there would be an Ecumenical Council, he had also announced that the code of canon law would have to be revised. The Pope presided over the meeting for a while, then once more exhorted all present to continue their work with enthusiasm, repeating his hopes that the Council would bear rich fruit. After imparting his Apostolic blessing, he left the hall.

The next major event in the pontificate of Pope John, now slowly drawing to a close, was his signing of his eighth encyclical, *Pacem in Terris* ("Peace on Earth"), on April 9, 1963.

On Easter Sunday, April 14, a very disturbing close-up photograph of the Pope appeared on the front page of *L'Osservatore Romano*. It had been taken during the Good Friday afternoon service in St. Peter's, and it showed him bending down to kiss the crucifix during the Veneration of the Cross. From the expression on the Pope's face, he appeared to be in terrible agony. But the only answer given at the Vatican to inquiries was that the Pope had been very "fatigued" during the ceremony. As I later learned, the Pope's immediate associates had been fearful that he might not get through the strenuous Holy Week services, but on Holy Saturday his condition had improved.

Some days later, on April 22, Pope John approved the texts of twelve schemas and ordered that they should be sent to the Council Fathers. They were the product of the numerous meetings held by the Coordinating Commission and the Council commissions. Pope John had been relentless in his insistence on speed. He had given no one any rest. He knew that his life was running out, and he worked all the more feverishly to move his Council ahead.

On April 25, I had an appointment with Dr. Luciano Casimirri, the Director of the Vatican Press Office, who told me—unofficially, and with great sadness—that the Pope was a very sick man. Consequently immediate preparations had to be made for press coverage of his final illness and death, and for the subsequent conclave. Once his condition became known, Dr. Casimirri said, reporters would flock to Rome to report the Pope's death and the election of a new Pope. He asked, since he did not speak English fluently, and since English-language reporters were always the largest group, whether I might be able to assist him in case of need.

Later that day, from another source, I learned that the Pope was hemorrhaging every other day, and his condition was rapidly deteriorating.

On April 30, Cardinal Cicognani wrote to all the Council Fathers to say that he was doing everything in his power to have the first twelve schemas sent to them as soon as possible. In the letter he added that by the end of June he hoped to have another set of schemas ready for distribution by the Secretary General. "I have the honor to inform you," he wrote, "that the Most Holy Father is extremely concerned that these schemas should be given serious study. Then, if you judge that certain things still need reconsideration, you are invited to send your observations, advice, and amendments, written clearly and in proper form, to the General Secretariat of the Council, before the end of July. In this way, the Council commissions will have sufficient time to study these considerations attentively and to prepare their reports, which will accompany the schemas when they are presented in amended form to the General Congregation."

As May advanced, Pope John could not understand why the twelve texts which he had approved on April 22 were not yet ready for mailing. Not even half of them were ready. Archbishop Felici then felt himself obliged to send a letter to all the Council Fathers on May 8, just one week after Cardinal Cicognani's letter, informing them that the first six schemas would be sent "within a few days."

The very next day, May 9, Cardinal Cicognani sent yet another letter to all the Council Fathers, containing this one sentence: "His Holiness Pope John XXIII desires to inform the Fathers of the Second Vatican Council that he has himself attentively examined the schemas which are being sent to the same Council Fathers, and intends to examine them anew after they have been discussed by the Council Fathers, before giving them his final approval."

Pope John gave no one any rest. He had one driving desire: to see the Second Vatican Council complete its work. He wanted to be sure that the documents would be in the hands of the Council Fathers, so that there should be no excuse for the Council's not continuing.

He forced himself to go through the ceremonies connected with the reception of the Balzan Peace Prize on May 11. On the following day, he paid a state visit to the Quirinal. Two days later, a copy of *Pacem in Terris*, autographed by Pope John, was personally delivered by Cardinal Suenens to Secretary General U Thant of the United Nations in New York.

On May 18, I met Dr. Casimirri again, and he said that Pope John's condition was "very bad."

Pope John wrote another long letter, on May 20, to all the bishops of the world, announcing that he would make his annual spiritual retreat, in recollection and solitude, during the Pentecostal novena from May 25 to June 2,

Pentecost Sunday. He explained that he was informing the Council Fathers that he was going into spiritual retreat "so that you may accompany us in those days with your prayers and with your recollection." He had chosen this time to make his retreat "because, as is our custom, we are acting promptly on a good inspiration."

On May 21, Archbishop Felici finally mailed the first six schemas. On the next day, May 22, Pope John was scheduled to give one of his usual Wednesday audiences in St. Peter's basilica at 10 A.M. At 9:55 A.M., it was announced that the Pope would not come to the basilica, but would bless everyone from his window at 10:30. Pope John, I learned, had been hemorrhaging again, and had received blood transfusions throughout the night.

The following Sunday morning, the Pope told those around his bedside that he wanted to go to his window at noon as usual to bless the crowds in St. Peter's Square, even though his spiritual retreat had begun. His doctors, however, forbade this, saying that he must refrain from all physical exertion. The next day, Italian priests in Rome were quoting Gustavo Cardinal Testa, who had access to the Pope's room, as saying that blood had issued from the Pope's mouth. Informed sources said that he was receiving blood transfusions every four hours.

On May 28, when Cardinal Cicognani told him that the entire world was praying for him, the Pope smiled and, after a short silence, said, "Since the whole world is praying for the sick Pope, it is only natural that some intention should be given to this prayer. If God should wish the sacrifice of the life of the Pope, then may that sacrifice succeed in obtaining abundant favors for the Ecumenical

Council, for the Holy Church, and for mankind, which longs for peace."

On Thursday, May 30, Pope John said to his doctor, "They say that I have a tumor. But this means nothing, as long as God's will is done. I hope to bring the Council to a conclusion, and to see peace in the world."

Near midnight on the same day, the final crisis set in. On being informed of his condition on the following day, Pope John requested that he be given the Last Sacraments immediately. His confessor came to his bedside, and then brought him the Holy Viaticum. At his own request, Pope John received the holy anointings, and asked his confessor to remain near his bed with the Blessed Sacrament, while he said a few words. This he did in a clear and strong voice, once again offering his life for the successful outcome of the Second Vatican Council, and for peace among men. He said, too, that he wanted all Council Fathers throughout the world to know that the great work which had been started would certainly be completed.

After addressing all of those around him, he turned to his nephew, Monsignor Giovanni Baptista Roncalli, and called him to his side. "Look, you arrive here, and you find me in bed! The doctors say that I am suffering from a stomach malady. But let us hope that everything will turn out for the best, and that soon I shall be able again to dedicate myself to the Council and to the Church."

On Friday afternoon, the long vigil began in St. Peter's Square. Day and night on Friday, Saturday, Pentecost Sunday and Monday, the crowds waited and prayed. Then, on Monday evening, June 3, at 7:49 P.M., Pope John died.

"The Council!" he had said. "God knows that with simplicity I have opened the smallness of my soul to the greatness of this inspiration. Will he allow me to finish it? Should he do so, may he be blessed. And if he does not allow me to finish it? . . . Then I shall watch its joyful conclusion from heaven, where I hope—rather, where I am certain—the Divine Mercy will draw me."

A SECRETARIAT FOR NON-CHRISTIAN RELIGIONS

On Tuesday, April 2, 1963, Archbishop Zoa of Yaoundé, Cameroun, a member of the Council Commission on the Missions, gave a press conference in which he stated his views on the schema on the missions.

He had felt, he said, that the first session of the Council had had only two main preoccupations: a pastoral preoccupation, causing it to study ways whereby the Church might better foster the spiritual growth of its own members; and an ecumenical preoccupation, dictating what was to be done or omitted in order to improve relations with other Christian bodies. What seemed to have been forgotten was that the Catholic Church was by definition a missionary Church. Its message, said the Archbishop, was not only to its own members, or to other Christians, but to all men.

Pondering over the Archbishop's words that night, in a dimly lit chapel, I thought of the immense good that had been accomplished by the Secretariat for Promoting Christian Unity, and wondered if a similar secretariat might not also be founded for non-Christian religions.

There were over a billion members of Judaism, Islam, Brahmanism, Vedaism, Hinduism, Jainism, Buddhism, Confucianism, Taoism and Shintoism. Such a new secretariat might initiate and foster dialogue with these great world religions with as much success as the already existing Secretariat for Promoting Christian Unity had done for non-Catholic Christian churches. The more I thought about it, the more necessary such a secretariat seemed. And should there not be observers from these non-Christian religions at the Council?

Early the next morning I telephoned Archbishop Zoa, believing that his reaction would be significant, since he had so many Muslims in his archdiocese. When he favored the project, the next question was, could a bishop be found who might be willing to launch the idea at a press conference?

It so happened that Bishop Anthony Thijssen of Larantuka, Indonesia, was spending a few days in Rome in the same house as I. We discussed the idea of another secretariat, and he told me that, while lecturing in Northern Europe in the previous weeks, he had advocated inviting observers from non-Christian religions to the next ecumenical council, although not to the present one.

Chinese-born Thomas Cardinal Tien was also in Rome at this time, and reacted very favorably to the proposal. He felt that, since the major non-Christian religions were mainly concentrated in Asia, the idea should not be launched by an Indian bishop, as planned, but by a European. "In the East we have a saying," he said, "that you should not invite yourself." He also believed that the Vatican would more readily accept the proposal if it were made by a European, and he agreed to make a statement to the press in support of the secretariat, once a Council Father had come out publicly in favor of it.

Bishop Thijssen was then contacted again and, after further consultation, agreed to hold a press conference on the subject on April 6. The conference was attended by representatives of all the international news agencies with Rome bureaus, as well as by members of the embassies of India, Sudan, and Saudi Arabia.

Bishop Thijssen explained that he was Dutch by birth, but had been an Indonesian citizen since 1949. "Indonesia is known all over the world for its religious tolerance," he said. "And I myself have many personal friends whom I respect highly, who are Muslims and Hindus." The Bishop said that he would like to see "a special secretariat founded in Rome for the major non-Christian religions of the world." The advantage of such a secretariat would not be one-sided. "We Catholics, for example, could learn much from the liturgy, culture, and philosophy of these non-Christian religions." He was not proposing some kind of religious syncretism, he said. "No, not at all! We shall all simply come to understand each other better."

The Bishop believed that the world would welcome the establishment of such a secretariat. He felt that it was in line with the aspirations of the major non-Christian religions of the world, and in harmony with the spirit of Pope John XXIII, who had said that he wished to be regarded as "a true and sincere friend of all nations."

Bishop Thijssen was asked to comment on a statement by a Buddhist priest—reported in a Tokyo paper on January 18, 1963—to the effect that, while the Ecumenical

Council would do much to promote religious and international harmony, the presence of observers from Buddhism and the other great non-Christian religions "would make the Council even more effective as an instrument of world peace and religious cordiality." The Bishop replied that, while appreciating the views of the Buddhist priest, he personally considered the proposal premature in relation to the current Council, which was concerned with the internal reform of the Church and unity among Christians. "There would be little of very direct interest" to non-Christian observers, he said. He was deeply convinced, however, "that the formation of a special secretariat for the major non-Christian religions would be of inestimable worldwide value, and would indirectly enrich the religious life of all of us."

Asked by the representative of the Middle East News Agency whether he had already spoken to the Pope on the subject, the Bishop said that he had not, and that he had wished first to get the reaction of the press, which had its finger on the pulse of the world. He said, too, that he would appreciate the assistance of the press in making the idea known throughout the world.

Another reporter asked the Bishop whether he knew of other Council Fathers who might favor the plan. The Bishop answered that he had spoken on the subject in general terms during the Council with the two Jesuit Indonesian archbishops of Semarang and Djakarta, as well as with Bishop van Bekkum of Ruteng. "All three were in favor of the idea," he said.

Immediately after the press conference, Bishop Thijssen attempted to speak on the matter with Gregorio Cardinal

Agagianian, at the headquarters of the Congregation for the Propagation of the Faith. In the Cardinal's absence, he was received by Archbishop Pietro Sigismondi, who expressed his pleasure that the Bishop had spoken to the press about a special secretariat for non-Christian religions. He assured the Bishop that he would inform Cardinal Agagianian about it, and that the Cardinal would likewise be very pleased about the press conference. Bishop Thijssen explained to Archbishop Sigismondi that he had not advocated inviting representatives of the non-Christian religions to the Council hall, since so much of the terminology used there would be incomprehensible to them. They would derive more benefit, he felt, from explanations given by the special secretariat outside Council meetings, if the secretariat were to function in conjunction with the Council at all.

On April 8, before leaving Rome for Madrid, Cardinal Tien issued a statement for the press in which he made further suggestions. After pledging his full support for Bishop Thijssen's proposal, he said, "It is most important that the Catholic Church come to understand better the major non-Christian religions of the world, and that the non-Christian religions come to understand the Catholic Church better." This could best be done "by establishing a secretariat where outstanding scholars of non-Christian religions could meet and confer with outstanding scholars of the Catholic Church." As to the date of its establishment, the Cardinal said, "I would like to see it established very soon, so that, when the next session of the Ecumenical Council opens in September, we may have here in Rome representatives of the major non-Christian religions." He wanted such representatives to be allowed to attend a few meetings inside St. Peter's basilica, but added that he felt it would be of little value for them to be present regularly.

The two statements of Cardinal Tien and Bishop Thijssen came in the wake of Pope John's encyclical *Pacem in Terris*. Many commentators looked upon the proposed secretariat as a practical means of implementing Pope John's desire for better international understanding among "all men of good will."

Father Edmund Farhat, a Lebanese priest in charge of the daily newscast in Arabic on Vatican Radio, had attended Bishop Thijssen's press conference and had become as interested in the project as I. We both felt that no cardinal in the Church was better qualified to head such a secretariat than Cardinal König of Vienna. He was internationally known as an expert on non-Christian religions, had written copiously on the subject, and had at one time taught comparative religion at the university level. We decided to seek out an opportunity to put the idea to him.

All action in the matter was suspended on June 3, with the death of Pope John XXIII. In the weeks that followed, the great question was whether the Council would continue at all.

The world did not have long to wait. On June 22, 1963, the day following his election, Pope Paul VI delivered his first radio message to the city of Rome and to the world, and stated: "The preeminent part of our pontificate will be occupied with the continuation of the Second Vatican Ecumenical Council, on which the eyes of all men of good will are fixed. This will be our principal task, on which we intend to spend all the energies which Our Lord has given us." The Council would be "the first thought of our Apostolic ministry," and he pledged to do all in his power "to continue the work of promoting Christian unity so auspiciously begun, with such high hopes, by Pope John XXIII."

All the cardinals could be expected to remain in Rome until the coronation ceremonies, scheduled for June 30. On June 25, copies of the statements of Cardinal Tien and Bishop Thijssen on the proposed secretariat were mailed to Cardinals Alfrink, Cushing, Frings, Gilroy, Gracias, König, Liénart, Meyer, Ritter, Rugambwa, Spellman, Suenens, and Wyszynski. On June 27, Cardinal Frings permitted me to question him on his reactions to the proposed secretariat. He agreed that it might well prove a source of as many blessings to the world as was the Secretariat for Promoting Christian Unity, and added that he could think of no one more qualified to direct it than Cardinal König. He undertook to approach Cardinal König in the matter.

Father Farhat and I were able to speak to Cardinal König on the day of the coronation, June 30. He had already discussed the matter with Cardinal Frings and felt that this was certainly the right time for the establishment of such a body, since the non-Christian religions were bound to show less interest in the Catholic Church after the Council ended. Cardinal König said that he would speak to Cardinal Bea about it that afternoon at the coronation ceremonies.

Cardinal Bea, too, was in sympathy with the idea, as was Cardinal Gracias of Bombay. A few days later,

Cardinal Liénart wrote that he had read the statements on the proposed secretariat "with very great interest." In his view, "the idea of establishing a secretariat for non-Christian religions seems opportune, but the decision in this regard pertains to the Sovereign Pontiff."

With the Cardinal of China and the Cardinal of India favoring the project, as well as Cardinals Bea, Frings, Liénart, König, and, presumably, Cardinal Agagianian, the next step was to bring the matter to the attention of Pope Paul VI. And since the matter had to be presented by a cardinal, the logical choice seemed to be Cardinal Tien, who had first given public support to the idea. I therefore approached him on July 3, and asked whether he would write to Pope Paul VI, proposing this new secretariat and suggesting Cardinal König as best qualified to act as its president.

The Cardinal agreed, had me write a preliminary draft of the letter, and then asked me to read it back to him. When I was halfway through, he put his hand on my arm and stopped me. Sitting back in his chair, and folding his hands over his chest, he said with a mischievous smile, "I think we should do it the Chinese way." He explained that it was difficult for him to send such a letter to the new Pope, whom he hardly knew, or to propose the name of one particular cardinal as most suitable to head the new organization. "However," he suggested, "if you were to write a letter to me, you could explain at length what the functions of such a secretariat might be, mention the names of cardinals and bishops who have expressed their interest in it, and indicate the qualifications of Cardinal König for directing the secretariat. You could also say that you have reason to believe that Cardinal König would not be averse to being assigned such a task."

After reaching Taiwan, where he was to fly on the following day, Cardinal Tien would write to Pope Paul, enclosing my letter and stating that he heartily approved of the project. He had one last bit of advice: My letter to him, and his to the Pope, were both to be written in Italian, so that the members of the Roman Curia might be able to read them without difficulty.

On July 21, Cardinal Tien wrote me from Taipei, saying that he had mailed the two letters to the Holy Father as planned. "In my opinion, the Holy Father will not act quickly," he wrote. "He will first have to ponder the matter, and then confer with other cardinals."

But on September 12, less than eight weeks after Cardinal Tien's letter, Pope Paul VI announced that "a secretariat will also be founded in due time for those who are members of non-Christian religions." There was no indication as to the name of the president of the new secretariat.

THE FULDA CONFERENCE AND ITS IMPLICATIONS

After Pope Paul's announcement that the second session would open on September 29, 1963, the Council Fathers throughout the world resumed their study of the various schemas. In some countries, such study was undertaken by the episcopal conference as a whole. In the United States, some 125 bishops gathered in Chicago in early August 1963 for an unofficial review of Council questions. The bishops of Argentina met in plenary session from August

6 to 10 to decide their stand on particular Council issues. The Italian episcopal conference met in Rome on August 27 and 28. The South African bishops met in Pretoria, also in August, and the Spanish episcopal conference met in Madrid in mid-September.

The meeting that drew most attention, however, was the one held at Fulda, Germany, from August 26 to 29.

The Coordinating Commission of the Council convened in Rome on July 3 for a two-day session. It examined and approved the schemas on the missions and matrimony; and on the second day, Cardinal Suenens reported on the schemas on the Church (Part II) and the Church in the Modern World. A proposal for improved press relations during the second session, put forward by Monsignor Vallainc, was also discussed and accepted in principle.

Immediately after that meeting, Cardinal Döpfner contacted Cardinal Frings and Cardinal König, with a view to arranging a mutually acceptable schedule for the Fulda conference. The opening date was fixed for August 26.

On July 9, Cardinal Döpfner sent a detailed letter to all Council Fathers in Germany and Austria, inviting them to the conference. As in February, he told them, the Council Fathers of Switzerland and Scandinavia would also be invited, as would Council Fathers "from neighboring lands to the west."

The letter contained a twelve-point program. It listed successively the twelve schemas approved by Pope John XXIII on April 22, and distributed to Council Fathers, together with the names and addresses of the German or Austrian bishops belonging to the commissions responsible for the schemas concerned. Observations on a particular schema were to be sent to the appropriate bishop, who was to prepare an analysis of the schema and mail it to all participants two weeks before the opening of the conference. At the conference, the author of the analysis was to lead the discussion. On the basis of such discussion, a new and expanded analysis of the schema would be drafted, indicating its positive and negative aspects. That final text would be forwarded to the General Secretariat of the Council as the common stand taken by the German-speaking Council Fathers assembled at Fulda. Each member and guest of the conference would also receive a printed copy of that final text.

Cardinal Döpfner also wrote that he would endeavor to obtain exact information from Rome as to the order in which the schemas were to be treated. Depending on the answer, he explained, the twelve-point program might be considerably shortened. "As soon as I receive definite word from Rome, I shall pass it on to you."

When the conference opened on August 26, there were present four cardinals and seventy archbishops and bishops, representing ten countries. Germany, Austria, Switzerland, and the Scandinavian countries were represented by nearly all of their archbishops and bishops. France, Belgium, and Holland had representatives; Cardinal Alfrink himself represented Holland. Cardinal Frings presided.

The work carried out by the European alliance at Fulda was very impressive, and it is to be regretted that all national and regional episcopal conferences did not work with the same intensity and purpose. Had they done so, they would not have found it necessary to accept the

107

positions of the European alliance with so little questioning. The Council would then have been less one-sided, and its achievements would truly have been the result of a worldwide theological effort.

Since the position of the German-language bishops was regularly adopted by the European alliance, and since the alliance position was generally adopted by the Council, a single theologian might have his views accepted by the whole Council if they had been accepted by the German-speaking bishops. There was such a theologian: Father Karl Rahner, S.J.

Technically, Father Rahner was Cardinal König's consultant theologian. In practice, he was consulted by many members of the German and Austrian hierarchy, and he might well be called the most influential mind at the Fulda conference. Cardinal Frings, in private conversation, called Father Rahner "the greatest theologian of the century."

Bishop Schröffer of Eichstätt, who had been elected to the Theological Commission by the highest number of votes received by any candidate to that Commission, was responsible at Fulda for the three schemas produced by the Theological Commission, namely, the schemas on revelation, the Blessed Virgin Mary, and the Church. In mid-August, he sent separate analyses of these schemas to each of the Council Fathers invited to Fulda. He explained that these analyses had been prepared by Father Rahner and subsequently examined and commented on by three other German theologians—Father Ratzinger, consultant theologian to Cardinal Frings; Father Aloys Grillmeier, S.J.; and Father Otto Semmelroth, S.J. It had been impossible, the Bishop wrote, to find other theologians to examine the text in the short time available, but those three theologians had fully endorsed Father Rahner's analyses, expressing only "a few wishes," which had been incorporated in the text. The extent to which the bishops of Germany and Austria, and the entire Fulda conference, leaned on Father Rahner may be gauged by comparing his original observations with those submitted to the General Secretariat of the Council.

Numerous other criticisms of schemas, as well as some substitute schemas, were distributed either shortly before or immediately following the conference. Abbot Johannes Hoeck, President of the Benedictines of Bavaria, and a member of the Commission on Oriental Churches, wrote to all who attended the Fulda conference, asking for a "yes" or "no" reply to four specific points, so that he would know what stand to take on behalf of the German-speaking and Scandinavian Council Fathers at the meeting of his Commission, which was to begin one week before the opening of the second session.

Each of the German-speaking Council Fathers had been supplied with a total of 480 mimeographed pages of comment, criticism, and substitute schemas by the time he left for the second session. All this work was accomplished in connection with the Munich conference in February and the Fulda conference in August.

A meeting of Council Fathers from so many nations was bound to interest the press, and a succession of newspaper stories appeared with references to a "conspiracy" and an "attack" upon the Roman Curia and some of its representatives. Some of the Council Fathers were styled "progressives," others "traditionalists," still others "anti-progressives." It was insinuated that the Fulda conference was intended to counteract the possible "personal inclinations" of the new Pontiff in regard to the direction to be taken by the Council, which might make it deviate from the path which Pope John had indicated.

Such statements produced a prompt and authoritative reaction. Cardinal Frings gave a press conference at which he said that the conference had been held to discuss the Council schemas. He pointed out that all observations had been transmitted in writing to the competent authorities in Rome. The word "conspiracy" as applied to the Fulda meetings was "an unjust stupidity." And the German episcopal conference issued a statement expressing "profound consternation" at the "completely absurd" conclusions drawn from the Fulda conference.

On August 26 and 27, the Fulda conference completed its examination of three of the most important Council schemas, those on the Church, divine revelation, and the Blessed Virgin Mary. The numerous proposals were quickly drawn up; they filled a total of fifty-four long typewritten pages. These Cardinal Döpfner took to Rome on August 31, when he left for the fourth meeting of the Coordinating Commission. They were presented to the General Secretariat in the name of the German-speaking Council Fathers and the Episcopal Conference of Scandinavia.

Cardinal Döpfner took this opportunity to visit Pope Paul VI at Castel Gandolfo on September 2. Among other things, they spoke of the Fulda conference. "It was a great relief to me," Cardinal Döpfner said later, "when I saw that His Holiness had not taken seriously the reports which had appeared in the Italian press about Fulda." The audience had been "very cordial." In order to counteract "these press reports, which have received much attention in Italy," Cardinal Döpfner had discussed with Archbishop Felici an explanation to clarify the issue, which was subsequently published by the Council Press Office in *L'Osservatore Romano*, on September 4, 1963.

This "explanation" stated that the presence at Fulda of representatives from neighboring episcopal conferences had not been an innovation, but merely a continuation of a practice initiated in Rome during the first session. The purpose of the meeting had been to guarantee "a more careful and serious preparation for the coming Council meetings." It was also stated that the German-speaking bishops, after their Munich conference and again after their Fulda conference, "had transmitted the results of their studies to others."

Cardinal Döpfner informed the bishops of Germany, Austria, Switzerland, and Scandinavia in a letter dated September 7, 1963, of his audience with Pope Paul and of the article published in *L'Osservatore Romano* through the cooperation of Archbishop Felici. He took the opportunity to inform the Council Fathers that "at the moment the sequence of schemas to be treated at the coming session of the Council is as follows: (1) the Church; (2) the Blessed Virgin Mary; (3) the bishops; (4) the laity; (5) ecumenism."

Meanwhile, major changes were being prepared in the organization and procedure governing the Council. These were announced by Pope Paul VI on September 13. "On the advice of certain venerable Council Fathers," he said, he was revising the Rules of Procedure which had been approved thirteen months earlier by Pope John. Under the revised rules, the Presidency received an increase in membership but suffered a loss of power. The number of Cardinal Presidents was raised from ten to twelve, and their function reduced to that of policing the Council, enforcing the rules, and "solving doubts and difficulties." They were no longer to have any authority in the matter of the direction of Council discussions.

The new rules placed the responsibility for "directing the activities of the Council and determining the sequence in which topics would be discussed at the business meetings" in the hands of four Cardinal Moderators chosen from the membership of the Coordinating Commission, which had been expanded from six to nine by Pope Paul. The four Moderators chosen by the Pope were Cardinals Döpfner, Suenens, Lercaro, and Agagianian. Cardinal Döpfner was well known for his organizational ability; during the preparatory stages of the Council he had served on the technical-organizational preparatory commission together with then-Cardinal Montini, and throughout the first session he and Cardinal Suenens had served with Cardinal Montini on the seven-member Secretariat for Extraordinary Council Affairs. Cardinal Lercaro was known to be a liberal, an active supporter of the European alliance, and a close personal friend of the Pontiff. Cardinal Agagianian was regarded by the liberals as the most acceptable of the Curial cardinals. It therefore appeared that the Pope, in selecting these four men, was supporting the liberal element in the Council, as his predecessor had done.

By these papal appointments the European alliance grew in power and influence, advancing from control of 30 percent of the Council Presidency and control of 50 percent of the Coordinating Commission to control of 75 percent of the board of Cardinal Moderators. And since Cardinal Agagianian was not a forceful person, the three liberal Cardinal Moderators often had 100-percent control.

In addition to this structural reorganization, there were many procedural changes. One of them, for example, provided that, if three commission members so desired, they might invite one or more *periti* not attached to that commission to attend its meetings. Pope John's rules had provided that all such *periti* must be designated by the president of the commission concerned.

At Vatican I, the German, Austrian, and Hungarian Council Fathers had asked Pope Pius IX to authorize a minority group to defend its position before a Council commission, but the Pope had denied the request. Under the new Rules of Procedure approved by Pope Paul VI, "Council Fathers may request a hearing from any commission in order to give their views on the schema under discussion either in their own names, or in the names of a certain number of Council Fathers, or in the name of some region." The commission was to set aside a special meeting at which such representatives could be heard.

The rules authorized by Pope John left it to the president of the commission to determine who should read the commission report on the Council floor. The new rules provided that this decision rested with the commission as a whole, and not simply with its president. As for the report itself, a new provision ruled that it must represent the majority view of the commission, but also that another *relator* might be designated to present the minority view.

Still another revision permitted as few as five members of a commission "to substitute another form of a proposed amendment," and stated that "this new form, together with the original one, or in its place, must be examined by the commission." Why was the figure set at five? It may have been mere coincidence, but the European alliance had a minimum of five members on every commission.

To preclude the possibility of a procedural deadlock (as had happened in the vote on the schema on the sources of revelation), the new rules provided that a vote on the rejection of a schema, or the postponement of its discussion, required a simple majority only (50 percent plus one). A two-thirds majority was still required for the approval of schemas, or parts of schemas, or amendments.

The Moderator for the day was empowered, when the list of speakers was exhausted, to give the floor to other Council Fathers who requested it at the same meeting, especially to those *relators* who asked permission "to illustrate the issue before the Council more clearly, or to refute objections" that had been made. Like the Presidents before them, the Moderators might intervene and have the assembly vote on whether or not discussion on a topic should be discontinued. After such a vote, cardinals, and other Council Fathers as well, were still to be permitted to speak on request, "if they request permission to speak not only in their own names, but also in the names of at least five other Council Fathers." Even after the discussion was completed, a minority was entitled "to designate an additional three speakers, even among the *periti*, who are to be granted the privilege of exceeding the ten-minute time limit."

With a definite policy laid down at Munich and Fulda, which could be revised at the weekly meetings held in the Collegio dell'Anima; with 480 pages of comment and substitute schemas; with a German-speaking Council Father on every commission (the Bishop of Fulda was appointed by the Pope to the Commission on Missions when an elected member died in the interim between sessions); with Cardinal Frings on the Council Presidency and Cardinal Döpfner on the Coordinating Commission and serving as one of the Moderators—no other episcopal conference was so well prepared to assume and maintain the leadership at the second session.

It was clear at this point how the discussions would develop. There would be a strong German influence which would make itself felt in nearly every Council decision and statement of any importance. In every Council commission, German and Austrian members and *periti* would be highly articulate in presenting the conclusions reached at Munich and Fulda. With the Munich and Fulda conferences, the drastic changes that Pope Paul VI had made in the Rules of Procedure, and the promotion of Cardinals Döpfner, Suenens, and Lercaro to the position of Moderators, domination by the European alliance was assured.

Opening the Second Session

In his opening address, on September 29, 1963, Pope Paul VI enumerated four specific objectives of the Second Vatican Council: greater self-awareness by the Church, and understanding of its own nature; renewal within the Church; promotion of Christian unity; and promotion of dialogue with modern man.

The Pope then addressed the observer delegates directly: "We speak now to the representatives of the Christian denominations separated from the Catholic Church, who have nevertheless been invited to take part as observers in this solemn assembly. We greet them from our heart. We thank them for their participation. We transmit through them our message—as a father and a brother—to the venerable Christian communities which they represent.

"Our voice trembles and our heart beats the faster, both because of the inexpressible consolation and reasonable hope that their presence stirs up within us, as well as because of the deep sadness we feel at their prolonged separation."

Pope Paul also spoke out against religious persecution and political, racial and religious intolerance. Instead of uttering bitter words, however, he preferred "a frank and human exhortation to all who may be responsible for these evils to put aside with a noble heart their unjustified hostility toward the Catholic religion." He said that Catholics "ought to be considered neither as enemies nor as disloyal citizens, but rather as upright and hard-working members of that civil society to which they belong." At the same time, he lamented that "atheism is pervading a part of the human race and is bringing in its wake the derangement of the intellectual, moral and social order."

He also had some words for the great non-Christian religions of the world. "From the window of the Council, opened wide to the world," the Church looks "beyond its own sphere and sees those other religions which preserve the sense and notion of the one, supreme, transcendent God, Creator and Sustainer, and which worship him with acts of sincere piety and base their moral and social life on their beliefs and religious practices.

"It is true that the Catholic Church sees in such religions omissions, insufficiencies and errors which cause it sadness. Yet it cannot exclude them from its thoughts, and would have them know that it esteems the truth and goodness and humanity which they contain."

The principal concern of the second session, said Pope Paul, was "to examine the intimate nature of the Church and to express in human language, so far as that is possible, a definition which will best reveal the Church's really fundamental constitution and explain its manifold mission of salvation." It should not come as a surprise, he said, that after twenty centuries there should still be need for the Catholic Church to enunciate a more precise definition of its true, profound and complete nature. Since the Church is "a mystery," "a reality imbued with the Divine Presence," it is "ever susceptible of new and deeper investigation."

The notion of collegiality was the most important aspect of the Church before the Council, said the Pope. He looked forward "with great expectations and confidence to this discussion which, taking for granted the dogmatic declarations of the First Vatican Council regarding the Roman Pontiff, will go on to develop the doctrine regarding the episcopate, its function, and its relationship with Peter." For him personally, this study, and the conclusions to be drawn from it, would "provide doctrinal and practical standards by which our Apostolic office, endowed though it is by Christ with the fullness and sufficiency of power, may receive more help and support, in ways to be determined, from a more effective and responsible collaboration with our beloved and venerable brothers in the episcopate."

The thirty-seventh General Congregation—the first business meeting of the second session—opened on the following day, September 30. The first schema before it was the schema on the Church.

At the end of the first session, when that schema had been referred back to the Theological Commission, it had consisted of eleven chapters. Now it consisted of four, headed as follows: "The Mystery of the Church," "The Hierarchic Constitution of the Church, with Special Reference to the Episcopate," "The People of God and the Laity," and "The Vocation to Sanctity in the Church."

One of the first items to come up for discussion was the notion of episcopal collegiality, or government of the Universal Church by the Pope in conjunction with the bishops of the world. This was really the core of the entire Second Vatican Council, which was intended to complement the First Vatican Council, in which the primacy of the Pope had been studied in detail and solemnly defined.

In defining the notion of episcopal collegiality, the Council Fathers had to decide: first, whether Christ had intended that, alongside the universal teaching and governing authority of the Pope, there should exist in the Church another body endowed with universal teaching and governing authority—namely, the body of bishops— as successors of the Apostles, according to the constant teaching of the Church; second, if the answer was "yes," whether all bishops constituted this collegial authority, or only those with dioceses of their own; third, the conditions under which such collegial authority functioned; fourth, the relation between the collegial authority of the bishops and the personal authority proper to the Roman Pontiff.

A problem so complex and many-faceted was bound to elicit various reactions on the Council floor.

Cardinal Siri of Genoa, for instance, maintained that the bishops, "under certain conditions," certainly constituted a college together with the Roman Pontiff; that was evident from Sacred Scripture and tradition. However, the concept of a college was "strictly juridical" and therefore much more complex than that of a simple association. It implied, in fact, "a juridical solidarity both in being and in action." Cardinal Siri felt that the wording of the schema should be clearer and better organized, and should be harmonized with what the First Vatican Council had already defined on the papal primacy.

Albert Cardinal Meyer of Chicago supported the statement in the schema that Christ had entrusted his Church to the twelve Apostles as a college, or group. In his view, the text should also state that the office of the Apostles was a permanent one, because of Christ's words "I am with you all days, even unto the consummation of the world" (Mt 28:20), and "the Father . . . will give you another Advocate to dwell with you forever" (Jn 14:16). The Cardinal cited numerous scriptural texts to show that episcopal collegiality was as clearly stated in the New Testament as was the foundation of the Church on Peter.

Cardinal Léger of Montreal told the assembly that

119

the concept of episcopal collegiality did not weaken the doctrine of the primacy of Peter, since collegiate action required a head, for the sake of unity. He called for a statement in the text that membership in the episcopal college flowed from episcopal consecration; all bishops, whether residential or only titular, belonged to the episcopal college.

Bishop De Smedt, of Bruges, said that episcopal collegiality "had always existed in the Church" and should be emphasized more than ever today in order that "Peter"—the Pope—might more effectively carry out his function of strengthening his brethren. Former barriers to rapid communication had been removed by scientific progress, he said, and it was therefore desirable and even imperative that the Holy Father, "in matters of graver importance," should communicate with the other bishops and with episcopal conferences.

Archbishop Staffa, of the Roman Curia, addressed the assembly on the "full and supreme power of the episcopal college." The question at issue, he said, was whether this power belonged to only one person, or to the entire college. The reply to the question had already been given, he pointed out, by the First Vatican Council, which had defined that only Peter had supreme jurisdiction over the whole Church. He recalled, in that connection, that the *relator* at Vatican I had said, in explanation of the text on the primacy, that the power of the Pope over the bishops was at all times supreme, immediate, and complete, and that the Pope had that power independently of the bishops. Archbishop Staffa also pointed out that the *relator* had rejected proposals which would have limited the

Pope's power by placing supreme power in the episcopal college, which included the Pope. The monarchic structure of the Church would thereby have been replaced by an aristocratic structure. As long ago as the thirteenth century, Pope Innocent III (1198-1216) had written to the Patriarch of Constantinople, saying that Christ had given power in the Church not to others without Peter, but to Peter without others.

At the forty-fourth General Congregation, on October 9, Archbishop Sigaud, of Diamantina, Brazil, called for special caution in the phrasing of episcopal collegiality. The Archbishop, who called himself a traditionalist, said that a comparison of Articles 12, 13, and 16 of the schema made it appear that "some new doctrine" was being taught—namely, that the twelve Apostles, with Peter as head, constituted together a true and permanent college strictly so called, and "even by divine institution."

The Archbishop feared that most serious consequences would flow from this doctrine. "If by divine institution the bishops and the Pope constitute a true and permanent college, strictly so called, then the Church must habitually and ordinarily (not extraordinarily) be ruled by the Pope with the college of bishops. In other words, the government of the Church, by divine institution, is not monarchical or personal, but collegial." But the exercise of collegial authority by bishops, as in ecumenical councils, was a rare event in the history of the Church, and must therefore be regarded as an extraordinary—not an ordinary—manner of governing the Universal Church.

The traditional Catholic teaching in the matter, he said, was that every bishop, on his appointment to office by the

Pope, "receives the duty and, consequently, the authority of exercising the episcopal office among the faithful committed to him, within the territorial limits indicated to him by the competent authority." There was a distinction, he pointed out, between acts performed by bishops collectively, and those performed collegially. An example of collective action was the gathering of many bishops of one ecclesiastical province or nation, the efficacy of which was not derived from divine institution and could not be said to have been collegially produced. The decisions of such gatherings had only "a juridical efficacy, that is, they oblige within a diocese only if the Roman Pontiff approves of such decisions as binding by virtue of his own full and universal power; or if the bishop of the diocese concerned, by virtue of his own jurisdiction, approves such decisions as binding for his own diocese."

Two "very dangerous precipices" must be avoided, said Archbishop Sigaud. In the first place, "we must avoid the establishment of some world institution which would be like a permanent ecumenical council, to which some bishops would be elected or delegated by others, and who would carry out the duties of the entire episcopal college. In this way, together with the Roman Pontiff, they would perform acts which were truly collegial, in a habitual and ordinary manner, and their efficacy would be extended by divine institution to the Universal Church." Such an organism, said the Archbishop, would be a kind of "world parliament" within the Church. But, he pointed out, Christ had most certainly not established such an organism, because for twenty centuries the Roman Pontiffs and bishops had been wholly unaware of it. "On the contrary, it is clear to all that Christ the Lord conferred the supreme government of his Church upon the person of Peter, to be personally exercised, first, indeed, by Peter himself, and then by Peter's successors."

Another form of organism was also to be avoided, namely, "some kind of permanent national or regional council, in which a number of bishops of one nation or region would make juridical or doctrinal decisions. The Roman Pontiff would be unable, in practice, to deny assent to these judgments, and thus all bishops of the same nation or region would be bound." It was clear that "such bodies would present very serious impediments . . . to the exercise of the supreme ordinary power by the Holy Father, and also to that of ordinary power by the individual bishop."

Archbishop Sigaud had scarcely returned to his place in the Council hall when he received a message from Bishop Carli, of Segni, congratulating him on his address. This was the beginning of a firm friendship between the two prelates. Archbishop Sigaud subsequently introduced Bishop Carli to French-born Archbishop Marcel Lefebvre, Superior General of the Holy Ghost Fathers. The two archbishops had met in the first week of the first session and had formed a *piccolo comitato* (small committee) aimed at opposing certain ideas which they considered extreme, and which, they felt, were being forced upon many of the Council Fathers by the strong episcopal conferences, especially those of the European alliance. They now invited Bishop Carli to join their midget alliance; the bishop accepted the invitation. Cardinal Döpfner later admitted that there was no bishop at the Council whom he feared more.

In an exclusive interview, Archbishop Lefebvre told me that he saw no threat to the papacy in powerful episcopal conferences, but that he did regard them as a threat to the teaching authority and pastoral responsibility of individual bishops. He could speak on the matter with authority, having founded the national episcopal conferences of Madagascar, Congo-Brazzaville, Cameroun, and French West Africa while serving as Apostolic Delegate for French-Speaking Africa from 1948 to 1959.

It was easy to conceive, said the Archbishop, that "three, four, or five bishops in a national episcopal conference will have more influence than the rest and will take over leadership." This he called "a danger to the teaching and pastoral authority of the individual bishop, who is the divinely constituted teacher and pastor of his flock." Referring specifically to the conference of archbishops of France, he said that at times this conference would issue a joint statement on social or pastoral questions. "It is then very difficult for an individual bishop to disagree with the public stand that has been taken, and he is simply reduced to silence." Archbishop Lefebvre called this "a new and undesirable power over the diocesan bishop."

He went further, saying that it was "a new kind of collectivism invading the Church." The present tendency in the Council hall, he said, was to make national episcopal conferences so strong that "individual bishops would be so restricted in the government of their dioceses as to lose their initiative." An individual bishop might contradict a national episcopal conference, "but then his clergy and laity would be in a quandary, not knowing whether to follow their own bishop or the conference."

A restrictive influence was already at work in the Council, the Archbishop maintained, "because minority groups in various nations are not speaking out as they should, but are silently going along with their national episcopal conferences." What was needed, he said, "at this Catholic Council," was not a grouping of Council Fathers on national or linguistic lines, as hitherto, "but a grouping . . . on international lines, by schools of thought and special tendencies." In that way, it would be possible to see what the bishops thought, rather than what the nations thought. "For it is the bishops, not the nations, that make up the Council."

The outstanding French theologian Father Yves Congar, O.P., agreed that episcopal conferences raised a difficult problem affecting the Church in very vital areas. Such conferences, he maintained, must not obliterate the personal responsibility of bishops by imposing on them the dictates of an organization, nor must they even remotely threaten Catholic unity.

Once more, the Council was headed for conflict.

THE SCHEMA ON THE BLESSED VIRGIN MARY

Throughout the preparatory stages of the Council, the schema on the Blessed Virgin Mary was alternately treated independently and as a chapter of another schema.

In January, 1963, following the close of the first session, the Coordinating Commission ruled at its first meeting that the schema "on the Blessed Virgin Mary, Mother of the Church, is to be treated independently of the schema on the Church." Because of this decision, the schema was reprinted and distributed to the Council Fathers, together with eleven others, before the second session. The only difference was in the wording of the title. Originally the title had read, "On the Blessed Virgin Mary, Mother of God and Mother of Men"; now it read, "On the Blessed Virgin Mary, Mother of the Church." An additional note on the title page specified that "the text will be changed only after suggestions are made by the Council Fathers."

When the German and Austrian Council Fathers received their copies of the schema, they asked Father Rahner to prepare comments on it for presentation at the forthcoming Fulda conference.

According to Father Rahner, whose written comments were distributed to all participants in the conference, the schema as then drafted was "a source of the greatest concern" for himself and for Fathers Grillmeier, Semmelroth, and Ratzinger, who had also examined it from a theological point of view. Were the text to be accepted as it stood, he contended, "unimaginable harm would result from an ecumenical point of view, in relation to both Orientals and Protestants." It could not be too strongly stressed, he said, "that all the success achieved in the field of ecumenism through the Council and in connection with the Council will be rendered worthless by the retention of the schema as it stands."

It would be too much to expect, continued Father Rahner, that the schema on the Blessed Virgin could be rejected as simply as the schema on the sources of revelation. It should therefore be urged "with all possible insistence" that the schema on the Blessed Virgin be made either a chapter or an epilogue of the schema on the Church. "This would be the easiest way to delete from the schema statements which, theologically, are not sufficiently developed and which could only do incalculable harm from an ecumenical point of view. It would also prevent bitter discussion."

Father Rahner contended further that the schema as it stood used "tactics which objectively are not honorable," since "it declares that there is no intention of defining new dogmas, and at the same time presents certain teachings as though they already belonged to the doctrine of the Church, although they are not as yet dogmas and, from a modern theological standpoint, cannot become dogmas."

What he attacked especially was the schema's teaching on the mediation of the Blessed Virgin Mary, and the title "Mediatrix of all graces," which it gave the Blessed Virgin. This teaching was not proposed as a dogma of faith, but rather as a doctrine commonly held by Catholics. Although the teaching was supported by many pronouncements of the ordinary teaching authority of the Church, especially by recent papal encyclicals, "this doctrine must nonetheless be carefully pondered anew," for the schema would have "great influence on Mariology and on the devotion of the faithful to Mary." If the word "mediation" were to be used at all, it must be most clearly defined.

Father Rahner painstakingly listed for the German and Austrian Council Fathers precisely what he felt should be changed or omitted in the existing schema. The whole substance of the schema, he contended, could be stated "without stirring up these difficulties and dangers." And he suggested by way of conclusion that "the bishops of Austria, Germany and Switzerland" should consider themselves "forced to declare openly" that they could not accept the schema in its present form.

The Fulda conference adopted his suggestions with one major exception. He had been opposed to leaving the title "Mediatrix" in the text. But the proposals eventually submitted to the General Secretariat of the Council by the Fulda conference read as follows: "By far the greater part of the Council Fathers of Austria, Germany, Switzerland and Scandinavia are not absolutely opposed to retaining the words 'Mediatrix' and 'mediation' in the schema. However, it seems desirable that the expression, 'Mediatrix of all graces' should not be used." These expressions, the Council Fathers explained, would raise the problem as to how the Virgin could be the Mediatrix of the sacramental graces flowing from the very nature of the sacraments themselves, "a question which might well be avoided." They added, nevertheless, that the Theological Commission should weigh the reasons given by the minority for excluding the terms "Mediatrix" and "mediation" from the schema altogether.

The proposal officially submitted by the Fulda conference to the General Secretariat of the Council also quoted from Protestant writings. Bishop Dibelius, of the German Evangelical Church, was quoted as saying in 1962 that the Catholic Church's teaching on Mary was one of the major impediments to union. Other German Protestant authorities, such as Hampe and Künneth, were quoted as saying that the Council Fathers in Rome should remember that they would be erecting a new wall of division by approving a schema on Mary. Therefore, these writers had concluded, the Council should either keep silence on the subject, or reprehend those guilty of excesses. More moderate Protestant writers, such as Professor Meinhold, were quoted as expressing the hope that, if the Council treated of the Blessed Virgin Mary at all, it would do so in the schema on the Church, since then "a new approach could be made to the doctrine on the Blessed Virgin."

The topic before the thirty-seventh General Congregation, held on September 30, the first working meeting of the second session, was the revised schema on the Church. As the first speaker on this topic, Cardinal Frings, of Cologne, stated that it would be most fitting to include in the schema on the Church everything pertaining to the Blessed Virgin Mary. Among other considerations, such action would do much to foster dialogue with the separated Christians. The Cardinal pointed out that his stand was endorsed by sixty-five German-speaking and Scandinavian Council Fathers.

Cardinal Silva Henríquez, of Santiago de Chile, was the first speaker on the following day. Speaking in the name of forty-four Latin American bishops, he said that devotion to the Virgin Mary in those countries at times went beyond the bounds of Christian devotion. If a separate dogmatic constitution were adopted on the Virgin Mary, it would be difficult for the faithful to relate the doctrine contained therein to the doctrine on Christian salvation as a whole. He therefore supported Cardinal Frings' proposal that Catholic teaching on the Blessed Virgin be included in the schema on the Church. The same morning, Archbishop Gabriel Garrone, of Toulouse, speaking on behalf of "many French bishops," also supported Cardinal Frings' proposal. The theological image of the Church, he said, would be completed by the inclusion of all teaching on the Blessed Virgin in the teaching on the Church as a whole. Moreover, this would prove an anti-dote to devotional excesses, since the Virgin would not appear to be outside the providential plan of salvation, but rather as participating therein.

Two days later, Benjamin Cardinal de Arriba y Castro, of Tarragona, took the floor on behalf of sixty bishops, most of them from Spain. He argued that, contrary to what had been suggested at previous meetings, it would be preferable to adopt a separate schema on the Blessed Virgin, because of the importance of the Mother of God in the economy of redemption. However, if it should be decided to include this text in the schema on the Church, then an entire chapter should be devoted to it, preferably the second.

On October 4, the hierarchy of England and Wales cir-culated a letter drawing attention to a "draft for a chapter or epilogue on the Blessed Virgin Mary, to be included in the constitution on the Church." This draft had been prepared as a substitute for the existing schema by Abbot Christopher Butler of Downside, Superior General of the English Benedictines, "on the principle that the Council, especially in view of the ecumenical orientation set before it by the Holy Father, should as far as possible base the full modern Catholic understanding of Our Lady, including the dogmas defined in 1854 and 1950, on Holy Scripture and on the traditional evidence preceding the East-West rupture." If fifty Council Fathers endorsed this substitute schema, according to a new procedural rule, it could be presented to the Cardinal Moderators, who would then be obliged to transmit it to the Coordinating Commission for consideration and a decision.

A booklet dated October 4 was circulated by the Servites (Order of the Servants of Mary) suggesting, among other things, that, if the reference to the "titles" of Mary was to be retained in the schema, then more than one such title should be given; in addition to the title of "Mediatrix" used in the schema, the title "Coredemptrix" would be appropriate.

Another booklet, bearing the same date, was circulated by Father Carolus Balić, a *peritus* on the Theological Commission, citing many reasons for retaining the schema on the Blessed Virgin Mary as a separate document. Numerous Council Fathers were quoted, including Cardinal Spellman, who had asked in a written intervention whether the schema could pass over in silence titles like Coredemptrix, Reparatrix, and others used by the Supreme Pontiffs, simply "because they would be rather difficult for Protestants to understand." The Cardinal was opposed to this sort of reasoning, he said, because "the task of the Ecumenical Council is to teach the members of the Church, rather than those outside of it."

On October 17, Cardinal Silva Henríquez officially submitted his own substitute schema on the Blessed Virgin Mary. He was aware, he said, that the hierarchy of England and Wales had also proposed a text. The one that he was submitting was intended simply as "a help in producing the definitive text." Four days later, he circulated another draft, explaining that it had been produced by the

Chilean bishops by combining their own schema with that of Abbot Butler and also with that of Canon René Laurentin of France, one of the *periti*.

On October 24, the Cardinal Moderators announced that so many Council Fathers had requested the inclusion of the schema on the Blessed Virgin Mary in the schema on the Church that a debate on the motives for and against such a proposal would be held that morning. Rufino Cardinal Santos, of Manila, Philippines, spoke first, giving reasons why the two schemas should be treated separately. "I humbly beg the Cardinal Moderators not to allow the vote to be taken on this question immediately," he said, "but to grant a suitable amount of time to the Council Fathers for pondering over the matter and giving it prudent consideration." Cardinal König of Vienna, a member of the Theological Commission like Cardinal Santos, then stressed the advantages of uniting the two schemas.

On the following day, a letter signed by five Eastern Rite Council Fathers was circulated, pointing out that "among the Orientals united to the Apostolic See, as well as among those separated from it, the Blessed Virgin Mary is very greatly honored," and urging the Council Fathers to vote in favor of an independent schema on Our Lady.

A rebuttal to all arguments in favor of combining the schemas was circulated on October 27 by Servite Bishop Giocondo Grotti, of Acre e Purus, Brazil. As for the argument that a special schema should not be devoted to Mary because she was a member of the Church, the Bishop pointed out that she was not like other members; "because of her singular mission and singular privileges, she should receive singular treatment." Turning to the argument that a separate schema on Mary would be taken as defining something new on Mary, the Bishop pointed out that the Council Fathers had many schemas before them, and no one claimed that those schemas were defining anything new. Another objection, he recalled, was that more honor would be given to Mary than to Christ. But from the text of the schema it was clear that Mary was "neither above nor against Christ." He added that abuses in the devotion to Mary were not an argument against a separate schema, but rather in favor of it, since in a separate schema the truth could be more clearly presented. Bishop Grotti then asked: "Does ecumenism consist in confessing or in hiding the truth? Ought the Council to explain Catholic doctrine, or the doctrine of our separated brethren? . . . Hiding the truth hurts both us and those separated from us. It hurts us, because we appear as hypocrites. It hurts those who are separated from us because it makes them appear weak and capable of being offended by the truth." Bishop Grotti concluded his rebuttal with the plea, "Let the schemas be separated. Let us profess our faith openly. Let us be the teachers we are in the Church by teaching with clarity, and not hiding what is true."

On October 29, a vote was taken on the following statement: "Does it please the Council Fathers that the schema on the Blessed Virgin Mary, Mother of the Church, should be so arranged that it may become Chapter 6 of the schema on the Church?" When the votes were counted, there were 1,114 in favor of combining the two schemas; the required majority was only 1,097. Father Rahner—and the European alliance—had won by a margin of seventeen votes.

THE DIACONATE

One of the arguments offered by the European alliance toward the close of the first session for the rejection of the schema on the Church was that it made no mention of the diaconate. Chapter 3 of the schema contained merely one paragraph on bishops and one on priests.

At the conference of German-speaking Council Fathers held in Munich on February 5 and 6, 1963, the discussion centered around an alternate schema prepared by Monsignor Philips and Father Rahner. In this draft, the section on the priesthood was lengthened, and two paragraphs added on the diaconate and the minor orders. The text was officially submitted to Pope John XXIII and Cardinal Ottaviani in mid-February, 1963, and the section on deacons was incorporated in the revised official schema; the section on minor orders was not included.

One of the sentences in the new paragraph read: "Although today in the Church, the diaconate is generally considered to be only a step on the way to the priesthood, this has not always been the practice, nor is it everywhere the practice today." The revised text provided further that "the diaconate can in the future be restored as a proper and permanent rank of the hierarchy wherever the Church may consider this expedient for the care of souls." It would be up to the competent ecclesiastical authorities to decide whether such deacons were to be bound by the law of celibacy or not. A footnote accompanying the text pointed out that something similar had been presented for consideration at the Council of Trent on July 6, 1563.

This addition to the schema on the Church was strongly

contested when this last revision was made by the Theological Commission. Asked to comment on the revised schema on the Church for the benefit of the Council Fathers assembled in Fulda, Father Rahner devoted thirty-three lines in defense of the fourteen lines on the diaconate, stating that it was most desirable, in spite of certain objections raised, that the section on deacons should be retained in its entirety. His commentary was accepted verbatim by the Fulda Fathers, and officially presented to the General Secretariat of the Council prior to the opening of the second session.

The topic was raised in the Council on October 4 by Francis Cardinal Spellman, of New York. After expressing general satisfaction with Chapter 2 of the revised schema on the Church, he argued against the retention in it of the section concerning the diaconate. The matter, he said, was a disciplinary one and should not, therefore, be included in a dogmatic constitution. As to whether it should be treated in any other constitution, he felt that it should not, and he proceeded to explain his position.

In the first place, he said, deacons would have to be adequately prepared for their functions. In many places, however, it was scarcely possible, or even impossible, to establish seminaries for candidates to the priesthood. How, then, could other houses be provided for deacons? Again, if those men who were already deacons were to remain so permanently, there would automatically be fewer priests. The idea of a permanent diaconate had originated mainly with liturgists, who wished to restore ancient practices without taking modern conditions into account. With the passage of time, he pointed out, the diaconate as a permanent rank in the hierarchy had in fact become obsolete. No steps, therefore, should be taken to restore it without careful consideration of the reasons leading to its abandonment. The role of the diaconate in the modern Church was being fulfilled by many lay religious, members of secular institutes, and lay apostles who were living lives of service to the Church; one of the purposes of the Council, he recalled, was precisely the fostering of the growth of this type of lay activity.

At the next General Congregation, Cardinal Döpfner answered some of Cardinal Spellman's objections. As for seminaries for the training of deacons, they would not be necessary; it was a question of "sacramentalizing functions that already exist," not introducing new ones. Those who were already trained for these functions, or were exercising them, he said, like married catechists in mission lands, should receive the corresponding sacramental grace to help them carry them out more perfectly. In conclusion, he pointed out that the purpose of the text was "simply to give a dogmatic basis for a permanent diaconate and to open the door to a further examination of the question."

Cardinal Suenens, of Belgium, also proceeded to refute Cardinal Spellman's objections. Because the diaconate was sacramental, it pertained to the very constitution of the Church and must be treated on a supernatural level, he said. Certain functions in the Church should be entrusted only to those with the necessary supernatural grace. God had established certain ministries and graces, and these ought not to be neglected in building up a Christian community; the community had a right to them. The Cardinal rejected the contention that a married diaconate would undermine priestly celibacy or result in a decline in vocations. The diaconate itself was a gift of divine grace and would strengthen Christian communities, thereby aiding the growth of the Church.

Cardinal Suenens asked, in conclusion, that a vote be taken at the end of the discussion in order to determine the consensus on the subject.

Archbishop Bernard Yago, of Abidjan, Ivory Coast, suggested that the Council Fathers might be interested in hearing a voice from Africa on this matter. He supported the establishment of a permanent diaconate; deacons could play an important role, especially in missionary countries, since many communities seldom saw a priest. To the objection that a practice dating from the first centuries of Christianity and long since discarded should not be revived, he replied that Africa was in fact experiencing its first century of Christianity.

Archbishop Paul Zoungrana, of Ouagadougou, Upper Volta, accepted the principle of a permanent diaconate, but he argued that a married diaconate would be altogether undesirable in West Africa. A strong reason for insisting on celibacy, he said, was that the modern world needed a firm witness to the possibility of a life of chastity. However, since circumstances might suggest that a noncelibate diaconate was more useful in some regions, episcopal conferences should be able to obtain the necessary powers from the Holy See to dispense with the obligation of celibacy.

Cardinal Bacci, of the Roman Curia, spoke out against the principle of a married diaconate; it was both inopportune and dangerous. If the law of celibacy were relaxed for deacons, the number of priests would certainly decline, since youth "would choose the easier way." Moreover, if the Council waived the obligation of celibacy for deacons, the plea would soon be heard that the same should be done for priests.

Bishop Jorge Kémérer, of Posadas, Argentina, addressed the assembly in the name of twenty bishops from Argentina, Uruguay, Paraguay, and various mission lands. "Something serious must be done," he said, "to solve the great and urgent problem of the shortage of priests around the world." Although theoretically there was one priest for every 6,000 souls in Latin America, in fact "nearly every diocese has many parishes with a single priest caring for 10,000, 20,000, or even 30,000 souls!" The solution was not to import priests from abroad, he said, since the population of Latin America was close to 200 million and was expected to be double that by the end of the century. "What we need is the restoration of the order of the diaconate in the hierarchy, without the obligation of celibacy." He then made this earnest and eloquent appeal: "The restoration of the diaconate is our great hope. And it is the wish of many bishops in Latin America that you, venerable Fathers, do not deprive us of this hope when the matter comes up for a vote. The door is already open. If among you there are some who do not wish to enter, we shall not force you to enter. But we earnestly beg of you not to close the door on us, because we do want to enter. Allow us, please, to do so!" His plea was received with applause.

Archbishop Custodio Alvim Pereira, of Lourenço Marques, Mozambique, spoke on behalf of thirty-eight bishops from Portugal. He said that, if a candidate did not have the knowledge required of a priest and was not celibate, he was not fit for the diaconate; if, on the other hand, he did possess that knowledge and was celibate, he should become a priest. He contended that it was generally agreed that a married diaconate would undermine priestly celibacy.

Bishop Jean Gay, of Basse-Terre and Pointe-à-Pitre in the French West Indies, supported the restoration of a permanent diaconate, but he felt that a married diaconate would present difficulties. He recalled that Canon 17 of the Council of Trent had been designed to restore the minor orders in the Church and said that the present Council offered an opportunity to carry out such a step. Married men in minor orders could help in the liturgy, in Catholic Action, in catechetics, and in administrative work. The restoration of minor orders, he said, deserved attention, "and should be given a place in the schema alongside the diaconate."

Bishop Paul Sani, of Bali, Indonesia, told a press conference that on an ordinary Sunday in Flores it took a priest a half hour to distribute Holy Communion. "This annoys the congregation," he said, "and we could use some help from deacons here." Nevertheless, he said, "I am not in favor of a diaconate by Orders. This may have been well and good in the first centuries, when the Church was not yet organized. But many of the functions performed by ordained deacons in the early Church are today performed by teachers, catechists, and church board members." Ordained deacons, moreover, would have to be paid salaries for performing services similar to those rendered gratis by church board members. "This would be a blow to the lay apostolate movement, in which people render their services spontaneously and without remuneration."

The Bishop was especially concerned with the fact that the sacrament of Orders, by which the diaconate was conferred, imprinted an indelible mark on the soul of the recipient. "But if an ordained deacon is involved in a scandal or a village quarrel, what will you do with him? People will no longer come to him to receive Communion. And linguistic, cultural, property, and family ties make his transfer from one parish to another more or less impossible. So his services cease, but you must still continue to support him." On the other hand, a diaconate by jurisdiction, or faculties, was much more suited to mission needs. "Bishops or ordinaries in charge of dioceses should receive faculties or jurisdiction from the Holy See to appoint an individual or individuals, married or unmarried, on a temporary basis, to do the work or perform the functions of deacons on specific occasions." The Bishop said that lay brothers, as well as catechists, whether married or not, and other married men, should be eligible to the diaconate, but always on a temporary basis. He believed that, if lay brothers were given priority in serving as deacons, that would change their role in the mission apostolate and would result in an increase in vocations to the brotherhood.

Other Council Fathers, however, insisted that the diaconate must be conferred by the sacrament of Orders, so that the deacon in performing his duties might receive the grace of that sacrament. Bishop Ermann Tillemans, a Dutch-born missionary on the island of New Guinea for thirty-four years, was of this opinion. "Having an unordained catechist or layman teaching the faith is not the same as having an ordained man. The ordained man will have the help of the grace of his ordination."

In conformity with the suggestion made earlier by Cardinal Suenens, an exploratory vote was taken on October 30 to determine the thinking of the assembly. The Council Fathers were asked whether the schema should be revised in such a way as to take into consideration the opportuneness of restoring the diaconate as a distinct and permanent grade in the sacred ministry, depending upon its usefulness for the Church in particular places. The vote prescinded from the question whether deacons would be allowed to marry.

The result of the exploratory vote was a 75 percent majority in favor of establishing the diaconate as a permanent and distinct grade in the sacred ministry.

THE LAITY

In the schema on the Church that was presented to the Council Fathers during the first session, Church membership was divided into three categories with a chapter devoted to each: hierarchy (i.e., bishops and priests), religious (i.e., members of religious orders and congregations), and laity. When the Council called for a revision of the schema, the Coordinating Commission in January, 1963, ordered that these three chapters should be retained, but changed their sequence: hierarchy, laity, and religious. Less than one month later at Munich, the German-speaking bishops asked that the chapter on religious be considerably shortened, and that it more explicitly identify the perfection sought by religious as "nothing else but the perfection sought by all Christians." These views, favored by the European alliance theologians, became so strong in the Theological Commission that the chapter on religious was changed to "The Vocation to Sanctity in the Church."

At the last minute, in early July, Cardinal Suenens succeeded in having the Coordinating Commission partially alter its orders of January, and call for an additional chapter on "The People of God." This chapter, which carefully avoided the word "member," was to be so phrased as to include not only Catholics, but everyone who in any way might be called a Christian. By July, however, it was much too late for the already revised schema to be revised once again, since it had to be sent through the mails to the Council Fathers for their study without further delay. The solution was to print a footnote informing the Council Fathers that, "according to a recent ruling by the Coordinating Commission," the chapter on the laity would be divided into two parts, constituting Chapter 2 on the People of God, and Chapter 4 on the laity. The phrase "the People of God" had been copied from the first page of the rejected schema of Cardinal Ottaviani and his Theological Preparatory Commission.

In this way, the number of chapters in the schema on the Church was increased from four to five. The schema structure and content were now precisely what the German-speaking bishops had called for in their official resolutions taken at Munich in February of that year, when they had studied a five-chapter substitute schema on the Church prepared principally by Monsignor Philips of Belgium and Father Rahner of Germany. The other chapters indicated in the footnote of Cardinal Suenens were Chapter 1: the mystery of the Church; Chapter 3: the hierarchical constitution of the Church; and Chapter 5: the vocation to sanctity in the Church.

Examination of the two chapters on the laity and on the People of God, discussed as a unit—and not altogether without confusion—as a result of the last-minute change, began at the forty-ninth General Congregation, on October 16.

Bishop Wright of Pittsburgh spoke on the historical and theological importance of the chapter on the laity. "The faithful have been waiting for four hundred years," he said, "for a positive conciliar statement on the place, dignity and vocation of the layman." He found fault with the traditional notion of the laity as defined in Church law as being too negative; the layman was defined as "neither a cleric nor a religious." Once the Council had declared "the theological nature of the laity," he said, "the juridical bones of the Church would come alive with theological flesh and blood."

Abbot Godefroi Dayez, President of the Benedictine Congregation of Belgium, also drew attention to the faulty definition of the laity in the schema. According to the text, "the Sacred Council in using the word 'laity' understands it to mean those faithful who, through Baptism, have been united to the People of God. They serve God in the ordinary state of the Christian faithful. . . . But they belong neither to the hierarchical rank, nor to the religious state sanctioned by the Church." The Abbot contended that this definition was incorrect. Strictly speaking, he said, the laity formed a group separate from the clergy, but not separate from religious. For many in the religious life—nuns, brothers, certain monks—were in fact members of the laity, even though they were members of religious orders. "Unfortunately, many do not know that the religious life is neither clerical nor lay, but is based on a special charism." He called for the insertion of a new passage in the text which would state that the layman was a "noncleric." Moreover, the text should distinguish between the laity in general, those members of the laity who were in religious orders, and those who belonged to secular institutes.

Cardinal Meyer of Chicago contended that the text was "neither adequate nor realistic, because it neglects two fundamental facts." Instead of speaking only of the graces, gifts, and privileges of the People of God, the schema should also emphasize that "we are all sinners as members of a fallen race," and that "even after our entrance into the Church, we remain aware of our weakness and have lapses into sin." The difficulties in living a good Christian life, the Cardinal said, sprang from both internal and external sources. The internal source was the tendency to evil in man's fallen nature, combined with his actual lapses into sin. The external source was the Devil, as was abundantly clear from Scripture. (Cardinal Meyer thus became one of the few Council Fathers to refer to the Devil.) Therefore, he said, if the Council document was to reach the hearts of men, weighed down by a sense of sin and moral incapacity, a new paragraph should be inserted in the text to describe the Church as the home of the Father of Mercies, where the sins of the prodigal son were forgiven.

The U.S. bishops were particularly concerned that the

schema should make specific mention of racial equality. Bishop Robert Tracy, of Baton Rouge, Louisiana, speaking in the name of 147 United States bishops, said that a reference to racial equality by the Council would bring consolation to people around the world who were deprived of rights and liberties, and subjected to sufferings and discrimination, not because of any transgression on their part, but simply because they belonged to a certain race. Although only countries such as the United States, South Africa, Rhodesia, and to some extent, also, Australia, were generally affected by racial problems, said Bishop Tracy, "their repercussions and effects today are international and are therefore proper matter for conciliar concern. We therefore ask," he concluded, "that a solemn dogmatic declaration on the equality of all men, with respect to nation and race, be included in the chapter on the People of God." His proposal was greeted with applause, and incorporated in the final text.

Cardinal Siri, of Genoa, took exception to the footnote on the first page of the chapter on the laity which announced that the Coordinating Commission had recently decided to make two chapters out of it, one on the People of God, and the other on the laity. He said that he was very much in favor of the biblical expression "People of God" but opposed to devoting a separate chapter to it. "From such a chapter, it might be inferred that the People of God can subsist, or can achieve something, even without the Church. That would be contrary to the teaching that the Church is necessary for salvation." This proposal, however, was not supported, and the order indicated in the footnote was adopted.

The examination of the chapter on the laity stretched from the forty-ninth General Congregation on October 16 to the fifty-fifth General Congregation on October 24. In that time 82 speakers had addressed the assembly: 13 cardinals, 1 patriarch, 16 archbishops, 49 bishops, and 3 superiors general. The chapter was sent back to the Theological Commission for a further revision.

RELIGIOUS ORDERS AND THE UNIVERSAL VOCATION TO SANCTITY

One of the unpublicized minority groups at the Council was the Roman Union of Superiors General, comprising 125 Council Fathers, some bishops, but most of them priests. These Fathers were particularly disturbed by the fact that, in the interim between the first and second sessions, the members of the European alliance had succeeded in prevailing upon the Coordinating Commission of the Council to delete the chapter on religious life from the schema on the Church, and to replace it by a new chapter entitled, "The Vocation to Sanctity in the Church."

The position of the European alliance was based on the arguments advanced by Father Rahner and Monsignor Philips, and submitted to the German-speaking Fathers meeting in Munich in February, 1963. Those arguments were that the inclusion of the chapter on the religious life would "confirm Protestants in their objections, namely, that in the Church, through the religious state, there exist two essentially diverse paths to salvation; that the laity are not called to evangelical perfection and automatically are always on a lower level of sanctity; and that those who are members of religious orders are automatically considered better than those who are joined in marriage."

The Munich Fathers forwarded these considerations to the Theological Commission; and, in the process of the revision of the schema, the chapter on religious was duly dropped, and a new chapter included instead on the universal vocation to sanctity in the Church. When news of this revision reached the German-speaking and Scandinavian Council Fathers gathered at Fulda in August, they wrote to Rome expressing their satisfaction at "the victory that has finally been won—after long discussions—for the view that this chapter should treat of sanctity in the entire Church, and should make special but not exclusive mention in that context of those in religious life."

It was against this background that the Roman Union of Superiors General decided on October 14 to request a detailed report on the matter from Bishop Enrico Compagnone of Anagni, a Discalced Carmelite whom Pope John had appointed to the Commission on Religious; he had previously been a member of the Preparatory Commission on Religious.

Bishop Compagnone explained that the preparatory commission had expressed the desire that the schema on the Church should contain something on religious orders, "since they constitute an integral part of the Church." In consequence, the Theological Preparatory Commission had included in its schema a chapter entitled "On the States of Life Devoted to Achieving Evangelical Perfection." Immediately after the first session, the Coordinating Commission had instructed a joint commission made up of members of both the Theological Commission and the Commission on Religious to review that chapter. The joint commission had agreed on a new title, namely, "On Those Who Profess the Evangelical Counsels." However, after the text had been returned to the Theological Commission, the title had been changed to read "On the Vocation to Sanctity in the Church," and the text had also been "substantially altered." He labeled as "perplexing" these steps taken by the Theological Commission on its own initiative.

While there were positive elements in the new chapter, said Bishop Compagnone, such as the emphasis on the fact that all members of the Church were called to holiness, it was defective in its presentation of the nature of the religious life. It stated merely that the purpose of the religious life was to bear witness to the fact that the evangelical counsels were followed in the Church. That, however, was only one aspect of the religious life. Those in the religious life, he said, constituted "a vital part of the Church." Various forms of the apostolate would perhaps never have come into existence but for the religious orders: for example, the missionary apostolate, which was an essential function of the Church, and which had in practice been carried out solely by religious, at least up to modern times.

Bishop Compagnone proposed that a chapter should be included headed "On Religious," in which it would be clearly stated, as had been agreed in the joint commission, that "Christ wished to have in his Church consecrated souls who would follow the evangelical counsels." Precisely because this was Christ's will, the schema on the

Church ought to speak of the religious life, and to clarify the position effectively occupied by members of religious orders in the Church.

The Council's Commission on Religious had decided that all statements on the vocation to sanctity in general should be transferred to the chapter "On the People of God." The schema would then have this logical sequence: 1. The Mystery of the Church; 2. The People of God; 3. The Hierarchy; 4. The Laity; 5. Religious. Bishop Compagnone urged the superiors general to make oral and written representations to secure this order and formulation.

After further discussion, the Roman Union of Superiors General decided to request the introduction in the schema of a new chapter on religious.

On October 22, Father Schütte, Superior General of the Society of the Divine Word, officially proposed in the Council hall the sequence of chapters for the schema on the Church which had been advocated by Bishop Compagnone. Father Schütte suggested further that everything pertaining to the universal call to holiness should be treated in the chapter on the People of God. That chapter dealt with all members of the Church as a whole, and it should therefore treat of the call which all received to holiness. "If in this schema on the Church," he said, "we have a special chapter on the hierarchy . . . , even though there is another entire schema on bishops, and if we have an entire chapter on the laity, although still another schema is going to treat of the lay apostolate, then why can we not have a special chapter which properly treats of religious?"

Religious, said Father Schütte, should not be considered in the schema on the Church "only from the

149

viewpoint of their vocation to sanctity, but also from the viewpoint of their educational, charitable, social, pastoral, and especially missionary work, which is of the greatest importance for the life of the whole Church." Over one third of all those entitled to attend the Council, he pointed out, were members of religious orders. Moreover, one third of all priests in the world were members of religious orders, and there were altogether some 2 million men and women in the world who had consecrated themselves to Christ in the religious state. "Why, therefore, do we appear to be ashamed to speak out about members of religious orders properly and clearly, distinctly and explicitly, not only about their vocation to sanctity, but also about their fruitful activity which is so necessary to the life of the Church?"

Some days later, Cardinal Döpfner addressed the Council on behalf of seventy-nine German-speaking and Scandinavian Council Fathers. He praised the new chapter on the vocation to sanctity, because it laid down that all the People of God were called upon to practice the evangelical counsels, thereby refuting the false notion that there were different classes of Christians, more or less perfect by reason of their state of life. He suggested that the Council should warn religious not to live for themselves and remind them that they were called upon, together with other groups of the faithful, to form a united Christian people.

Cardinal Léger of Montreal recalled that the monastic ideal of holiness had long been the prototype on which all Christian life had been modeled. But since the life of lay people was so different from that of monks and other members of religious orders, sanctity had seemed to them to be unattainable. Many of the faithful, the Cardinal continued, had searched in vain for a life modeled on the Gospels and suited to their needs. A great loss of spiritual forces in the Church had resulted. Consequently, he said, the laity would welcome the propositions contained in the chapter on the universal call to holiness.

The Cardinal pointed out, further, that the only specific aspect of lay life mentioned in the text was the conjugal life. But the search for holiness must be pursued by people regardless of their age, and whether or not they were married. He asked that mention be made of "all the activities of human life: daily work, political affairs, cultural activities, leisure, and recreation, since through them and in them holiness must be developed."

Cardinal Bea contended that the schema was not realistic enough, since the Church included sinners as well as holy persons. He therefore called for a distinction "between the Church in heaven which is perfectly holy, and the Church on earth which tends dynamically to sanctity, but is never perfectly holy." The way in which the schema cited Scripture was "unworthy of the Council," he said, in referring to several examples where Scripture texts were used to support statements to which they had no reference.

Bishop Frane Franić, of Split-Makarska, Yugoslavia, spoke of poverty as a necessary condition for holiness of bishops. "When the Church was poor, it was holy. When it became rich, sanctity diminished accordingly." Bishops, he said, had a much greater obligation to be holy than all other members of the Church, "because as bishops we must sanctify others." But, he pointed out, since the Middle Ages, most saints had come from the ranks of the religious orders, not from the ranks of the bishops. "This would seem to indicate a lack of heroic sanctity among bishops," he said, "and I believe the reason for it is a lack of evangelical poverty." Diocesan priests and religious orders also needed to reform themselves in the matter of poverty, he added.

A good number of bishops belonging to religious orders, as well as some superiors general, had prepared statements in favor of the inclusion of an entire chapter on the religious life in the schema on the Church, and had given due notice of their desire to speak. But day after day of discussion passed, and their names were not called out by the Cardinal Moderators.

On October 30, the assembly voted to close the discussion, but many of those scheduled to speak took advantage of the rule which allowed one to address the assembly after cloture, provided five Council Fathers had endorsed the request.

Cardinal Döpfner was Moderator at the fifty-ninth General Congregation, on October 31. Before permitting any speakers to come to the microphone, he announced that many Council Fathers were complaining that the Council was proceeding too slowly. In order to preserve the right to speak of those Council Fathers who had obtained five signatures, and at the same time to satisfy the general desire of the assembly to close the discussion and keep moving, he asked speakers "to confine their remarks to pertinent matter, to avoid repetitions, to stay within an eight-minute time limit instead of the usual ten, and to remember that statements not delivered in the Council hall but presented in writing have equal weight before the Commissions."

This latter recommendation, which the Cardinal himself did not follow, was followed consistently by Archbishop Felici, the Secretary General, who because of his position had renounced his right to deliver interventions.

Cardinal Döpfner intervened frequently during the speeches on that day, reminding the Council Fathers of the points that he had mentioned. At least three speakers were interrupted twice. Three others were interrupted once, or were told when they had finished that what they had said was not pertinent to the matter at hand. Many Council Fathers found it hard to understand the Cardinal's hasty manner and his seemingly arbitrary reduction of the time allowed to speakers.

Father Agostino Sepinski, Superior General of the Franciscans and President of the Roman Union of Superiors General, was the nineteenth speaker to take the floor that day. He suggested that the text on the universal call to holiness in the Church should be transferred from Chapter 4 to the chapter on the People of God. Chapter 4, he said, should treat only of the religious state, according to the logical sequence of chapters. He informed the assembly that the superiors general, at one of their meetings, had unanimously decided to request the inclusion of a special chapter on the religious state in the schema on the Church.

Bishops from religious orders waiting to speak were not invited to the microphone. At the same time, others whose names had been handed in only that morning were called upon to speak. The silenced Council Fathers were so indignant that they decided to send Cardinal Döpfner a private warning, stating that they would not allow the matter to rest and would ask for an official investigation if there was no change. But when they tried to contact him, they found that he had left for Capri for a long weekend and was not due back until the evening of November 4.

On his return, Cardinal Döpfner found a message from the offended Council Fathers waiting for him. He called them together, apologized for what had happened, promised that it would never happen again, and asked them to renounce their right to speak. They refused. He then agreed to read a summary of their speeches in the Council hall and asked them to indicate the points they considered essential. At the sixty-second General Congregation, on November 7, he read a summary, but not the one that they had been asked to prepare. It was extremely short, obscure, and in many places inaccurate.

The immediate result was that seven bishops from different religious orders met to decide on action to neutralize the German and Belgian element which they felt was exerting a "dictatorship" in the Council. They drew up a series of propositions, or *postulata*, concerning the schema on the Church, including, in particular, a demand for a separate chapter on the religious life. The *postulata* were printed in large numbers to be distributed to individual Council Fathers for their study and signatures.

On November 11, the seven bishops met with thirty-five other bishops from thirty-five other religious congregations, and it was decided to give the organization permanency and elect a board of seven presidents. The first of these was Archbishop Pacifico Perantoni of Lanciano, Italy, a former Superior General of the Franciscans and a close acquaintance of Pope Paul VI. Bishop Richard Lester Guilly, S.J., of Georgetown, British Guiana, was elected secretary. The name decided upon for the organization was "The Bishops' Secretariat," and its offices were set up in the international headquarters of the Jesuit order.

When the Roman Union of Superiors General held its regular meeting two days later, it decided to establish immediate liaison with this new group, and to give full support to the project of collecting signatures for the *postulata*. For the balance of the Council, the Bishops' Secretariat and the Roman Union of Superiors General worked hand in hand. Because of the disdain shown by many diocesan bishops and Roman Curia bishops for religious orders, it would not have been possible for the Roman Union of Superiors General alone to conduct a program at the Council with anything near the success that the Bishops' Secretariat could hope for.

Within two weeks, the *postulata* had been signed by 679 Council Fathers, including seventeen cardinals. The seven presidents of the Bishops' Secretariat then personally presented the signed *postulata* to the Secretary General of the Council and to Cardinal Browne, Vice-President of the Theological Commission, at the same time giving them an oral explanation of the background of the matter. Both the Secretary General and Cardinal Browne said that they would take the matter up with Pope Paul. The Pope subsequently referred the *postulata* to the Theological Commission with a personal note saying that he was sending them "for diligent and careful study." In a separate letter to Archbishop Perantoni, of the Bishops' Secretariat, Pope Paul explained what he had done, expressed his thanks for the interest shown by the Bishops' Secretariat, said he hoped it would continue its work, and applauded the fact that religious were collaborating in so positive a way in the work of the Council.

When the Theological Commission revised the schema on the Church once more between the second and third sessions, it added a new chapter "On Religious." The reason it gave in its report was that "very many Council Fathers, including the 679, have explicitly and formally requested a chapter to be reserved for religious." This was the first defeat for the European alliance. Its iron grip on the Council had been broken, because a group had come into being with comparable powers of organization.

THE ROMAN CURIA UNDER FIRE: SCHEMA ON BISHOPS AND THE GOVERNMENT OF DIOCESES

The discussion of the schema on bishops and the government of dioceses opened on Tuesday, November 5, at the sixtieth General Congregation.

That morning I had a special pass to attend the meeting. At 9 A.M. chimes tinkled softly, inviting the Council Fathers who filled the broad aisle between the two banks of tiered seats to take their places. They did so quickly, and five minutes later the chimes tinkled again and a voice announced in distinct Latin over the crystal-clear public address system that His Beatitude, Paul II Cheikho, Babylonian Patriarch of Baghdad, Iraq, was about to celebrate Mass in Aramaic in the Chaldaean rite. When the bishops lowered their private kneelers, it sounded like thunder rumbling through the basilica.

Half an hour later, when Mass was over, the hushed basilica burst into life as Council Fathers adjusted their collapsible tables, reached into portfolios for notes and official documents, glanced at the morning newspaper, or exchanged comment with those sitting around them. Latecomers hurried through the center aisle to their places. Five minutes later the Book of the Gospels was solemnly enthroned, and then one of the Presidents said: "In the name of the Father, and of the Son, and of the Holy Spirit. Amen." Immediately afterwards all Council Fathers and the *periti* prayed together the "*Adsumus*" ("We are here before You, O Holy Spirit") prayer, and then the day's business began, with one speaker following the other at the microphone without a break.

The new schema was presented by Paolo Cardinal Marella, President of the Commission concerned, and Bishop Carli, of Segni, followed with a report on the origin, development, and content of the schema. One of the five chapters was titled, "Relationships between Bishops and the Roman Curia."

Paul Cardinal Richaud, of Bordeaux, France, made a brief speech in which he said that the Roman Curia should be reorganized with a view to a better distribution of functions, a clearer definition of competency, and a more satisfactory degree of coordination. The membership of the Roman Curia should become international, and it should include diocesan bishops.

These points were also emphasized by the next speaker, Bishop Giuseppe Gargitter, of Bressanone, Italy. Just as the bishops were in the service of the People of God, so too the Roman Curia should be in the service of the bishops, he said. The mere concession of faculties was not enough; effective decentralization was needed. He called for the internationalization of the Curia, saying that no Western nation or nations should have a privileged position in that body. The schema should include a reference to the function of international and even intercontinental episcopal conferences, as well as to national ones.

Bishop Jean Rupp, of the Principality of Monaco, humorously referred to the schema as a "model of Roman brevity"—so short that important questions such as the compulsory retirement of bishops for reasons of age were developed up to a certain point and then left hanging up in the air. The principle laid down for the reorganization of dioceses was much too general, since the schema indicated merely that "dioceses should be neither too large nor too small." He suggested, further, that bishops had been so careful about clearly stating their rights in the schema on the Church that in this schema it would be well to set out clearly the rights of others in the Church, especially of priests.

Following the example of many Council Fathers, I left my seat halfway through the meeting and went to the coffee shop which the Council Fathers had christened "Bar Jona." (Coffee shops in Rome are known as bars.) This one was set up in a sacristy, and inside I had to elbow my way through noisy groups of bishops and *periti* drinking coffee and soft drinks. Archbishop D'Souza, of Bhopal (formerly of Nagpur), whom I met that day in the coffee shop, assured me that criticism of the schema would increase as the days went by. "No one has anything to fear from giving us bishops more power; we are not children," he said.

The Indian prelate was right. In a fiery address, Patri- arch Maximos IV charged that the schema envisaged "only a slight and timid reform in the central government of the Church," since it provided that "bishops might *possibly* be invited from the entire world to become members or consultants of the Sacred Congregations of the Roman Curia." The Patriarch maintained that restricting the bishops' collaboration to the Sacred Congregations corresponded "neither to the actual needs of the Church in our times, nor to the collegial responsibility that the episcopate has toward the Church." His suggestion was that "the task of assisting the Pope in the general government of the Church should be given to a limited number of bishops representing their colleagues." These representatives should be "the residential and apostolic patriarchs, the cardinal-archbishops by virtue of their archiepiscopal sees . . . , and finally, bishops chosen by the episcopal conferences of every country." This group, he said, should constitute the new Sacred College to be convoked by the Pope at fixed times, "whenever the need is felt for discussion on the general affairs of the Church."

Cardinal König, of Vienna, made a similar proposal. The schema should contain practical suggestions on the manner in which the bishops, with and under the Roman Pontiff, might collaborate in the government of the Universal Church. "Once or twice a year," he said, "if the world is at peace, the Roman Pontiff might call together the presidents of episcopal conferences, and also certain other bishops, to take counsel with them and find out what they think about matters affecting the Universal Church . . . . In this, or some similar way, unity will be established between the center and the periphery through closer contact between the Supreme Pontiff and the Episcopal College; real assistance will be rendered by bishops in the government of the Universal Church; and there will be more communication between mission territories and other countries."

Dutch-born Bishop Francis Simons of Indore, India, speaking in the name of thirteen bishops, said that Christ had entrusted the Church not only to the Pope, but also to all the bishops under the primacy of the Pope, because of the diversity of peoples, languages, and cultures in the world. The Roman Curia in its present form, he said, "is not aware of local conditions, nor does it sufficiently represent the bishops of the whole world"; it was therefore not a suitable instrument for the exercise of universal jurisdiction over the Church. "Often," he added, "it is not an instrument of the Pope, but a barrier between him and the bishops."

Cardinal Alfrink, of Utrecht, speaking on behalf of the Dutch bishops, pointed out that, if collegiality was by divine right, then the episcopal college took precedence over the Curia, and the Curia was not entitled to stand between the Pope and the bishops. This was a theological as well as a juridical question, he said, and one which did not lessen the dignity of the Curia or the respect and gratitude owed to it.

Cardinal Spellman, of New York, drew attention to articles appearing in newspapers and periodicals with interpretations of Council discussions; these, he said, were often misleading, and detrimental to the welfare of souls. "The authority of the Pope is full and supreme," he said. "It is neither necessary nor essential that the Pope share this authority with the bishops, although he may do so if he wills." And since the Roman Curia was in fact the executive instrument of the Pope, only the Pope was competent to judge and reform it. "This is something that he has already indicated he will do."

Bishop Pablo Correa Leòn, of Cúcuta, Colombia, speaking on behalf of sixty bishops from Latin American countries, proposed a structural change in the schema. In its existing form, he said, it treated only of matters pertaining to the bishop's role as "ruler of a community." Another schema, on the care of souls, considered the bishop's role as sanctifier and teacher. "But these three roles of ruler, teacher, and sanctifier are three different aspects of the same pastoral office of bishops, and they are complementary." For "the only reason why a bishop has any power to rule at all, or to prohibit, or even to punish, is precisely in order that he may be able effectively to carry out his pastoral office, which obliges him to lead souls, endowed with faith and vivified by grace, to eternal salvation. Consequently, the power to rule is intimately and logically bound up with the bishop's role as sanctifier and teacher." He therefore urged that the schema should show clearly that the power to rule flowed from the very nature of the pastoral office of the bishop.

Italian-born Bishop Edoardo Mason, of El Obeid,

161

Sudan, rose in defense of the Roman Curia. "My personal experience," he said, "has shown me that the Roman Curia as well as papal delegates are always a great help in difficulties and a good friend at all times." Everyone was aware that an *aggiornamento* was needed in the Curia, and the Pope himself had said so. "But we are all in need of this *aggiornamento*," said Bishop Mason. "Perhaps the patriarchate needs an *aggiornamento* too!" And instead of bishops being eager to obtain more faculties, perhaps they should abandon some of those they already possessed, such as wearing a special cape and having the title "Excellency."

Patriarch Ignace Pierre XVI Batanian, Armenian Patriarch of Cilicia, with residence in Beirut, Lebanon, begged the Council Fathers to be "objective and calm in making their observations on the present form of the central administration of the Church, giving due consideration to the merits of the Supreme Pontiff's collaborators, and to the obligation of avoiding scandal." The bishops, he said, were certainly free to suggest whatever they considered effective and useful for the Church. But he asked that "while we do this, we should not give others occasion to think that the Church through its present method of administration has been reduced to a lamentable condition." A tree must be judged by its fruits, "and we must say that the Church, notwithstanding the calamities that plague the world, is experiencing a glorious era, if you consider the Christian life of the clergy and of the faithful, the propagation of the faith, and the salutary universal influence possessed by the Church in the world today."

It was difficult for the public to understand how the bishops could pour such severe criticism upon the Roman

Curia which had given those bishops, the Pope, and the Church so many decades, generations, and centuries of service.

COLLEGIALITY *N. B*

In the minds of many Council Fathers, the purpose of the Second Vatican Council was to balance the teaching of the First Vatican Council on the papal primacy by an explicit doctrine on episcopal collegiality. Just as the doctrine of the papal primacy clarified the right of the Pope to rule over the Universal Church alone, so too collegiality was to establish the right of bishops to rule the Universal Church in union with the Pope. It was to be expected that collegiality should be differently interpreted by different groups in the Council.

Among the adherents of the European alliance, for example, some theologians took the view that the Pope was bound in conscience to consult the College of Bishops on important matters. But not all Council Fathers shared this view. In fact, it was not even clear whether a majority of Council Fathers favored the principle of collegiality in any form, even after the matter had been discussed for nine days.

On the final day of discussion, Tuesday, October 15, the Cardinal Moderators announced that four points would be presented to the Council Fathers in writing on the following day to determine the four principal arguments of Chapter 2 of the schema on the Church, and that these points would be put to the vote one day later. On Wednesday, however, the Moderators announced that the distribution of the four points would take place "on another day." Day after day passed, and no further mention was made of the matter.

The action suggested by the Moderators had been an innovation, not provided for by the Rules of Procedure, and had been overruled by the Presidency.

Subsequently, on October 23, a compromise solution was finally worked out by the Presidency, the Coordinating Commission, and the Moderators, and on October 29 the printed text of the four points was distributed to the Council Fathers.

The text asked the Council Fathers whether they wished to have Chapter 2 of the schema on the Church revised to state:

1. That episcopal consecration was the highest grade of the sacrament of Holy Orders;

2. That every bishop legitimately consecrated and in communion with other bishops and the Roman Pontiff, their head and principle of unity, was a member of the College of Bishops;

3. That this College of Bishops succeeded the College of Apostles in its role of teaching, sanctifying, and caring for souls, and that this college, together with its head, the Roman Pontiff, and never without him (whose primacy over all bishops and faithful remained complete and intact), enjoyed full and supreme power over the Universal Church; and

4. That that power belonged by divine right to the College of Bishops united with its head.

An accompanying note informed the Council Fathers that these points would be put to the vote the following day. It explained further that by their votes the Council Fathers would "neither approve nor reject any text" contained in the schema, since the voting had no other purpose than to "make it possible for the Theological Commission to determine the feelings of the assembly concerning the proposed points." The Commission expressly obliged itself, in accordance with the Rules of Procedure of the Council, to "give due consideration to the individual interventions of Council Fathers"; furthermore, it would submit the text of the schema in its entirety for a vote by the Council Fathers in a General Congregation. It was explained further that the Moderators were taking this action because it had been requested by many Council Fathers, and even by entire episcopal conferences.

These carefully phrased qualifications on the significance of the vote indicated clearly that there were some influential Council Fathers who feared that the vote might be used by the controlling liberal element in the Theological Commission as a reason for ignoring all arguments to the contrary that had been presented in oral and written interventions.

The voting which took place on October 30 was another brilliant victory for the liberals. The first point was carried by 2,123 votes to 34; the second by 2,049 to 104; the third by 1,808 to 336; and the fourth by 1,717 to 408.

Bishop Wright of Pittsburgh, a liberal member of the Theological Commission, said that the vote was of the greatest importance because it showed that an overwhelming majority of Council Fathers shared "the tendencies of the Council in this important matter." He did not attach any importance to the 408 negative votes on the question of collegiality, saying that those who had voted against the point had done so for many different reasons, and this did not necessarily signify that they did not have "faith in this project." They might be against the formulation, or they might consider the moment inopportune.

Father Gregory Baum of Toronto, one of the *periti*, hailed the voting results as "support of the position of the Moderators." He also said that the successful use of this procedural device would enable the Cardinal Moderators in the future to discover the majority feeling of the Council Fathers on a particular subject without the need to hear an interminable stream of speakers.

On November 5, when the schema on bishops and the government of dioceses came up for discussion, at least six Council Fathers found fault with it because it appeared to ignore the notion of collegiality.

The next day, Cardinal Browne of the Roman Curia, Vice-President of the Theological Commission, said that there was no foundation for the objections made the previous day, "because the notion of collegiality has not yet been determined accurately by the Council or by the Theological Commission." He stated that it would be necessary to await the report of the Theological Commission for clarification of this basic point before taking any practical action.

Two days later, Cardinal Frings referred to Cardinal Browne's remarks as "indeed amazing." Those remarks, he said, would seem to imply that the Theological Commission had access to sources of truth unknown to the rest of the Council Fathers. Such observations, he went on, lost sight of the fact that the Council commissions were intended to function only as instruments of the General Congregations, and to execute the will of the Council Fathers. While the October 30 vote had been merely indicative, "an almost unanimous assent should not be considered as of no value at all."

In another part of his address, Cardinal Frings called for a clear distinction between administrative and judicial practice in the Roman Curia. "This distinction should also be applied to the Holy Office," he declared. "Its methods in many cases no longer correspond to modern conditions, and as a result many are scandalized." The task of safeguarding the faith was extremely difficult, he said, but even in the Holy Office "no one should be judged and condemned without a hearing, and without an opportunity to correct his book or his action." The Cardinal was applauded several times during his address.

Cardinal Ottaviani, of the Holy Office, happened to be on the list of speakers on the same day. "I must protest most strongly concerning what has just been said against the Holy Office, whose President is the Supreme Pontiff," he began. "Such words were spoken out of lack of knowledge—I do not use another word lest I offend—of Holy Office procedure." He explained that experts in the Catholic universities of Rome were always called in to study cases carefully, so that the cardinals who made up the Congregation of the Holy Office might be able to base their judgment on certain knowledge. Their resolutions were then submitted to the Supreme Pontiff for his approval.

As for the votes which had been taken in the Council hall on October 30, they had been "only an indication of the thinking of the Council Fathers." It was unfortunate, he said, that the points voted on had been proposed by the four Moderators without first being submitted to the Theological Commission, which was competent in the matter, since it touched on dogma. Those points had contained equivocal terms which should have been clarified. In particular, the point on collegiality had presumed the existence of the Apostolic College, of which the present College of Bishops was said to be the successor. "But this is a case of confusion on the nature of episcopal succession," he said. "It is true that the bishops succeed the Apostles, but they do not succeed the College of Apostles as a college, because the College of Apostles as such did not exist, at least not in a juridical sense." There had been only one example of collegiality among the Apostles, and that had been at the Council of Jerusalem. No one doubted that at Jerusalem the Apostles had acted as a college, he said, "just as no one doubts that the bishops today, in Council, are acting as a college with and under the Pope." Christ's words "Feed my sheep" had been addressed only to his vicar, "and therefore whoever wants to be counted among the sheep of Christ must be under the universal pastor appointed by Christ." There were no exceptions to this rule, "not even bishops."

Archbishop D'Souza of India charged Cardinals Browne and Ottaviani with acting as though the indicative votes taken on October 30 "were null and void because the collegiality of bishops had not yet been juridically established. . . . Does this not seem like an act of derision of the Council, to say that there is no obligation to take into consideration the views which 85 percent of the Council Fathers have clearly expressed by vote?" He found it difficult to see how a few bishops from around the world "scattered among the various Sacred Congregations," as called for by the schema on bishops and the government of dioceses, could have any real influence on the Roman Curia "when 2,200 bishops from all parts of the world, gathered together for an Ecumenical Council, find it difficult at times to resist certain pressures."

The common good of the Church, continued the Archbishop, would be greatly promoted "if some Senate, so to say, were formed of bishops from various countries, who might rule the Church with the Supreme Pontiff." But it would be even more desirable "if on the one hand the power of the Roman Curia were limited, and if on the other hand the bishops were granted all the faculties for the exercise of their office which belong to them by common law and by divine law." The Apostolic See, he said, would always "retain the right to reserve to itself those things which are opportune for the good of the entire Church." Archbishop D'Souza's address was greeted with tremendous applause.

At the next General Congregation, on November 11, the October 30 vote was again brought up, this time by Cardinal Döpfner. The impression was being created, he said, that while the Holy Spirit was working elsewhere, some enemy had sown in the Council hall the points presented for a vote on October 30. But collegiality had not been inserted "by stealth," he said. It was after a fifteen-day study that "the competent authority, that is, the Moderators," had presented propositions based in wording and sense upon the schema on the Church. The voting had served as a helpful indication not only for the

Theological Commission but also for the Council Fathers in discussing the schema. While the votes were not definitive, "what is clear should not be made obscure."

That evening, by coincidence, I had an appointment with Cardinal Ottaviani in his home to check out a story. When he came into the room and sat down, he seemed disturbed and said distractedly: "I have just come from a meeting of the Theological Commission and things look very bad; the French and the Germans have united everyone against us. . . ."

Ten days after the Frings-Ottaviani exchange, which received extensive and prolonged coverage in the press, I was approached by Bishop Dino Romoli, O.P., who had served in the Sacred Congregation of the Holy Office for eight years. He asked me whether I would be interested in carrying a report in the Divine Word News Service on the conduct of condemnation procedures in the Holy Office. He had informed Cardinal Ottaviani of his desire to have such a report published, and the Cardinal had readily agreed. I assured the Bishop that we would welcome his report.

To my question whether it was true that the Church's highest tribunal would condemn an accused person without a hearing, Bishop Romoli replied: "You have to distinguish. If one member of the Church accuses another of a crime for which the Holy Office is the competent tribunal, then the accused is always given a full hearing and has every opportunity of defending himself. He receives the assistance of a lawyer and may himself present the lawyer of his choice to the tribunal. The precautions taken to safeguard the accused in such a case are so extensive and elaborate as to appear at times even excessive."

Bishop Romoli pointed out that the condemnation of publications was an altogether different matter, "since here it is a question of a theory which, considered in itself, might be injurious to the integrity of Catholic doctrine and to souls." In such a case, he said, "where the orthodoxy of Catholic doctrine does not appear clear, or where orthodoxy is put in doubt, the Holy Office does not always listen to the interested party before pronouncing its verdict." In such condemnations, he said, the author's intentions were not called into question or condemned; the tribunal was concerned only with the author's theories.

To the question whether it would not be more humane to consult with an author before condemning his writings, the Bishop said that that could readily be done in the case of an unpublished manuscript. "But once the uncertain or false doctrines have already been published, what purpose would such interrogation serve?" It could not alter the impact of his writings on the Catholic world. "Before the Holy Office condemns a published work or issues a solemn warning to an author," the Bishop explained, "it makes a vast, accurate, and intensive investigation by consulting with highly qualified experts from various linguistic and national groups in order to be incontestably objective and secure in its judgment. At times such investigations take several years, so great is the delicacy with which the Holy Office treats this matter."

Observer-Delegates and Guests

On September 8, 1868, fifteen months before the opening of the First Vatican Council, Pope Pius IX sent an Apostolic Letter to all patriarchs and bishops of the Orthodox Church, inviting them to end their state of separation. If they agreed, they were to have the same rights at the Council as all other bishops, since the Catholic Church considered them to be validly consecrated. If they did not, they were to have the opportunity of sitting on special Council commissions composed of Catholic bishops and theologians, to discuss Council affairs, as at the Council of Florence in 1439. But the wording of the letter was offensive to the patriarchs and bishops. And they were further annoyed by the fact that the entire text was published in a Roman newspaper before they had received their personal copies. As a result, not a single Orthodox patriarch or bishop accepted the invitation.

Five days after writing the above letter, Pope Pius IX invited "all Protestants and other non-Catholics" to use the occasion of the Ecumenical Council "to return to the Catholic Church." A careful examination, his letter stated, would prove that not one of their groups, or all of them together, "constitute and are in any way that one Catholic Church which Jesus Christ founded, constituted, and willed to be; nor can these groups in any way be called a member or a part of this Church, as long as they are visibly separated from Catholic unity." He invited them "to strive to free themselves from that state in which they cannot be certain about their own salvation."

This letter, too, proved offensive, and achieved very little.

The failures of the First Vatican Council in promoting Christian unity hung like an ominous cloud over the second. But Pope John XXIII, in his optimism, appeared to ignore them. When he informed the world of his intention to convoke an Ecumenical Council, he immediately spoke of "a renewed invitation to the faithful of the separated Churches to follow us in friendship in this search for unity and grace, desired by so many souls in all parts of the world." And among the numerous commissions and secretariats that he established on June 5, 1960, to take in hand the more immediate work of preparation for the Council, was the Secretariat for Promoting Christian Unity. Its purpose was to establish contact with the Orthodox, Old Catholic, Anglican, and Protestant Churches, and to invite them all to send official representatives to the Council.

The religious climate in the world of Pope John XXIII was very different from what it had been in the days of Pope Pius IX. In the intervening years, the ecumenical movement, for the promotion of Christian unity, had taken firm hold of Christian communities around the world.

Many factors had contributed to the development of this truly providential movement. One was biblical research, which brought together Protestant, Anglican, Orthodox, and Catholic scholars. This was the first area of fellowship among the Christian churches.

Next came the World Council of Churches, founded specifically to promote Christian fellowship in all possible fields, which in less than thirty years saw its membership grow to 214 full-member and eight associate-member churches of the Protestant, Anglican, Orthodox, and Old Catholic communions.

Another contributing factor was the neo-pagan threat of Nazism in Europe during World War II, which threw Catholics and Christians of all other denominations together in defense of religion. This explains why Catholic interest in the ecumenical movement was first apparent in Germany, France, and Holland. Among the most active leaders of Catholic ecumenism were members of the Jesuit and Dominican orders.

The initial successes in these three countries were given added impetus when the Sacred Congregation of the Holy Office issued its lengthy "Instruction on the Ecumenical Movement" of December 20, 1949. This "Instruction" urged bishops throughout the world "not only to use diligence and care in watching over all these activities, but also to promote and direct them prudently, in order that those who are seeking for the truth and the true Church may be helped, and that the faithful may be shielded from the dangers which might so easily result from the activities of this movement."

Pope John's choice of Cardinal Bea—a German, a Jesuit, and a biblical scholar—was therefore not surprising; the fact that the Cardinal was seventy-nine years old seemed to be negligible.

With thousands of separated Christian churches around the world, it was impossible for each of them to be represented at the Council. Cardinal Bea's solution was to contact larger groups and invite them to send delegations which might represent all their affiliated churches.

Thus invitations were sent to the Lutheran World Federation, the World Alliance of Reformed and Presbyterian Churches, the World Convention of Churches of Christ (Disciples of Christ), the Friends' World Committee for Consultation, the International Congregational Council, the World Methodist Council, the International Association for Liberal Christianity and Religious Freedom, the World Council of Churches, the Australian Council of Churches, and other groups.

Archbishop John C. Heenan, of Liverpool, a member of Cardinal Bea's Secretariat, said in 1962: "It is not too much to say that the personality of the Pope has altered the outlook of non-Catholics in England to the Vatican. In the jargon of our day, we could say that Pope John has given a 'new image' to the Catholic Church in the minds of Protestants. . . . Dr. Fisher [former Archbishop of Canterbury] has told me that the attitude of Pope John inspired him to take the initiative of proposing a visit to the Vatican. This would have been unthinkable even so short a time ago as five years."

Cardinal Bea invited the Archbishop of Canterbury to send a representative delegation on behalf of the Anglican Church. The invitation was accepted. He then approached the Ecumenical Patriarch of Constantinople, Athenagoras, asking him to send a delegation representing the various branches of the Orthodox Church. But when the Patriarch approached the Russian Orthodox Church (Moscow Patriarchate), it showed no interest, maintaining that the Ecumenical Council was a private affair of the Catholic Church, which did not concern it. As international interest in the Council grew, however, so did that of the Russian Orthodox Church, and when Bishop Nikodim Rotow was asked at the New Delhi Assembly of the World Council of Churches, in November, 1961, whether the Russian Orthodox Church would send delegates to the Second Vatican Council, he replied that this was an embarrassing question, since it had not been invited.

Technically this was true, since the Russian Orthodox Church had not been directly invited by Cardinal Bea, but through the Ecumenical Patriarch in Constantinople, who considered himself to have the right of initiative in proposing to the other patriarchs a common delegation. And when Monsignor Jan Willebrands, Secretary of the Secretariat for Promoting Christian Unity, visited the patriarchal sees of the Middle East to explain to the patriarchs and their synods the matters to be treated by the Council, he learned that they too were all averse to being invited through the Ecumenical Patriarch at Constantinople. To their way of thinking, no one patriarch was superior to another; they were all on the same level. Cardinal Bea therefore issued invitations directly to each group in the Orthodox Church.

When Bishop Nikodim met Monsignor Willebrands in Paris in August, 1962, he told him that his Church would react favorably to an invitation if Monsignor Willebrands would go to Moscow and invite Patriarch Alexius personally. This Monsignor Willebrands did, visiting Moscow from September 27 to October 2. He explained the items on the Council agenda to the Patriarch, and issued a verbal invitation. He received no immediate reply, however, because the written invitation had not yet arrived.

The matter of Communism did not come up directly at either the Paris or the Moscow meetings. No request was made by the Russian Orthodox Church that the subject should not be treated at the Council, and no assurance was given by Monsignor Willebrands that it would not. In explaining the Council agenda, Monsignor Willebrands simply stated that the problem was treated positively in the Council program. However, he made it clear that, once the Council had opened, the Council Fathers were free to alter the program and introduce any topic they wished.

Cardinal Bea's written invitation arrived after Monsignor Willebrands' departure. On October 10, the day before the Council opened, Patriarch Alexius and his Synod telegraphed acceptance of the invitation. On the same day, Patriarch Athenagoras, of Constantinople, informed Cardinal Bea that he had been unable to assemble a representative delegation of the Orthodox Church as a whole, and that he was reluctant to send a delegation representing only his Ecumenical Patriarchate. (Neither his patriarchate, nor the Greek Orthodox patriarchate of Alexandria, sent representatives to the Council until the third session, and the patriarchates of Antioch, Athens, and Jerusalem never sent representatives at all.) Of the Orthodox present at the first session, in addition to the delegation from the Russian Orthodox Church, were representatives of the Coptic Orthodox Church of Egypt, the Syrian Orthodox Church, the Ethiopian Orthodox Church, the Armenian Orthodox Church, and the Russian Orthodox Church outside Russia.

Eleven days after the opening of the Council, it was

177

announced that Pope John had raised the Secretariat for Promoting Christian Unity to commission status. By refraining from publicizing this decision earlier, the Pope had in effect preserved intact the team of outstanding leaders in the ecumenical field whom Cardinal Bea had assembled in the previous two years. The Secretariat was the only "commission" which did not have sixteen elected members. Its new status meant that it was entitled to compose schemas, submit them to the general assembly, revise them where necessary, defend them, and perform all the other functions pertaining to Council commissions.

Before a month had passed, Cardinal Bea publicly expressed his great satisfaction with the reactions of the observer-delegates. It was "a true miracle," he said, that so many non-Catholic Christian churches had asked their members to pray for the Council, as contrasted with the atmosphere prevailing at the time of the First Vatican Council.

Professor Oscar Cullmann, of the Universities of Basel and Paris, who was a guest of the Secretariat for Promoting Christian Unity, gave a lengthy press conference at the end of the first six weeks of the first session to explain his reactions and those of other guests and observers. He said that they had received all the Council texts, were able to attend all General Congregations, could make their views known at special weekly meetings of the Secretariat, and had personal contact with Council Fathers, *periti*, and other leading personalities in Rome. The activities of the Secretariat for Promoting Christian Unity, he said, "daily reveal to us how truly its existence serves to draw us closer together."

Professor Cullmann pointed out that mistaken conclusions were being drawn from the presence of observers
and guests at the Council. He was receiving letters from
both Catholics and Protestants who appeared to think
that the purpose of the Council was to bring about union
between the Catholic and other Christian churches. That,
however, was not the immediate purpose of the Council, he said, and he feared that many such people would
be disillusioned when, after the end of the Council, they
found that the churches remained distinct.

Among the ecumenical achievements of the Council,
Professor Cullmann mentioned in the very first place
the existence of the Secretariat for Promoting Christian Unity. "If it continues to be full of respect for other
churches, and to work in a sincere ecumenical spirit such
as now characterizes all its actions and attitudes, one may
justly consider its existence as of extreme importance for
the future of ecumenism," he said. Another achievement
was the presence of observers and guests in the Council
hall. "I am more and more amazed every morning at the
way we really form a part of the Council," he said.

In preparation for the General Congregations, the
observers studied the schemas which had been distributed
to them. "We make notes on them, compare them with
the Bible, and check them with the writings of the Fathers
of the Church and the decisions of previous Councils.
Our reactions to the schemas which have been shown to
us so far have obviously been very varied: some we like,
others we don't; some really encourage us, others we find
disappointing."

Professor Cullmann noted that any future historian of

the Second Vatican Council must refer to the "ecumenical import" of the coffee shop installed for all members of the Council. "Not only does it refresh us, but it also enables us to meet bishops from all over the world in a way that would otherwise be impossible. . . . And if the dialogue is continued by both sides in the spirit which has animated it thus far, that in itself will be an element of unity capable of bearing still more fruit."

The experiment worked so well during the first session that it continued throughout the duration of the Council. When Pope Paul, early in the second session, received the observers and guests in audience, Cardinal Bea was able to announce that their number had increased from forty-nine to sixty-six, and that the number of churches or communities which they represented had grown from seventeen to twenty-two.

The observer-delegate of the Lutheran World Federation, Dr. Kristen Skydsgaard, addressed the Pope in French on behalf of all the observers and guests present, and expressed their "deep gratitude for the renewal of the invitation to this second session of the Council." All were reassured, he said, to learn that Pope Paul did not share the naively optimistic or superficial ecumenism based on the assumption "that the visible union of Christians can be quickly achieved." He hoped that the light shed by a practical and historical theology, "that is, a theology nourished by the Bible and by the teaching of the Fathers, will shine more and more in the work of this Council." He also spoke of a new ecumenical spirit which was becoming manifest in the Council. "We find ourselves meeting together at the beginning of a road whose end only God knows."

In reply, Pope Paul spoke of "our desire to receive you not only on the threshold of our house, but in the very intimacy of our heart." After thanking the observers and guests for accepting the invitation to attend the second session, he asked them to be assured "of our respect, of our esteem, and of our desire to have with you, in Our Lord, the best possible relations. Our attitude does not hide any snare, nor is it intended to minimize the difficulties that stand in the way of a complete and final understanding. We do not fear the delicate nature of the discussion nor the pain of waiting." As for the history of separation, he preferred to focus his attention "not on what has been, but on what must be. We turn toward a new thing to be born, a dream to be realized."

On the following day, October 18, Cardinal Bea gave a reception for the observers and guests. Addressing them in French, he invited their criticisms, reminding them of Pope Paul's words to the Roman Curia only a few weeks earlier: "We must welcome criticism with humility, with reflection, and even with gratitude. Rome has no need to defend itself by turning a deaf ear to suggestions that come from honest voices, especially if the voices are those of friends and brothers." Cardinal Bea assured the observers and guests that their positive criticism, suggestions, and wishes would be greatly esteemed.

Archpriest Vitaly Borovoy, the observer-delegate of the Russian Orthodox Church and of the Orthodox Church of Georgia in the Caucasus, replied in Russian on behalf of the assembled observers and guests. "The whole history of Christianity in our era," he said, "is the history of the action of the Holy Spirit upon us and upon our churches, calling us to unity and helping us to understand the necessity and urgency of this task. . . . We are always ready to help our Roman Catholic brothers in anything which may contribute to harmony and unity among all Christians, so that, with a single tongue and a single heart, we may together glorify the most Holy Spirit."

Six weeks later he had an opportunity to prove how ready he was to contribute "to harmony and unity," when via telephone he was notified by Moscow to leave Rome immediately in protest because of a special religious service announced by the Vatican to honor St. Josaphat. This Catholic Saint, martyred in the year 1623 at Vitebsk, Poland (today, Russia), was considered by the Russian Orthodox Church responsible for the martyrdom of Orthodox Saints, and Archpriest Borovoy was ordered to conduct a religious service in Geneva in their honor while the religious service was being held in Rome. Archpriest Borovoy explained, however, that the order placed him in a dilemma since that same Monday, November 25, Cardinal Spellman was to conduct a Requiem service in St. John Lateran basilica for the recently assassinated President John F. Kennedy. His going to Geneva before this date would not only make ecumenical relations worse instead of better, he said, but the press could also be expected to interpret his going as an excuse not to participate in the Requiem service. His church headquarters in Moscow then rescinded the order.

The leader of the Anglican delegation, Bishop John Moorman, of Ripon, Britain, obligingly gave me a statement of his personal views on the primacy and collegiality. For 400 years, he said, the Anglican Church had lived in separation from the See of Rome, "and during that time the claims of the Pope have increased, especially with the decree of infallibility in 1870." However, if there was ever to be unity among Christians, "there will have to be a central head of the Church, and that head will certainly have to be the Bishop of Rome." It was his belief that the Anglican Communion as a whole "would be prepared to accept the fact of the papacy, though they would find great difficulty in recognizing the basis on which the primacy rests," since historically and exegetically "far too much has been made of the words of Our Lord to St. Peter." The Roman Catholic Church would be greatly strengthened, he said, "if the principle of collegiality of bishops were accepted, and some method were provided whereby representative bishops of the whole world could form a permanent council with the Pope." That, he said, would be "an improvement on the present system of a largely Italian Curia."

The observers and guests were particularly interested in the schema on ecumenism, which was taken up at the sixty-ninth General Congregation, on November 18. It comprised only three chapters, and it was presented to the assembly by Archbishop Joseph Martin of Rouen, France, a member of Cardinal Bea's Secretariat for Promoting Christian Unity. He explained that the schema was intended as a pastoral document for the instruction of Catholics, to help them to understand the significance and purpose of the ecumenical movement and its providential role in the Church.

Archbishop Casimiro Morcillo González, of Saragossa, Spain, said that one of the admirable qualities of the schema was its "positive tone," resulting from a reduction in the number of warnings and the complete disappearance of condemnations, such as had characterized previous documents on the subject. It would not be proper, he said, for the Catholic Church "to refuse to accept the collaboration now offered by our separated brethren in solving this very great question."

Cardinal de Arriba y Castro of Spain said that to foster dialogue, as was the intention of the schema, could be very dangerous "to the faith of our Catholics, especially those of low estate, who often are not prepared to answer the arguments presented by experts of the various sects or confessions." Endless proof existed, he said, that proselytizing by Protestants was on the increase. He therefore asked the Council Fathers "to include in the schema a request directed to the separated brethren that they abstain from all proselytism among Catholics, lest the faith of our people be obscured through confusion."

Cardinal Bea admitted on the Council floor that indifferentism and doubts concerning the faith might arise if ecumenical questions were treated by those whose good faith was not matched by learning and caution. The remedy was not to avoid all ecumenical efforts, he said, but rather to have them carried out under the direction of the bishop concerned. "We hope to issue an ecumenical directory," he explained, "but these rules and principles issued by the Holy See will have to be adapted to local conditions by the bishops themselves." Cardinal Bea recalled that the "Instruction" issued by the Holy Office in 1949 required that those who engaged in dialogue should be well versed in theology and should follow the norms laid down by the Church.

Archbishop Heenan said that the hierarchy of England and Wales were prepared "to do anything outside of denying the faith" to obtain the union of Christians. "We desire fuller and more frequent dialogues with all Christian denominations," he said.

Auxiliary Bishop Stephen Leven of San Antonio, Texas, told the assembly, on November 26, that "every day it becomes more clear that we need the dialogue, not only with Protestants, but also among us bishops." There were some Council Fathers, he said, who "preach to us and chastize us as though we were against Peter and his successors, or as though we desired to steal away the faith of our flocks and to promote indifferentism." Such bishops "prefer to blame non-Catholics, whom perhaps they have never seen, rather than instruct the children of their parishes. Otherwise, why are they so afraid that the effects of ecumenism would not be good? Why are their people not better instructed? Why are their people not visited in their homes? Why is there not an active and working Confraternity of Christian Doctrine in their parishes?"

Bishop Leven concluded in most solemn tones, "I pray you, Venerable Conciliar Brothers, let us put an end to the scandal of mutual recrimination. Let us proceed in an orderly way with the examination and study of this providential movement called ecumenism, so that with patience and humility we may achieve that unity for which the Lord Christ prayed at the Last Supper."

No voting took place during the eleven days of the discussion on the schema on ecumenism. But, on the basis of the numerous interventions made, a revision was to be prepared by the Secretariat for Promoting Christian

Unity; the revised text was to be presented to the Council at its third session.

WORLD ALLIANCE

On November 15, when Cardinal Lercaro, in the presence of the other Moderators, the Coordinating Commission, and the Council Presidency, read a progress report on the second session to Pope Paul VI, he said that the Council could move ahead with much greater speed "if we Moderators can use the same method that we used at the conclusion of the debate on Chapter 2 of the schema on the Church." According to this method, which had been used in voting on the four points and was now being requested "by many episcopal conferences," the Moderators—as the Cardinal said—would be empowered to determine "the major aspects of each debate," and would put them in the form of questions for voting, "so that directive norms could be provided for the commissions."

The requested authorization was not granted to the Moderators, who very likely could have obtained a majority vote on the Council floor for whatever proposals they might make. If adopted, this method would have given them the power to decide what was the majority opinion, and likewise would have made it possible for them to determine policy for the individual commissions. The Moderators, technically, were supposed to have only administrative authority, with the policy being determined by the general assembly after—not before—the commissions had thoroughly studied both the oral and written interventions, and had revised the schema in accordance with what it considered the mind of the Council Fathers to be. There were no further cases of "points" being formulated by the Moderators.

Having failed in getting this suggestion officially adopted, the Moderators—and the liberals whom they represented—sought other ways to gain more control over the individual commissions. The struggle for theological power was becoming more and more evident.

After November 15, there was increased agitation against so-called "Curia-controlled commissions." The solution for the problem, presented to the Pope in letters signed by individual Council Fathers and by entire episcopal conferences, was to hold new elections for all presidents, secretaries, and members of all Council commissions. The aim was to increase the number of liberal members on each commission. The European alliance by this time had full control of the Council majority and was confident that it could replace all conservative members on Council commissions if only it were given the opportunity. Less extreme proposals suggested that elections be held at least for new presidents and secretaries. Still another proposal was that the number of members on the individual Council commissions should be increased, since this would make more personnel available for subcommissions and then, theoretically, the work of the commissions could be accomplished more quickly.

On November 21, at the seventy-second General Congregation, the Secretary General announced that the Pope had decided to allow the number of members on each commission to be increased from twenty-five to thirty, "in order that the work of the Council commissions may be carried out more expeditiously and quickly." In doing so the Pope was responding "to the requests of many Council Fathers." It was further announced that the Council Fathers were to elect four members and the fifth would be appointed by the Pope, who also authorized each commission to choose from its members an additional vice president and from its *periti* an additional secretary.

The lengthy announcement also suggested that the presidents of episcopal conferences should assemble their members and name not more than three of them for each commission. These lists were to be submitted to the Secretary General by Monday, November 25, for printing and distribution, so that the election could take place on Thursday, November 28, one week after the announcement was made.

Most significant in the General Secretary's announcement was this sentence: "It is highly desirable that several conferences should unite and present a combined list."

With each member of a thirty-man commission representing 3⅓ percent of the commission's voting power, and with four members to be elected, there was at stake in this election 13⅓ percent of each commission's voting power. Realizing this, the European alliance set to work drawing up an unbeatable international list. This work was greatly facilitated since by this time, late in the second session, the European alliance had expanded into a world alliance. In point of fact, the origins of the world alliance went back to the beginning of the first session, and from that time it was always under the dominating influence of the European alliance.

The world alliance during the first session was an

undercover group of five or six bishops and archbishops, representing national, regional, or continental episcopal conferences, who met periodically. From the beginning of the second session, when they considered themselves strong enough to act more openly, they held meetings at Domus Mariae each Friday evening and saw their membership grow to twenty-four bishops and archbishops, who represented approximately sixty-five episcopal conferences.

The one who presided over the meetings was Coadjutor Archbishop Pierre Veuillot of Paris, whenever he was in Rome.

Although not juridically organized, the world alliance was able to determine the policy of the controlling liberal majority, and prepared sample letters which individual episcopal conferences then submitted to the Pope, requesting him to take specific action on specific issues. The secretaries of these twenty-four members held a meeting of their own every Tuesday night, thus making possible top level intercommunication twice every week.

When the lists of candidates for Council commissions were ready for distribution by the General Secretariat on November 27, they contained in the first place the combined list presented by the sixty-five episcopal conferences of the world alliance. Other lists were presented by eight national hierarchies, the superiors general, and three groups of Eastern Rite Churches.

When the results of the November 28 election were announced the next day, it was no surprise that all candidates elected to office came from the list proposed by the world alliance. Germans and Austrians had been so well

189

placed on the list that six of them were elected to office. France had to be satisfied with only two.

All candidates presented by the world alliance, however, did not fulfill Pope Paul's condition of being "truly skilled" in the material to be studied by their commissions. There was the case of the Council Father placed second on the list of candidates for the Theological Commission, who was elected to office with 1,448 votes. Some days before the election he presented a substitute schema on the Blessed Virgin Mary to sixty bishops meeting in the Columbus Hotel. When they raised objections against it, he could not answer them and admitted repeatedly that he was no theologian, but was simply presenting to the group a schema which had been drawn up for him by others.

After this election there was no longer need for anyone to doubt about the direction in which the Council was headed. Strangely enough, Pope Paul waited six weeks before publishing the names of his lone candidates for each commission.

ADOPTION OF THE SCHEMA ON COMMUNICATIONS MEDIA

The schema on communications media was presented at the first session on November 23 by Archbishop René Stourm of Sens, France, on behalf of the Commission on the Apostolate of the Laity, the Press and Information Media. After recalling that the press, radio, television, motion pictures, and other communications media were often sources of genuine pleasure and relaxation, he cited worldwide figures to illustrate their range: 8,000 daily newspapers with 300 million circulation; 22,000 other publications with 200 million circulation; 1,000 television stations and 120 million television sets; 6,000 radio stations and 400 million radio sets; 2,500 new motion pictures produced annually and shown to 17 billion viewers in 170,000 theaters. He therefore judged that these were "the most universal and most effective" vehicles of opinion, doctrine, and human communication.

The Church, he said, could not ignore the problem of mass media, since "by its very mission and nature it must make known the one and only message necessary for men, the message of salvation." For the first time in history, the Church had the possibility of making its message known to the whole world. Should it not regard the mass media as "a providential means for transmitting the Christian message more rapidly, more universally, and more effectively?" A profound scrutiny of modern communications media would reveal an invitation from God himself, "asking us to assume the task of guiding them." Yet instead of providing leadership in this field, and thus bringing others to Christ, he pointed out, the Church was experiencing more difficulty than ever before, and was seeing even its own sons "neglect the voices of their pastors to follow mercenaries imbued with a pagan or materialistic concept of life."

In order to remedy this situation, said the Archbishop, the Church must "establish norms for the faithful which will make it possible for them to enjoy such wonderful inventions with advantage." For the Church realized that modern man "would be nourished, educated, and formed by these media." Therefore the Church requested of the faithful "that they should work together with it to perfect them and bring about their righteous and honest use, so that through them the Christian concept of life and of the world might be more extensively and vigorously promoted." Those had been the underlying considerations in the preparation of the schema now before the Council.

By way of conclusion he referred to weaknesses in the schema, pointing out at the same time that the priests who specialized in this field were nearly all absorbed in the production aspect of communications, and stressing the fact that "the theologians have not yet made the contribution desired of them in this particular field." There had been a liturgical movement in the Church, a biblical movement, and an ecumenical movement, but there had not been an enduring communications movement.

Archbishop Stourm's address was aimed at rousing the bishops of the world from their lethargy, but relatively little constructive reaction to the schema resulted. Some Fathers pointed out that the schema was too long, too diffuse, too specific on points that were subject to daily change. They maintained that the schema should simply enunciate certain fundamental principles of permanent validity and leave the practical application to the experts. It was repeatedly stressed that laymen rather than clergy should be urged to take the leadership in the field of mass communications.

On the third day, after fifty-four Council Fathers had spoken on the schema, the assembly voted to close the discussion. And on the following day, by a vote of 2,138 to 15, a three-point statement on the schema was adopted. First, the assembled Fathers declared the substance of the schema satisfactory; it was fitting, they said, for the Church in view of its teaching office to treat explicitly of a matter of such great pastoral importance. Secondly, they instructed the Commission on communications media to review and summarize the essential principles and pastoral guidelines contained in the schema, and to submit the schema in shortened form. Thirdly, the balance of the existing schema should be revised and published in the form of a pastoral instruction.

The schema on communications media, as revised after the first session, was presented at the second session on November 14. It had been reduced from eleven chapters to two, from 114 articles to twenty-four, and from forty pages to nine.

When the vote was taken, 92 negative votes were cast on Chapter 1, and 103 on Chapter 2. The Secretary General announced that under the Rules of Procedure the schema in its revised form had received the necessary approval of the assembly. Nevertheless, the Moderators had decided to invoke Section 7 of Article 61 of the rules, which "in special cases" permitted another vote on the schema as a whole. No specific date was set for that vote, as the Commission concerned wished to examine the schema once more in the light of the new amendments that had been submitted.

That afternoon, at the U.S. Bishops' Press Panel, the revised schema came up for discussion. Wary journalists asked panel members for a full explanation of Article 12, which provided that the civil authority had the duty "to defend and protect a true and just availability of information; the progress of modern society utterly depends on this, especially as regards freedom of the press." They were particularly disturbed at the statement that the civil authority had "the duty of seeing to it in a just and vigilant manner that serious danger to public morals and social progress do not result from a perverted use" of communications media. This appeared to open the door to state censorship of the press.

Three Catholic newsmen, Mr. Robert Kaiser of *Time*, Mr. John Cogley of *Commonweal*, and Mr. Michael Novak of the *Catholic Reporter*, decided to alert the Council Fathers. They set out their views in a short statement and had four *periti* attest that their statement was "worthy of consideration"; the *periti* were Father John Courtney Murray, S.J., Father Jean Danielou, S.J., Father Jorge Mejia, and Father Bernard Häring, C.SS.R. The statement termed the proposed decree on communications media "not an *aggiornamento*, but a step backward," which might "one day be cited as a classic example of how the Second Vatican Ecumenical Council failed to come to grips with the world around it." In two important passages, said the authors, the schema seemed to give the state "an authority over mass media which is dangerous to political liberty everywhere and which in some countries like the United States is proscribed by constitutional law." Another passage could be interpreted as "endowing the Catholic press with a teaching authority and near infallibility that is neither proper to journalism nor helpful to the formation of public opinion in the Church."

The action taken by the three newsmen prompted some

of the *periti* to undertake a campaign of their own against the schema before the crucial vote, which had meanwhile been set for November 25. A Latin text was circulated, stating that the Council Fathers "ought to cast a negative vote" because the revised schema was no longer substantially the one discussed at the first session but really "a new schema." Since it might be difficult to persuade Council Fathers who had already voted in favor of the schema now to vote against it, it was suggested that the Moderators should place the following proposal before the general assembly: "Would it please the Council Fathers to have the Coordinating Commission incorporate this schema in the schema on the apostolate of the laity (on theological grounds), and in the schema on the Church in the modern world (on sociological grounds), so that the connection and force of the schema on communications media, which has been so worthily prepared by the Commission, may be more evident?" Thus an affirmative vote would in effect constitute a rejection of the schema.

Father Mejia, one of the *periti* who had endorsed the statement of the three newsmen, launched another drive of his own. He sent Council Fathers the following circular, printed in Latin and marked "Urgent": "On reading the schema on communications media once more before the final vote, many Council Fathers are of the opinion that the text of this schema is not fitting for a Council decree. The Council Fathers are therefore asked to consider seriously the advisability of casting a negative vote, because the schema does not conform to the expectation of Christians, especially of those who are skilled in this matter. Should it be promulgated as a decree, the authority of the Council would be jeopardized." Ample room was left on the paper for the signatures of Council Fathers. A brief letter accompanying the circular asked Council Fathers, if they were in agreement with the author, to obtain as many signatures as possible and to return them to the author by the evening of November 24. Cardinal Silva Henríquez, the letter said, would then deliver them the following morning to Cardinal Lercaro, who had indicated that he could make good use of them.

As was evident from the letter, Cardinal Lercaro, who was scheduled to direct that day's meeting, had a plan to block acceptance of the schema.

On the morning of November 25, Father Mejia stood on the steps of St. Peter's with a stack of printed copies of his petition bearing the names of twenty-five Council Fathers from fourteen countries who had signed and handed them to Council Fathers as they walked into the basilica. He was later relieved by Auxiliary Bishop Joseph Reuss of Mainz, Germany. The distribution proceeded peacefully until the huge, angry figure of Archbishop Felici appeared. The Archbishop tried to seize the papers from Bishop Reuss, a scuffle ensued, and the Bishop eventually surrendered them.

Before the voting took place that morning, Cardinal Tisserant, as Chairman of the Council Presidency and in the name of the Moderators, addressed the assembly on the matter. The distribution of circulars, he said, was "most vehemently to be deplored," particularly since the schema concerned had already been approved by more than the required two-thirds majority. He described the action as directed against conciliar tranquillity, as unworthy of an Ecumenical Council, and as an attack on the Council Fathers' freedom. Later the Secretary General announced that one of the Council Fathers named on the circular had deplored seeing his name published without his knowledge. In the face of this unfavorable publicity, the planned attempt at blocking the schema was dropped.

The result of the vote on the schema as a whole was 1,598 in favor and 503 opposed. In accordance with normal procedure, the Cardinal Moderator presented the schema to the Pope for promulgation as a decree, since it had received the required two-thirds majority.

On November 29, the following letter was sent to Cardinal Tisserant by eighteen of the twenty-five Council Fathers whose names had appeared on Father Mejia's circular:

"The President of the Sacred Council, together with the Moderators, at the General Congregation of the Council on November 25 of this year, deplored and designated as unworthy of the Council the fact that in St. Peter's Square papers signed by twenty-five Council Fathers were distributed, inviting other Council Fathers to consider seriously whether they should cast a negative vote on the schema on communications media. But there is no positive law of the Sacred Council forbidding the distribution of such papers; in fact, a short time earlier, a similar distribution took place without any mention of it being made by the President of the Sacred Council. Further, nowhere in the world where civil liberty flourishes is it forbidden to call the attention of those who are voting to the seriousness of their vote, nor is it even forbidden to win them over to one's own side.

"Therefore our manner of acting cannot be considered as a disturbance of the tranquillity of the Council, nor does it infringe upon its freedom. We took this action because no other way existed for us to appeal to the Council Fathers.

"Since that is how the matter stands, the Council Fathers who signed the aforementioned circular, and who sign below in their own hand, consider the statement made by the President of the Sacred Council as an offense, and they hope that the Most Eminent Chairman of the Council Presidency, when better informed about the affair, will discover some way of rectifying the matter."

Cardinal Tisserant answered with individual replies, dated December 2, as follows:

"I am very displeased that Your Excellency has taken offense. It was my intention, and likewise that of the Moderators, to provide for proper order in the Council, since this seemed to have been disturbed as a result of the distributed circulars. For, if the dignity of the Sacred Council and the liberty of the Council Fathers are to be safeguarded, it cannot be admitted that near the Council Hall, a few moments before a vote is to be taken, activity may be carried on against the text of a schema which has been properly prepared, properly presented, properly discussed, and properly approved, chapter by chapter, and which according to the norms governing Council procedure (Article 61, Section 6), can already be considered as being completely approved.

"Besides, it was the Most Eminent Moderators themselves who ordered me to deplore this affair, since complaints had been brought to them by Council Fathers.

"This, Your Excellency, is what I have to say in answer to your letter. For the rest be assured that I am filled with veneration toward Your Excellency, and I remain, your most devoted brother, ✠Eugenius Card. Tisserant."

At a public session in St. Peter's on December 4, the Council Fathers gave their formal approval to the decree on communications media by a final vote of 1,960 to 164. Pope Paul VI immediately promulgated the decree.

In that same month of December the Holy Father issued new norms for the *periti*, as follows:

"1. According to the work assigned, the reverend *periti* should answer with knowledge, prudence, and objectivity the questions which the commissions have proposed to them.

"2. They are forbidden to organize currents of opinions or ideas, to give interviews, or to defend publicly their personal ideas about the Council.

"3. They should not criticize the Council, nor communicate to outsiders news about the activities of the commissions, observing always in this regard the decree of the Holy Father about the secrecy to be observed concerning conciliar matters."

Before the opening of the third session, still another directive was issued: "Without the express permission of the President, which is to be obtained through the Secretary General, no one is permitted to distribute papers, treatises, printed matter, etc., of any kind whatsoever within the Council hall or in its vicinity. It is the duty of the Secretary General to see to it that this rule is observed."

These new norms and rules seemed to be aimed at pressure groups inside the Council.

Adoption of the Schema on the Liturgy, and Its Implementation

Bishop Zauner of Linz, Austria, was the best-known expert on liturgy among the Council Fathers. As a member of the Commission on the Sacred Liturgy, he was the logical choice to report to the Fulda conference in August, 1963, on the progress made by that commission.

The goal which the Liturgical Commission had always borne in mind during its discussion of the amendments proposed by Council Fathers, he said, was to produce a text which would be assured of gaining the support of two thirds of the Council assembly. For that reason, Bishop Zauner explained, many desirable points had been omitted. One such point was "the use of the vernacular in the breviary for a large part of the clergy in certain territories." He pointed out, however, that all "important issues that could be considered necessary for liturgical progress" had been accepted, and that the schema as drawn up by the Commission consequently deserved the support of all.

Bishop Zauner was disappointed with Article 57, which laid down the rules concerning concelebration. He explained that the numerous occasions for concelebration listed in an earlier draft, and which had been deleted by the subcommission on amendments during the preparatory stage of the Council, had not been restored. That was of little consequence, however, since "the opportunity for concelebration is practically extended to every group of priests."

He explained that in its meetings the Commission had

run into special difficulties regarding the language to be used when sacred rites were solemnized in song. There were some members who claimed that genuine Gregorian chant must necessarily be sung in Latin, whereas others maintained that this was not true. After lengthy discussion the commission decided to sidestep the issue, giving not even an implicit decision in the matter, so that—as the official commentary later said—"neither the true nature of the art of Gregorian chant may be disfigured, nor pastoral care may in any way be impeded." By referring in Article 113 of Chapter 6 to the general norms already listed elsewhere in the text, the Commission and subsequently the Council left bishops free to use either Latin or the vernacular when sacred rites were solemnized in song.

Bishop Zauner's hope that the Council Fathers would endorse the revised text was amply fulfilled at the second session. With approximately 2,200 Council Fathers voting, only 36 votes were cast against Chapter 2; 30 against Chapter 3; 43 against Chapter 4; and 21 against the combined Chapters 5, 6, and 7. The vote on the schema as a whole was 2,159 to 19; it took place in the morning of Friday, November 22, 1963, the sixtieth anniversary of the publication of the document, *Tra le sollecitudini*, issued by Pope St. Pius X, which had launched the whole liturgical movement.

In an interview following the vote, Bishop Zauner told me that four important aims or principles were reflected in the Constitution on the Sacred Liturgy. "The first is that divine worship must be a community action; that is, that the priest should do everything with the active participation of the people, and never alone." The use of the vernacular, he said, was a necessary condition for such participation.

A second principle was that the faithful must be enriched by Sacred Scripture directly, and not only through sermons. "Every liturgical function, including the marriage rite, will now include readings from Sacred Scripture."

A third principle was that, through liturgical worship, the people should not only pray but also learn. This was especially important, the Bishop said, in mission territories, where the priest could make only infrequent visits to his parishes. It was also necessary in countries suffering persecution, where religious instruction outside Mass was often forbidden. Even in free societies, the same need arose; the pace at which life moved was so rapid that if the faithful did not receive instruction at Mass, they often had no time for it at all.

The fourth principle applied specifically to mission territories. "Where there are tribal customs involving no superstitious elements, these may now be introduced in the liturgy," said Bishop Zauner. This process, known as adaptation, "may be carried out only by the authority of an episcopal conference assisted by experts from the linguistic areas concerned. Approval by the Holy See is required before such adaptation may be put into effect."

The Bishop said that he was "very well satisfied" with the Constitution on the Liturgy, and had never believed that "we would achieve so much."

The final, formal vote took place on December 4, the closing day of the second session, in the presence of Pope Paul VI. In his address, the Pope pointed out that the first schema to be discussed by the Council had been the one on the sacred liturgy; and the subject was also, "in a certain sense, the first in order of intrinsic excellence and importance for the life of the Church." The new Constitution on the Liturgy, he said, would simplify liturgical rites, make them more understandable to people, and accommodate the language used to that spoken by the people concerned. There was no question of impoverishing the liturgy, the Pope said; "on the contrary, we wish to render the liturgy more pure, more genuine, more in agreement with the Source of truth and grace, more suited to be transformed into a spiritual patrimony of the people."

Ballots had meanwhile been distributed, and the Council Fathers were asked to vote for or against the Constitution on the Sacred Liturgy. The results were speedily processed by electronic computer and announced: 2,147 votes in favor, 4 against. The announcement was greeted with an outburst of applause.

Pope Paul then rose and solemnly promulgated the Constitution, using a formula different from the one used at the First Vatican Council. Here, greater emphasis was placed on the role of the bishops: "In the Name of the Most Holy and Undivided Trinity, the Father, and the Son, and the Holy Spirit. The decrees which have now been read in this sacred and universal Second Vatican Council, lawfully assembled, have pleased the Council Fathers. And we, by the Apostolic power given to us by Christ, together with the Venerable Fathers, do approve, enact, and establish these decrees in the Holy Spirit, and command that what has been thus established in the Council be promulgated unto the glory of God." Once more, applause filled the hall.

Some, like Bishop Zauner, had believed that the Holy Father would put the Constitution on the Liturgy into effect immediately. Instead, it was announced that there would be a *vacatio legis*, or suspension of the law, until February 16, 1964, the first Sunday of Lent. In the interval, the Pope was to announce the manner in which the specific provisions of the Constitution were to be put into effect. This suspension of the law made it possible for bishops to instruct the priests and laity of their dioceses on the coming changes.

On January 29, 1964, *L'Osservatore Romano* published Pope Paul's *Motu proprio*, or directives, in the matter. In substance the Pope said that not all parts of the Constitution on the Liturgy could be put into effect at once, since new liturgical books must be prepared, and he announced that a special commission would be appointed to undertake this task.

On the following day, *L'Osservatore Romano* published a commentary by a Benedictine liturgist, Father Salvatore Marsili, expressing considerable disappointment with the *Motu proprio*, which, "while ostensibly ending the period of suspension of the Constitution, in practice lengthens it."

I had the good fortune to meet Father Marsili shortly thereafter, and learned that, in his eyes, the *Motu proprio* was a "disaster." The Constitution on the Liturgy, he said, had been so open, so expansive, "and now the Pope has closed it up again with his *Motu proprio*." Everyone on the Liturgical Commission was aware, he said, that three separate versions of the document had been prepared for the Pope. The one which eventually reached him had been so thoroughly altered by Archbishop Felici that in part it even contradicted the Constitution as promulgated. Unfortunately, Pope Paul, relying on the Secretary General, had permitted publication of the text.

In the twenty-four-hour period following the publication of the *Motu proprio*, there was pandemonium in the offices of the Vatican Secretariat of State. Telephone calls, telegrams, and cablegrams poured in from perplexed and angry bishops and episcopal conferences all over the world. Archbishop Angelo Dell'Acqua of the Secretariat of State later said that this department had never witnessed such a day in its entire history. The position was further aggravated on January 31, when *L'Osservatore Romano* published an Italian translation of the *Motu proprio* which did not tally with the Latin text published two days before.

Perhaps the major grievance against the *Motu proprio* was its failure to permit the introduction of the vernacular in the liturgy after February 16, 1964. It was soon reported in the press that the French hierarchy were going ahead with the vernacular regardless. The German hierarchy immediately sent one of their leading liturgists, Monsignor Johannes Wagner, to Rome, to see what had gone wrong. Cardinal Lercaro, of Bologna, was greatly displeased, and he announced that he was coming to Rome to see the Pope.

The jurists at the Vatican were busy, meanwhile, seeking a way out of the dilemma. The solution they found was to inform the episcopal conferences around the world, through the Apostolic nuncios or delegates, that the *Motu proprio* that had appeared in *L'Osservatore Romano* had

been revoked, and that another version was in preparation for publication in the *Acta Apostolicae Sedis*, the only
official journal of the Holy See. (Technically no Vatican
document is ever officially promulgated until it appears in
the *Acta Apostolicae Sedis*.)

On March 2, the official text of the *Motu proprio* as it
was to appear in the *Acta Apostolicae Sedis* was issued as a
brochure for distribution to bishops. Fifteen revisions had
been made. To many Council Fathers, those few sheets
of paper were a symbol of their victory over the Roman
Curia.

On March 5, *L'Osservatore Romano* announced the
establishment of a Commission for the Implementation
of the Constitution on the Sacred Liturgy, as promised by
Pope Paul in his *Motu proprio*. The new commission had
a membership of forty-two persons, representing twenty-
six countries, with Cardinal Lercaro as President. On this
commission were most of the Council Fathers who had
been members of the Liturgical Commission, as well as
many others; its Secretary was Father Annibale Bugnini,
C.M., who had acted in the same capacity on the preparatory commission on the liturgy.

The most surprising name of all on this commission was
that of Archbishop Felici, who had so thoroughly blue-
penciled the *Motu proprio* and caused such commotion
among the bishops and such embarrassment for the Holy
Father. What had he done to merit a seat on this commission? He was a canon lawyer, but not a liturgist. The
appointment had been promoted by Father Bugnini, who
felt that the Archbishop deserved to be rewarded for what
he had done in behalf of the schema in its early stages,

when eighty-year-old Gaetano Cardinal Cicognani, older brother of the Secretary of State and President of the Liturgical Preparatory Commission, had hesitated in giving the necessary approval. Strong conservative elements in the Sacred Congregation of Rites were urging him to withhold his signature. Archbishop Felici, who reported regularly on the progress of the schemas and their distribution to Pope John, explained the difficulty that he was having with Cardinal Cicognani, since without his signature the schema was blocked, even though the required majority of the commission had already approved it. Before the audience was over, a plan was devised to obtain the desired signature.

Pope John called for his Secretary of State and told him to visit his brother and not to return until the schema was duly signed. On February 1, 1962, he went to his brother's office, found Archbishop Felici and Father Bugnini in the corridor nearby, and informed his brother of Pope John's wish. Later a *peritus* of the Liturgical Preparatory Commission stated that the old Cardinal was almost in tears as he waved the document in the air and said, "They want me to sign this, but I don't know if I want to." Then he laid the document on his desk, picked up a pen, and signed it. Four days later he died.

THE THIRD SESSION

September 14 – November 21, 1964

SPEED IS OF THE ESSENCE

On January 4, 1964, shortly after the closing of the second session, Bishop Franz Hengsbach, of Essen, Germany, wrote in *America*: "After the Council has completed work on the five or six essential schemas, all remaining matters should be left for treatment in directories or handbooks to be assembled by post-conciliar commissions set up by the Council and following its basic directives." Such manuals would serve as guidelines, "but without the authority which comes from a decision of the Council itself."

At that time, there were still thirteen schemas on the agenda of the Council. The question was, Which were the five or six schemas regarded by the Bishop as essential? As a leading figure in the German hierarchy, he might well have been taking this occasion to announce a new policy of the European alliance. If so, it was to be expected that the Coordinating Commission of the Council would shortly take action along those lines.

And in fact, eleven days after the appearance of Bishop Hengsbach's article, the nine-member Coordinating Commission met in the Vatican and made decisions of so drastic and revolutionary a nature as to undo four years of work on six major Council documents.

It instructed the Commission on Oriental Churches to reduce its schema to "some fundamental points." It instructed the Commission on the Discipline of the Clergy and Faithful to reduce its decree on priests to a number of propositions. The decree was ultimately shortened to exactly one hundred lines. The Commission on Studies and Seminaries was instructed to reduce its constitution

on seminary training to "the essential points for presentation in the form of propositions . . . The rest of
the material will be used in the coming revision of the
Code of Canon Law, or in particular instructions to be
issued by the Holy See." The same Commission was also
instructed to shorten its constitution on Catholic schools.
The Commission on Religious was instructed to reduce
its thirty-four-page constitution to "its essential points."
The Commission on the Sacraments received similar
instructions concerning its decree on the sacrament of
Matrimony. Three months later, the Coordinating Commission instructed the Commission on the Missions to
reduce its decree on that subject "to a few sentences or
propositions." That raised to seven the number of schemas
affected.

When the Secretary General informed the Council
Fathers of these decisions by a letter dated May 11, 1964,
he also intimated that the shortened schemas would be put
to the vote in the Council hall but would not be discussed.

These, then, were clearly the schemas regarded as being
of secondary importance. The "essential" ones, therefore,
must have been those unaffected by the instructions mentioned—the schemas on divine revelation, on the Church,
on bishops, on ecumenism, on the apostolate of the laity,
and on the Church in the modern world. And those six
schemas were precisely the ones in which the German-
speaking Council Fathers, and the European alliance in
general, were most interested, and in regard to which they
had the most control. Two of them—on the apostolate of
the laity and on the Church in the modern world—were
within the competence of the Commission on the Apos-

tolate of the Laity, to which Bishop Hengsbach had been elected at the outset of the Council by the highest number of votes.

The reduction of seven schemas to the status of "propositions" was an attempt to speed up the work of the Council. Many formal petitions from individual Council Fathers, as well as from entire episcopal conferences, had requested that the Council should move faster; the United States hierarchy, for instance, had officially petitioned the Pope to make the third session of the Council the final one. On the other hand, the solution adopted by the Coordinating Commission was very unrealistic. All nine members could have anticipated that their decision would be overruled by the Council Fathers, at least in the case of the propositions on priests. For how could the bishops offer their priests a mere one hundred lines, never discussed in the Council hall, when they had spoken in detail and at such great length about their own role as bishops?

But perhaps there was some other reason behind the Coordinating Commission's decision. The controlling power in the individual Council commissions was in the hands of the European alliance. However, those commissions were not empowered to set aside a part or parts of individual schemas that they considered unsatisfactory. The Coordinating Commission, on the other hand, was so empowered, and it made use of its prerogative by instructing the various commissions to reduce their schemas, thereby ensuring that many, if not all, unsatisfactory elements would be eliminated. The seven schemas, as reduced to propositions, could then be expanded as a result of new suggestions from the Council floor.

In the latter part of April, Cardinal Döpfner wrote to the bishops of Germany, Austria, Luxembourg, Switzerland, and Scandinavia, inviting them to a conference on Council matters to be held at Innsbruck, Austria, from May 19 to May 22. Referring to the decision of the Coordinating Commission that the propositions should not be discussed, he indicated that the last word on the matter had not yet been said, and that it was also "an open question whether or not there will be a fourth session of the Council." The Cardinal said that the same observers from the hierarchies of neighboring countries would again be invited to attend. He announced further that, as in previous years, those "in our circle who are members of a Council commission will prepare drafts on the individual schemas with the help of the *periti* of their choice, and those drafts will serve as the basis for discussion." Holding the conference so early had a considerable advantage, he pointed out, for "in this way our proposals can be passed on in time to the Council Fathers of other countries who have requested them."

The Coordinating Commission took still further steps to speed up the Council's work at its next meeting, on June 26. These steps involved amendments to the Rules of Procedure and were approved by Pope Paul VI on July 2. From now on, all cardinals and Council Fathers who wished to speak had to submit written summaries of their proposed addresses to the Secretary General "at least five days before discussion of the topic begins." As a result, rebuttal was virtually impossible. According to the original Rules of Procedure approved by Pope John XXIII, any Council Father who wished to refute a statement could inform the Secretary General of his wish to speak, and was then to be given the floor as soon as the list of speakers was exhausted. During the second session, this request had to be supported by five signatures. Now, however, according to a new clause added to the rules, such a request had to be made in the name of at least seventy other Council Fathers. As might have been expected, the figure was such as to discourage anyone who did not belong to a highly organized group from asking for the floor; and the measure proved very effective in silencing minority views.

On July 7, the Secretary General informed the Council Fathers by mail that the sequence of schemas to be discussed and voted upon at the third session was as follows: on the Church, on bishops, on ecumenism, on divine revelation, on the apostolate of the laity, and on the Church in the modern world. The remaining schemas, which had been reduced to propositions and were not to be discussed, would be "submitted for voting in the sequence and manner to be determined by the Council Moderators in due course."

ORGANIZED OPPOSITION

For a long time it appeared as though the European alliance would have undisputed control over the Council. This could have proved unfortunate, because power, be it financial, political, military, academic or theological, has a way of being abused when a near monopoly is obtained over it. As the Council progressed, however, at least half a dozen organized opposition groups came into being and performed yeoman service by forcing the majority to take a closer and more careful look at schemas before accepting them.

We have already seen how the Bishops' Secretariat came into being to concentrate on texts concerning religious orders, and how it collaborated at all times with the Roman Union of Superiors General.

During the third session Archbishop Heenan of Westminster (formerly of Liverpool) founded the St. Paul's Conference, an English-language group which placed the chief emphasis on matters of a practical nature. Its members were drawn from the British Commonwealth, principally, and also from Ireland and the United States.

Another opposition group, to be treated in detail in a later chapter, consisted of thirty-five cardinals and five superiors general, who concerned themselves especially with the problem of collegiality.

Archbishop Philip Hannan of New Orleans, Louisiana, founded an opposition group at the very end of the Council to give weight to certain amendments that he wished included in the war section of the schema on the Church in the modern world.

Cardinal Siri of Genoa, working in collaboration with Monsignor Luigi Rossi, faculty member of the Genoa major seminary, prepared and printed numerous qualifications and commentaries on schemas which were widely circulated among conservative elements in the Italian hierarchy and in the Spanish- and Portuguese-speaking hierarchies of Europe and Latin America.

Besides these six organized opposition groups, which were either ignored by the press or unknown, there was the International Group of Fathers (in Latin, *Coetus Inter-*

nationalis Patrum), which—together with the Roman Curia—was depicted as the epitome of conservatism, holding back the progressive elements in the Council. This group received much unfavorable publicity in newspapers, reviews, and books. Its founder and driving force was Archbishop Geraldo de Proença Sigaud of Diamantina, Brazil, and the group was founded precisely to help gain a hearing for conservative minority views.

During the first and second sessions Archbishop Sigaud organized weekly conferences, but the Italian members left the group when it was rumored that Monsignor Loris Capovilla, the private secretary of Pope John XXIII, had stated that he would not consider attacks on the Roman Curia as an offense against the Pope. New impetus came from the number of votes against combining the schema on the Blessed Virgin Mary with the schema on the Church, since this proved, as Archbishop Sigaud said, that a very large number of Council Fathers were "trying to orientate the Council along doctrinal lines traditionally followed in the Church." But no conservative cardinal bold enough could be found to give the organization the needed backing until September 29, 1964, during the third session, when Cardinal Santos of Manila agreed to serve as the organization's vocal patron in the College of Cardinals.

This group then purchased a small offset press, installed it near the Vatican, and hired an office staff. Three days after the meeting with Cardinal Santos, Archbishop Sigaud issued a bulletin announcing that the International Group of Fathers would sponsor a conference every Tuesday evening open to all Council Fathers. The purpose of these meetings, the announcement said, was "to study the schemas of the Council—with the aid of theologians—in the light of the traditional doctrine of the Church and according to the teaching of the Sovereign Pontiffs." Patrons of the meetings were Cardinals Santos, Ruffini, Siri, Larraona, and Browne.

Soon the International Group of Fathers became so active and influential that it aroused the indignation of the European alliance, and one of the alliance cardinals stated that Archbishop Sigaud ought to be "shot to the moon." Katholische Nachrichten Agentur, the Catholic news agency subsidized by the German bishops, called him an archconservative and depicted him and his group as working covertly against the aims of the Council. In spite of this, an almost endless flow of circular letters, commentaries on schemas, interventions, and qualifications flowed from his pen and those of the bishops and theologians whom he united through his group. Long before a schema came up for discussion, a careful program had been worked out, indicating exactly what aspects of the schema should be supported or attacked in written or in oral interventions.

On November 9, 1963, during the second session, Bishop Carli, one of the group's most active members, drafted a letter to Pope Paul VI in which he appealed to him "to ask the Cardinal Moderators to abstain completely from making public interventions in their own name, both inside and outside the Council hall." In the eyes of all, he said, they appeared to be "interpreters of the mind of the Supreme Pontiff," and there was suspicion that they had leanings "in a certain definite direction." But

Cardinal Ruffini advised against making this appeal, and it was dropped.

Father Ratzinger, the personal theologian of Cardinal Frings, while dining one day with a group, mentioned that the liberals had thought they would have a free hand at the Council after obtaining the majority in the Council commissions. But in the speeches and voting in the Council hall, he said, they began to notice some resistance to their proposals, and consequently commissions had to take this into consideration when revising the schemas. Unknown to Father Ratzinger, one of those seated nearby and within hearing distance was Archbishop Sigaud, who chuckled at this public admission by a representative of the European alliance.

INFORMATION PLEASE!

Acoustics at the First Vatican Council, which began on December 8, 1869, were notoriously bad. All General Congregations took place in a transept of St. Peter's without the assistance of a public address system. At first not even the speakers who had powerful voices could be heard by all the Council Fathers, so the hall was reduced in size. But even then many of the seven hundred Fathers could still not hear everything that was said.

During the Second Vatican Council, thanks to the installation of a public address system which operated flawlessly, none of the more than two thousand Council Fathers ever had any difficulty hearing the speakers. Never once in the four sessions did the system fail, nor did it cause an interruption in a single meeting. The acoustical problems had been solved by the technicians of Vatican Radio, and the Latin which came over the loudspeakers was crystal clear.

In spite of the excellence of reproduction, however, many Council Fathers were disappointed that a simultaneous translation system had not been installed. Mr. Mauro Ercole, a Vatican Radio engineer, stated that the problem was not a technical one. Experiments had been carried out, and all technical problems had been solved. Nor was the problem a financial one, because Richard Cardinal Cushing of Boston had offered to finance a complete simultaneous translation system.

At a press conference on October 29, 1963, halfway through the second session, Archbishop John Krol of Philadelphia, an Undersecretary of the Council, said that there would be no simultaneous translation system operating during the Council "because of personnel problems."

By the time the fourth session began, this was an idea long since forgotten. But two American priests, Father Daniel J. O'Hanlon, a Jesuit from Los Gatos, California, and Father Frank B. Norris, a Sulpician from Menlo Park, California, found simultaneous translation an absolute necessity for their work. The number of English-speaking observers and guests for whom they provided translations of Council interventions during the meetings had grown so large by the fourth session that it was no longer possible to reach all of them with the unaided human voice. Although the two priests had received no previous formal training, they began providing simultaneous translation services on September 30, 1965, and continued them until the end of the Council.

Some bishops noticing the system in operation listened in and expressed the wish to have something similar. Father O'Hanlon, Father Norris, and Mr. Ercole all said that it would have been a simple matter to hook up headphones to the same microphone for the benefit of all Council Fathers who understood English. This system could have been used also for the five other languages.

The chief reason why simultaneous translation was not introduced on a large scale, however, was the objection by some Council Fathers that their interventions might not be correctly translated. Since doctrinal matters were at issue, they feared that a completely wrong interpretation might be placed upon their words through the incorrect translation of a word or phrase, and they therefore preferred to address the general assembly directly in Latin.

Another factor contributing to the poor state of internal communications at the Council was the complete lack of any official public record of the oral and written interventions submitted each day. Although the members of every responsible legislative body around the world have the right to obtain the full text of all speeches, this was not true at the Second Vatican Council.

Some questioned the advisability and even the possibility of printing the complete text of the written and oral interventions and giving them to the Council Fathers. This would have amounted to more than a hundred pages each day. Although it would have been impossible for everyone to read each intervention, those among the Council Fathers or among the *periti* who were experts in the subjects under discussion would have appreciated being able to make a careful study of the interventions, which in turn would have aided them to be more precise in submitting or preparing proposals and amendments.

An ideal arrangement would have been to print the entire texts of all oral and written interventions, in the Latin original, together with a Latin introduction of some fifteen lines in which the author of the intervention summarized his own proposals. In this way each Council Father could have had a reliable written summary of all interventions, and could have carefully examined the complete text of those which particularly interested him. Also, if the Council Fathers had been informed that their written interventions were to be placed in the hands of every member of the assembly, there would have been less reason for so many wanting to speak in the Council hall.

The lack of any official daily record for the Council Fathers was one of the great weaknesses of Vatican II. In seeking substitutes, large numbers of bishops subscribed to *L'Osservatore Romano*, which, during the first session, carried brief summaries of each General Congregation in Italian, English, German, French, and Spanish. But from the second session onward only the Italian version was published.

Father William K. Leahy, faculty member of St. Charles Seminary at Overbrook, Philadelphia, was a student of Sacred Scripture in Rome when Vatican II began. Personally convinced that a great theological reawakening was taking place at the Council, and dismayed that American bishops apparently had not been caught up in this fast-moving stream of theological thought, he decided that the reason for this was a lack of information on the precise nature of the discussions which were taking place in the Council hall. He then got the idea of producing for the American bishops a daily summary in English of all interventions read on the Council floor. He called it the *Council Digest* and, with the help of a handful of young priests, prepared the daily synopses of the oral interventions. The first issue appeared on September 30, 1963, the date of the opening business meeting of the second session, and the bulletins continued uninterruptedly until the final business meeting of the fourth session.

Publication of the *Council Digest* had been authorized by the Administrative Board of the United States Episcopal Conference "for the information of the Bishops of the United States." Since Father Leahy's team consisted of skilled theologians who used the actual texts of the oral interventions, the *Council Digest* became the most authentic public report available to bishops. From the beginning two hundred copies were printed for the American bishops, and seventy copies for the Canadian bishops. But it soon became necessary to print a total of 750 copies because English-speaking bishops from more than twenty-five countries were anxious to receive these authentic summaries.

It was very strange that the Council Fathers, who were able to pass any bill they wished, and who at the end of the second session solemnly promulgated a decree on communications media in which they spoke about the right to information, were unable for lack of united effort to properly and officially inform themselves about their own Council.

THE BLESSED VIRGIN AND THE CHURCH

Chapter 7 of the schema on the Church, entitled "The Eschatological Nature of the Pilgrim Church and Its Union with the Church in Heaven," was the first item to come up for discussion at the third session. This chapter had been introduced in the schema at the wish of Pope John XXIII. The "eschatological" character of a Christian's life was described as "a continuity of life which begins on earth and reaches perfection in heaven." The underlying doctrine is that the Church on earth and in heaven constitutes a single People of God and a single Mystical Body of Christ.

Cardinal Urbani, of Venice, called the structure of the chapter satisfactory, adding that it corresponded to the ideas expressed at the second session by Cardinal Frings on behalf of the bishops of Germany and Scandinavia.

The Latin Rite Patriarch of Jerusalem, Alberto Gori, objected strongly to the chapter, saying that the text should not be silent "on the existence of hell, on the eternity of hell," and on the possibility of "personal damnation." These were truths that had been explicitly revealed, he said, and should today be given their proper emphasis. So many, in their sermons, he said, seemed to shrink from expressing these doctrines openly and clearly.

Maronite Archbishop Ignace Ziadé, of Beirut, Lebanon, said that far too little prominence had been given to the Third Person of the Blessed Trinity. "The scope of my intervention is simple," he said. "How is it possible to speak of our eschatological calling without any reference to the Holy Spirit?" The Orientals, he declared, were not able to recognize their traditional doctrine on the Holy Spirit in "such a deficient profession of faith."

The eighth and final chapter was taken up on the following day. This was the text on the Blessed Virgin Mary, now included as a chapter in the schema on the Church instead of being treated as a separate schema. The chapter was a compromise text produced by two *periti*—Monsignor Philips and Father Balić—of widely differing views on the matter. Monsignor Philips insisted on leaving out the titles "Mother of the Church" and "Mediatrix," but the Theological Commission decided to include "Mediatrix," convinced that if neither of the two were in the text, it would not get the desired unanimous approval from the Council Fathers.

Thirty-three Council Fathers took the floor to discuss this chapter. Cardinal Ruffini, of Palermo, said that the schema "almost veiled" the cooperation of Mary in the work of redemption, which had been willed by God. And since the text also contained the unqualified statement that "Mediatrix" was a title given to the Blessed Virgin, it was necessary to explain clearly what that title meant, so that "non-Catholics will come to realize that the use of this title implies no lessening of the dignity of Christ, who is the one absolutely necessary Mediator."

Stefan Cardinal Wyszynski, of Warsaw, Poland, speaking on behalf of seventy Polish bishops, drew attention to Pope Paul's encyclical, *Ecclesiam suam*, published some six weeks earlier. In that encyclical, said the Cardinal, the Pope called attention to the fundamental importance of the Blessed Virgin in the life of the Church. On the basis of that affirmation, the Polish bishops had sent a memorandum to Pope Paul, requesting that he proclaim the Blessed Virgin "Mother of the Church." Cardinal Wyszynski also asked, on behalf of the same Polish bishops, that the chapter on the Blessed Virgin be numbered second instead of last in the schema, since in that way it would receive more attention and would better illustrate the role of the Blessed Virgin in relation to Christ and his Church.

Cardinal Léger, of Montreal, said that it was necessary "to renew the Marian doctrine and cult." This renewal, or reform, had already begun among the theologians, he said, "but it must also reach the pastors and the faithful, and this final chapter of the Constitution on the Church offers the best opportunity for promoting it." The desired renewal "consists in using accurate words and precise and sober terms to express Mary's role." In that connection, he questioned the use of the titles given to Mary in the schema—"Mother of Men," "Handmaid of the Lord Redeemer," "Generous Companion," and "Mediatrix." The origin and meaning of all these titles, he said, should be carefully studied in the light of the best theological research, before their use was endorsed in a conciliar text.

Cardinal Döpfner spoke next, in the name of ninety German-speaking and Scandinavian bishops, repeating what had been decided at the Innsbruck conference. He said that the chapter contained solid doctrine on the Blessed Virgin, without entering into disputed questions, and he felt that it would be best not to add anything more than was in the text concerning the role of Mary as Mediatrix.

Cardinal Bea, President of the Secretariat for Promoting Christian Unity, also objected to the title "Mediatrix." A Council text, he said, was not intended as a manual for personal devotion. What the Council Fathers had to decide was whether each and every affirmation made in the text was sufficiently thought out and theologically proven to be presented by the Council, as the highest Church authority. Since the role of Mary as Mediatrix was still disputed by some theologians, it should not be included in the text.

Archbishop Corrado Mingo, of Monreale, Italy, severely criticized the text. Contrary to what had been promised in the Council hall, the text had been "absolutely and radically mutilated" in the process of being turned into a chapter of the schema on the Church. The title "Mother of the Church" had been deleted without any justification whatsoever, he said, contrary to the wish expressed by Pope Paul in his discourses of October 11, 1963, in the Basilica of St. Mary Major, and December 4, 1963, at the closing of the second session of the Council. Not only should the title "Mediatrix" be retained in the text, he said, but it should be amplified to read "Mediatrix of all graces."

When the schema entitled "On the Blessed Virgin Mary, Mother of the Church" was incorporated as Chapter 8 in the schema on the Church, its title was changed to read "On the Blessed Virgin Mary, Mother of God, in the Mystery of Christ and the Church." Bishop Juan Hervás y Benet, of Ciudad Real, Spain, said that the original title should be restored. He also criticized the text severely, saying that it was not an adaptation but a completely new version of the original text, which did not correspond to the wishes expressed by the Council Fathers. The revised text had reduced the doctrine on the Virgin Mary to the absolute minimum; yet it had been stated in the Council hall at the time of the vote that "by inserting the schema on the Virgin Mary in the schema on the Church, no such diminution was intended or would be carried out."

Leo Cardinal Suenens, of Mechelen, Belgium, also objected to the revised text, saying that it appeared to minimize the importance of Mary, "a tendency which today constitutes a real danger." The text did not place the spiritual maternity "which Mary continues to exercise in the Church even today" in its proper light. It was also somewhat defective in its exposition of what the ordinary teaching authority of the Church had to say about Mary, and what the faithful believed regarding the cooperation of the Virgin in the work of redemption. It was necessary, he felt, that the schema should make the faithful realize that they were associated with the maternal action of Mary in carrying out their apostolate.

For this one brief moment Cardinal Suenens had the courage to break away from the party line of the European alliance and speak out his own mind. It would have been strange, indeed, if the Cardinal of Belgium—a land so noted in the Catholic Church for its great devotion to the Virgin Mary—had taken any other public stand.

Bishop Francisco Rendeiro, of Faro, Portugal, speaking on behalf of eighty-two bishops, expressly asked that the title "Mediatrix" should be retained in the text. Its omission would generate scandal among the faithful, since the public was by this time aware that the matter had been discussed in the Council hall.

Auxiliary Bishop Ancel, of Lyons, France, said that the

public was getting the false impression from the press that the Council Fathers did not have equal veneration for the Virgin. In order to offset this impression, it was necessary to obtain unanimous approval for the chapter. He attempted to show that the text was in fact a compromise, since it mentioned the title "Mediatrix" but at the same time gave it no endorsement, thus leaving the door open for further study. "Perhaps the title 'Mediatrix' might be listed with other titles, in order to avoid the impression that it is a privileged one."

Archbishop Rafael García y García de Castro, of Granada, Spain, speaking on behalf of eighty Spanish bishops, took the Theological Commission to task for "completely refashioning the text instead of adapting it, as the Council Fathers had desired." He was also of the opinion that the original title—"On the Blessed Virgin Mary, Mother of the Church"—should be restored, since it corresponded to the pontifical documents issued by Popes Benedict XIV, Leo XIII, St. Pius X, Benedict XV, John XXIII, and Paul VI, as well as to the writings of the Fathers of the Church, in particular SS. Irenaeus, Augustine, and Leo the Great. To change the title and to omit this doctrine would be an affront to the teaching of the popes, and would undermine the devotion shown by the Christian people to the Virgin, the Archbishop declared.

Archbishop Giuseppe Gawlina, director of the Polish hospice in Rome, said that devotion to Mary was evidently no obstacle to ecumenism, since Martin Luther had said in 1533—long after his break with Rome—that "the creature Mary cannot be praised enough." In 1521, in his dissertation on the *Magnificat*, Luther had written: "What can please her [Mary] more, than if in this way you come to God through her, and from her you learn to believe and hope in God. . . . Mary does not wish that you come to her, but that through her you should come to God." Four days later the Archbishop died suddenly of a heart attack.

The Moderators had decided that two days of discussion on this chapter would suffice. From the thirty interventions read at the General Congregations of September 16 and 17, it was quite clear that the assembly was still divided on the same lines as before, with large groups opposing and defending the two titles "Mother of the Church" and "Mediatrix." Concerned that these divisions might nullify everything that had been accomplished, Father Balić approached Cardinal Frings and begged him to address the general assembly the following day to urge acceptance of the compromise text as it stood.

The Cardinal agreed. In his address, he said that the chapter on the Blessed Virgin Mary contained nothing contrary to Catholic faith or to the rights of the separated brethren. It offered a middle road between diverse opinions "and in a certain way may be considered a compromise." It would be difficult to change the text, he said, since a two-thirds majority would be required. Therefore it seemed best that each one "sacrifice some personal ideas, even very right ones," and approve the schema after certain amendments had been made in the scriptural citations and particular passages, as requested in the course of the debate. "Theologians can then use this text as a starting point for making more profound studies of the doctrines which are not yet clear, and can better develop those which are still disputed."

Cardinal Alfrink, of the Netherlands, spoke next in the name of 124 Council Fathers from his own country, Africa, Latin America, Germany, Italy, and other countries. He repeated in substance the arguments put forward by Cardinal Frings, but he felt that the title "Mediatrix" should not be insisted upon, since it generated such great difficulties.

Bishop Laureano Castán Lacoma, of Sigüenza-Guadalajara, Spain, speaking on behalf of eighty Council Fathers, said that, since the Church was a family, the title of the chapter should read "On the Blessed Virgin Mary, Mother of the Church," as before. He saw no reason for its deletion by the Theological Commission.

The text was now referred back to the Theological Commission for revision. In addition to the texts of the oral interventions, the Commission had to take into account a number of written interventions and other comments submitted even before the opening of the third session. When the work of revision was completed, Archbishop Maurice Roy, of Quebec, announced to the assembled Fathers that the chapter would be put to the vote as a whole. The voting took place on October 29; the result was 1,559 affirmative votes, 521 qualified affirmative votes, and 10 negative votes. The required two-thirds majority had been achieved, and Father Balić credited the address of Cardinal Frings for this success.

Three weeks later, on November 18, the text as revised in the light of the qualifications submitted by the 521 Council Fathers was put to the vote again. When the assembly was asked if it was satisfied with the manner in which the qualifications had been handled, 99 percent replied "yes."

Archbishop Roy explained that, although the title "Mother of the Church" was omitted from the final text, it was equivalently expressed in Article 53, which stated, "Taught by the Holy Spirit, the Catholic Church honors her [Mary] with filial affection and piety as a most beloved mother."

As for the controversial title "Mediatrix," the solution proposed by Cardinal Ruffini, Bishop Ancel, and others had been adopted in Article 62, which stated: "Therefore the Blessed Virgin is invoked by the Church under the titles of Advocate, Auxiliatrix, Adjutrix, and Mediatrix. These, however, are to be so understood that they neither take away from nor add anything to the dignity and efficacy of Christ the one Mediator. For no creature could ever be classed with the Incarnate Word and Redeemer. . . . The Church does not hesitate to profess this subordinate role of Mary."

Professor Oscar Cullmann, a guest of the Secretariat for Promoting Christian Unity, gave a lengthy press conference at the end of the Council in the course of which he said: "We cannot pass over in silence the disappointment that we experienced at seeing the title of 'Mediatrix' given to Mary. . . . The fact that the text on Mary, after so much discussion as to where it should be placed, should have finally become the concluding chapter of the schema on the Church—a decision which was in fact intended to weaken Mariology—has in reality made it even stronger, because everything stated about the Church culminates, so to speak, in this chapter."

He went on to observe that, in the light of the many ceremonies honoring Mary during the Council, and also of the statements made about her by both Pope John and Pope Paul, it must be concluded "that Mariology at this Council has in general been intensified to a degree which is not in keeping with the ecumenical tendencies of Protestantism . . . and with a return to the Bible. Our expectations in this connection have not been fulfilled." It was clear, he said, "that we could not require the surrender of a teaching and tradition which belongs to the very kernel of Catholic piety." What he had expected, however, was "a weakening of emphasis, not some sort of revision of the fundamental relationship to the Virgin Mary."

Just as the attempt by some circles to bring about "a weakening of emphasis" had failed, so too the attempt to reduce the text in length had failed; the new chapter was one third longer than the original schema.

RELIGIOUS FREEDOM

No text was subjected to as many revisions by the Council as the one on religious freedom. Before its promulgation as a declaration on December 7, 1965, the day preceding the closing of the Second Vatican Council, six different drafts had been laid before the Council. One of the United States bishops said that, without their support, "this document would not have reached the floor."

The original schema on the Church, rejected by the Council at the end of the first session principally as a result of the efforts of the European alliance, had included a short chapter entitled "On the Relations Between Church and State." This chapter was suppressed altogether by the Coordinating Commission at its first meeting in January

1963. The action occasioned no little displeasure among a number of Council Fathers, particularly those from the United States.

Auxiliary Bishop Primo Gasbarri, of Velletri, a suburb of Rome, drew attention at the second meeting of the second session, on October 1, 1963, to the deletion of the chapter, and insisted that the matter must be treated because it was intimately bound up with the Church's right to fulfill its mission. A conciliar statement on the subject was necessary, furthermore, to counteract the propaganda conducted against the Church and to clarify the Church's position in countries where it was subjected to persecution.

Bishop Ernest Primeau, of Manchester, New Hampshire, expressed agreement with Bishop Gasbarri. The text, he said, should lay down general principles governing Church-state relations.

In an interview that Bishop Primeau gave me for the Divine Word News Service, he enlarged upon his ideas. "I do not think that the Council should go into particulars," he said, "or into the particular relationships that exist between the Church and the state, but some general principles should be laid down." As examples he mentioned freedom of conscience for individuals and freedom of action for the Church in carrying out its mission.

Bishop Primeau said that there would be little concern over such a statement in countries such as Spain, Italy, "or even England, curiously enough, which is a pluralistic society. But in our country, the Protestant intelligentsia are always asking for a definite statement on Church and state." Many Council Fathers were opposed to a Council declaration on Church-state relations, he said, because they felt it was a controversial matter. "But we have not come here just to rubber-stamp the status quo. There are knots to be cut."

Archbishop Lawrence Shehan, of Baltimore, speaking later in the name of the more than two hundred bishops of the United States, said that the question of Church and state was "entirely too important and too delicate to be treated only in passing, almost casually, in a discussion of the apostolate of the laity." He was referring to Chapter 3, on the laity, of the schema on the Church. The question required careful treatment, he said, and pertained not exclusively to the laity, but to the entire Church.

While religious freedom was only one aspect of the larger problem of Church-state relations, it was definitely one of the most important. A conciliar declaration on the matter was further necessary as a preliminary step before the Catholic Church could become seriously engaged in the ecumenical movement. Such a declaration, stating that the Catholic Church officially recognized the rights of members of other religions, would be considered by non-Catholics as a test of Catholic sincerity and would establish the basis for further contacts. Cardinal Bea's Secretariat, therefore, soon after it was founded in 1960, had set to work preparing a schema entitled "Freedom of Cult." This schema was examined by the Central Preparatory Commission in June 1962, and again by the Coordinating Commission at its first meeting, in January 1963, after the close of the first session. The Coordinating Commission authorized the Secretariat to incorporate in its schema on freedom of cult whatever it wished to take from the chapter on Church-state relations in the original schema on the Church.

Cardinal Bea's revised text was ready for presentation to the Council Fathers before the opening of the second session. But since doctrinal matters were involved, and since the chapter on Church-state relations had originally been within the competence of the Theological Commission, the schema had to be approved by that Commission before it could be presented on the Council floor. The long delay gave rise to accusations in the press that Cardinal Ottaviani, President of the Theological Commission, was deliberately blocking the document. Finally it was released with the necessary approval.

Cardinal Bea and his Secretariat decided to present the text as Chapter 5 of the schema on ecumenism, which had already been distributed. They felt that to introduce it as an independent schema might jeopardize its passage. It was entitled "On Religious Freedom" and was distributed on November 19, 1963.

Cardinal Ritter, of St. Louis, Missouri, addressing the assembly on November 18, said that he regarded religious freedom as "a basis and prerequisite for ecumenical contacts with other Christian bodies." He called for "an unequivocal declaration on religious freedom" and said that "without such a declaration, mutual confidence will be impossible, and serious dialogue will be precluded." He was also speaking for other American bishops when he said that such a declaration should include "considerations on the absolute freedom of the act of faith, the dignity of the human person and his inviolable conscience, and the total incompetence of the civil government in passing judgment on the Gospel of Christ and its interpretation. Such a declaration should also "reaffirm the complete independence of the Church of any civil government in fulfilling its mission."

The report on Chapter 5 was read on the following day by Bishop De Smedt, of Bruges, Belgium. He said that the Theological Commission had carefully examined the text and made "well-founded and useful observations and suggestions." He then listed the four chief reasons why "a very large number of Council Fathers have most insistently requested that this Sacred Synod openly express and proclaim man's right to religious freedom":

1. The Church must teach and defend the right of religious freedom because this is one of the truths committed to its custody by Christ;

2. The Church cannot keep silent today while nearly one half of humanity is deprived of religious freedom by various kinds of materialistic atheism;

3. The Church, using the light of truth, must show men how to live peacefully with their fellow men, at a time when people all over the world belong to different religions or have no religion at all; all are expected to live peacefully together in one and the same human society;

4. Many non-Catholics harbor resentment against the Church, or at least suspect it of some form of Machiavellianism, believing that it demands the free exercise of religion when Catholics are in the minority in a country and that it disregards the right to religious freedom when Catholics are in the majority.

Bishop De Smedt described religious freedom positively as "the right of a human person to the free exercise of religion according to the dictates of his own conscience." Negatively, it could be described as "immunity from all external force in those personal relationships with God which are proper to the conscience of man." Bishop De Smedt expressed the view that the entire matter could be discussed, voted upon, and approved before the end of the second session. "We shall work day and night," he declared.

Cardinal Léger, of Montreal, pointed out that, while the schema on ecumenism concerned the unity of Christians, religious freedom was a doctrine which concerned all religions; it should therefore not be a chapter of the schema on ecumenism, but should constitute a separate schema.

On the following day, Cardinal Meyer, of Chicago, expressed a contrary view. The question of religious freedom, he said, was intimately bound up with both theoretical and practical ecumenism, and he therefore urgently requested that the text be retained as Chapter 5 of the schema on ecumenism. On this point, he said, "I think I express the view of many bishops, especially from the United States."

In view of the considerable opposition to Chapter 5, the Moderators postponed the vote on the acceptability of the chapter as a topic of discussion.

Cardinal Bea was the last speaker at the final General Congregation of the second session, on December 2, 1963. Obviously aware of the discontent fomented by some bishops and *periti* who were wrongly blaming conservatives for holding back the vote, he stated in deliberate and solemn tones that the only reason why the chapter had not been debated was that time had run out. There was "no other reason," he asserted. And he repeated this for all to hear. "I think we should be grateful to the venerable Cardinal Moderators for wishing to give ample opportunity for discussion of the three fundamental chapters," he said.

"The new prophets of doom and gloom," as they were subsequently called by a bishop in an anonymous article in *America* after the second session, had made charges of "obstruction, foot-dragging, dirty pool in the committee," in explaining why the chapter on religious freedom had not come up for discussion. By way of rebuttal, the bishop cited Cardinal Bea's reason that time had simply run out, adding that nobody present could seriously say that there had been a filibuster.

In point of fact, however, there had been "foot-dragging" and "obstruction." Those responsible—by their own admission—were the Moderators. Cardinal Suenens made the admission on Sunday, December 1, 1963, the day before Cardinal Bea's speech in the Council hall. In a lecture at the Pontifical Canadian College, he said that the Moderators could have insisted that Chapter 4, on the Jews, and Chapter 5, on religious freedom, should be voted on, but they had decided against it. He explained that the Moderators believed that, after a cooling-off period and after the issues had been aired in the press, the two chapters would stand a much better chance of acceptance. The Moderators intended, he said, to present the two chapters for a vote early in the third session.

True to their word, the Moderators introduced the discussion on religious freedom on September 23, 1964, nine days after the opening of the third session. Bishop

De Smedt again presented a report, and said that in the interval between the second and third sessions no fewer than 380 written observations and amendments had been submitted by Council Fathers, and that these had been "most carefully examined by the Secretariat for Promoting Christian Unity." The new text still needed to be perfected in many points, he said, "since religious freedom, as you all know, has never been treated at an Ecumenical Council." The revised text was no longer presented as Chapter 5 of the schema on ecumenism, but as an independent declaration.

Three American cardinals spoke on that first day of debate. The first was Richard Cardinal Cushing, of Boston.

Speaking "in the name of almost all the bishops of the United States," he said that "the declaration on religious freedom in general is acceptable." He expressed the hope that amendments would make the text even stronger, rather than weaker. It was of the greatest importance, he said, that the Church in this declaration should "show itself to the entire modern world as the champion of liberty—of human liberty and of civil liberty—specifically in the matter of religion." He also said that "the substance of the doctrine as we have it here is true and solid, and is most appropriate for our times."

Cardinal Ritter, of St. Louis, called religious freedom a natural right of every man, one of the aspects of natural human freedom, a truth that was certain, and one that was limited only by the common good of society. However, he took exception to the proofs for religious freedom set out in the text, saying that they did not have the same simplicity, clarity, and certainty as religious freedom itself. He therefore asked that all argumentation be omitted from the declaration, since the nature of a declaration was simply to declare, and not to prove. The more simple and brief the document was, he said, the more effective it would be. There was a danger, moreover, that the Council Fathers, in rejecting the arguments proposed, might also reject the declaration itself. He therefore petitioned the Moderators to hold two distinct ballots on the two issues.

Cardinal Meyer, of Chicago, said that the declaration should be accepted, since it reaffirmed the teaching of recent popes, clarified traditional doctrine, and was especially needed at this time, when men greatly desired a statement from the Church encouraging religious freedom. By affirming the innate freedom of the person, he said, the Church would show that true religion consisted in the free and generous subjection of the individual to the Creator. This affirmation was essential, moreover, for a fruitful dialogue with non-Catholics. It was also a necessary prelude "if anything else that we have to say is to be accepted by the world."

Cardinal Silva Henríquez, of Santiago de Chile, speaking in the name of fifty-eight Latin American bishops, said that the great value of the declaration "consists in its being issued not as a chapter in some schema, but as an independent declaration intended for all mankind." That, he said, was one of the "special reasons why we approve of the text." There could be no real ecumenical movement in Latin America, he added, until non-Catholic Christians became aware of "our sincere recognition and defense of this fundamental liberty."

The next speaker was Cardinal Ottaviani. He said that the declaration stated a principle which had always been recognized, namely, that no one could be forced in religious matters. But the text was guilty of exaggeration in stating that "he is worthy of honor" who obeys his own conscience. It would be better to say that such a person was deserving of tolerance or of respect and charity. "The principle that each individual has the right to follow his own conscience must suppose that that conscience is not contrary to the divine law," he asserted. There was missing in the text "an explicit and solemn affirmation of the first and genuine right to religious freedom, which objectively belongs to those who are members of the true revealed religion." Their right was at once an objective and a subjective right, he said, while for those in error there was only a subjective right.

The Cardinal said that it was "a very serious matter" to assert that every kind of religion had the freedom to propagate itself. That would "clearly result in harm for those nations where the Catholic religion is the one generally adhered to by the people." He also said that an Ecumenical Council of the Catholic Church could not ignore the fact "that the rights of the true religion are based, not only on merely natural rights, but also, and to a much greater degree, on the rights which flow from revelation."

Cardinal Ruffini, of Palermo, pointed out that, although there was only one true religion, the world was in darkness and error, and consequently tolerance and patience must be practiced. Distinctions must be made in the text, lest the Council should appear to endorse religious indifferentism and to say no more than had the United Nations in its Universal Declaration of Human Rights of 1948. From certain statements in the text, he said further, it would seem that a state was not entitled to grant special favors to any one religion; if that were the case, then the papal agreements with Italy, Portugal, Spain, and the Dominican Republic would require revision.

Cardinal Quiroga y Palacios, of Santiago de Compostela, Spain, called for the complete revision of the text. From its style and language, its dominant preoccupation appeared to be to favor union with the separated brethren, without sufficient consideration of the very serious dangers to which it thereby exposed the Catholic faithful. The text was filled with ambiguities, he charged, new doctrine being favored at the expense of traditional doctrine, and the Council was being invited to give its solemn approval to that liberalism which the Church had so often condemned.

José Cardinal Bueno y Monreal, of Seville, Spain, said that the entire text was pervaded by a twofold ambiguity. Only the Catholic Church had received Christ's mandate to teach all nations. Objectively speaking, no other religious doctrine had the right to propagate itself, he said. In the social sphere, every freedom was subject to limitations, and these derived from the rights and freedoms of others, and from the requirements of law and order. The right to preach one's religion was valid, he maintained, as far as those who freely chose to listen were concerned, but not in relation to those who did not wish to listen. Those who were unwilling to accept the propagation of false religions or harmful moral teaching were undoubtedly entitled to demand that such public propagation not be allowed.

243

Bishop Smiljan Cekada, of Skoplje, Yugoslavia, pointed out that religious freedom had become the principal social problem for millions of men, because many countries were under the influence of Communism. He proposed that the Second Vatican Council should request the United Nations to remind public authorities throughout the world of their obligation to respect the religious freedom of all men and all groups.

As the first day of discussion on religious freedom came to an end, it was clear that it was not a matter which could be rushed through the Council.

On the following day, Cardinal König, of Vienna, said that the declaration was altogether acceptable as it stood, but he maintained that it should not keep silent regarding the tragic fact that nations existed where no religious freedom was enjoyed.

Cardinal Browne, of the Roman Curia, stated that the declaration could not be approved in its existing form. Archbishop Parente, also of the Roman Curia, made the same point, on the grounds that the rights of God were subordinated in the text to the rights of man and human liberty. It was an unfortunate suggestion, he said, that the Church should make use of its extraordinary teaching authority in a Council to proclaim absolute religious freedom.

Father Aniceto Fernandez, Superior General of the Dominicans, maintained that the text required complete revision because it was too naturalistic.

Bishop Carlo Colombo, chairman of the theological faculty of the major seminary of Milan, said that the declaration on religious freedom was "of the greatest importance," not only because of its practical consequences, but also and perhaps above all because of the judgment that would be passed on it by the well educated. They would look upon it as a key to the possibility of dialogue between Catholic doctrine and the modern mentality. He called for the further development and improved organization of the doctrinal content of the text, especially in regard to references to the fundamental principles of Catholic doctrine on religious freedom. Basically, he said, the text was making "a new application of unchangeable principles." Considerable importance was attached to Bishop Colombo's words, since he served as Pope Paul's personal theologian.

Immediately after this address, the discussion on religious freedom was closed by a standing vote. Nevertheless, at the next General Congregation, four more speakers addressed the assembly on this point in the name of seventy or more Council Fathers. All spoke out strongly in favor of the text, saying that a simple declaration on religious freedom was not enough. They insisted that the doctrinal foundations for religious freedom should be included in the text.

At this point the discussion on religious freedom came to an end, and once again the Secretariat for Promoting Christian Unity set about preparing a new revision, its third draft. There would also be a fourth, a fifth, and a sixth, before the document would be ready for promulgation.

JEWS AND MUSLIMS

Pope John XXIII received Cardinal Bea in private audience on September 18, 1960, three months after the foundation of the Secretariat for Promoting Christian Unity, and gave him an explicit oral mandate to prepare a special Council schema dealing with the Jews. The schema was ready for presentation to the Central Preparatory Commission in June 1962, but the Commission did not take it up. As Cardinal Bea explained later, this was "not because of ideas or doctrine expressed in the schema, but only because of certain unfortunate political circumstances existing at the time."

What had happened was that a member of the World Jewish Congress had given the impression to the press that he might attend the Second Vatican Council as an official observer. No official action had ever been taken in the matter, either by the World Jewish Congress or by the Secretariat for Promoting Christian Unity. Had the author of this story been an American or a European, little notice might have been taken of it; but he was from Israel and had served in the Ministry of Religion. The story was immediately taken up by the Arab press, and the Vatican was charged at great length with establishing political ties with Israel. The time was therefore judged inopportune for discussing and releasing a schema on the Jews.

The only mention made of the Jews at the first session was by Bishop Méndez Arceo, of Mexico, on December 6, 1962, two days before the session ended. He suggested that the Council should define the relationship between the Catholic Church and the Jews.

Later that same month, Cardinal Bea sent a long report to Pope John on the question. He stressed especially that the only point at issue in any document that the Council might prepare on the Jews would be a purely religious one. He maintained that there would be no danger of the Council's becoming involved in the grave political problems arising out of Zionism or the relations between the Arab nations and the state of Israel.

Pope John sent Cardinal Bea a reply in his own hand, dated December 23, 1962, saying, "We have carefully read this report of Cardinal Bea, and we agree with him completely on the importance of the matter and on the responsibility which we have to give it due consideration."

On the strength of Pope John's reaction, the Secretariat for Promoting Christian Unity set to work putting the final touches to its draft, entitled "A Document on the Purely Religious Relations Between Catholics and Jews." But no official action was taken in the matter before Pope John's death, early in June 1963.

Cardinal Bea submitted the final text to the Coordinating Commission after Pope Paul VI had declared, at the end of June, that the Council would be continued. But as late as October 18, 1963, three weeks after the opening of the second session, the Coordinating Commission still had made no decision about the distribution of the document or the manner in which it should be presented.

On November 8, 1963, a communiqué was issued by the Secretariat for Promoting Christian Unity, stating that that morning there had been distributed to the Council Fathers a draft on "the attitude of Catholics toward non-Christians, particularly toward the Jews." The communiqué went on to say that the draft would form Chapter 4 of the schema on ecumenism. The document, continued the communiqué, "cannot be called pro-Zionist or anti-Zionist, since it considers these as political questions and entirely outside its religious scope. In fact, any use of the text to support partisan discussion or particular claims, or to attack the political claims of others, would be completely unjustified and contrary to every intention of those who have composed it and presented it to the Council."

It was also pointed out in the communiqué that the part that the Jewish leaders of Christ's day had played in bringing about the crucifixion "does not exclude the guilt of all mankind. . . . The personal guilt of these leaders cannot be charged to the whole Jewish people either of Christ's time or of today." Therefore it was unjust, the communiqué said, to accuse the Jewish people of "deicide" or to consider them "accursed" by God.

The title of the draft, however, was misleading, because it spoke of "the attitude of Catholics toward non-Christians," whereas the draft itself dealt exclusively with the Jews.

On November 12, 1963, I arranged a press conference for Mr. Zachariah Shuster, the European director of the American Jewish Committee. He called the distribution of the draft on Catholic-Jewish relations "certainly one of the greatest moments in Jewish history." He was confident "that Jews of this generation will feel fortunate to have witnessed this historic step on the part of the Church." During the three years that the draft had been in preparation, he said, the Vatican had solicited the views of the most competent scholars and religious leaders, both Christians and Jews. "One may confidently say that there is not one Jewish group or trend or leading Jewish thinker that has not expressed his, or its, views, to the authorities in Rome at their request." He was particularly satisfied that the document contained "a total rejection of the myth of Jewish guilt for the crucifixion."

Before taking up the individual chapters of the schema on ecumenism, the Council discussed it in a general way, beginning on November 18.

The first speaker was Ignace Cardinal-Patriarch Tappouni, of the Syrian Patriarchate of Antioch, who said that the chapter on the Jews was especially inopportune. He did not understand why the Secretariat headed by Cardinal Bea had presented the chapter at all, since the purpose of the Secretariat was to foster the unity of Christians. In some regions where Christians were in a minority, he said, the chapter on the Jews would cause prejudice against the Church and the local hierarchy. Because of the current political situation and because of ignorance or indifference, the good intentions of the Council Fathers would not be understood, or would be misinterpreted by opposing factions, bringing harm to Christians. He felt that the explanations contained in the chapter would not suffice to counter these dangers.

Peter Cardinal Tatsuo Doi, of Tokyo, speaking on behalf of the Japanese bishops, said that the title of Chapter 4 should be amended to read, "On the Attitude of Catholics Toward Jews and Toward Other Non-Christians." He felt that the document should state that the Catholic Church respected the truths contained in the religions and ethical systems of non-Christians, and considered them as providential preparations for the Christian way of life.

Patriarch Stephanos I Sidarouss, of Cairo, head of the Coptic Patriarchate of Alexandria, said that a schema on

Christians was not the place to speak of the Jewish people. To treat of the Jews might hurt the cause of religion in a particular nation.

Patriarch Maximos IV Saigh also maintained that the chapter was out of place. And if it should be retained "for some reason of which I am not aware," then a separate section should be devoted to it. If mention was made of the Jews, he said, "then we should also mention other non-Christians—for example, the Muslims."

Cardinal Meyer, of Chicago, was the first speaker on November 20. He said he believed it was the view of many bishops, especially those from the United States, that the chapter on the Jews should remain right where it was. The questions treated in the chapter, he said, were "intimately connected with both theoretical and practical ecumenism."

Bishop Angelo Jelmini, of Lugano, Switzerland, speaking for all the bishops of Switzerland, said, "In these days of atheism we should speak not only of Jews, but also of Muslims and of all who believe in God." He said that the schema on ecumenism was the proper place to treat of the Jews, since the schism between the Synagogue and the Church was the source of all other schisms.

Since the chapter on the Jews had received as mixed a welcome on the Council floor as the chapter on religious freedom, the Moderators decided not to present it for a preliminary vote for fear that it might be rejected. They deferred the discussion until the third session.

It was obvious to all that there had been a threefold reaction to the chapter. One was, "Why treat of the Jews at all?" The second was, "Why treat of the Jews in a schema on ecumenism, which deals with Christian unity?" And the third was, "Why not include other non-Christian religions as well?" The Secretariat for Promoting Christian Unity and the Council as a whole realized that the only solution was to have a document, distinct from the schema on ecumenism, in which the Jewish and also other non-Christian religions would be mentioned, especially Islam (the religion of the Muslims).

The surprise announcement by Pope Paul at the end of the second session that he would make a pilgrimage to the Holy Land seemed like a stroke of genius calculated to help the Council Fathers resolve this particular problem more calmly. On that pilgrimage, the Pope would spend most of his time in the Arab state of Jordan and some of his time in the Jewish state of Israel. There were bound to be many occasions during that pilgrimage for the Pope to show the Muslims that the Catholic Church was as deeply interested in them as in the Jews.

Pope Paul's pilgrimage in this respect proved more than successful. He was back in Rome little over a month when Father Farhat, my Lebanese friend at Vatican Radio, on February 17, 1964, delivered a ten-page report to Monsignor William Carew at the Vatican Secretariat of State, entitled "Islam in the Middle East: Some Impressions on the Journey of the Holy Father to Palestine." The report stated that, by his attitudes, gestures, discourses, and prayers, the Pope had shown the Muslims, "who find it hard to distinguish between the temporal and the spiritual, the political and the religious orders," that he had come to Palestine for no other reason than "to show respect for the places where Jesus was born, where he lived, where he died, and where he rose from the dead for the salvation of the world." Father Farhat described Muslim reactions to the Pope's visit; he had experienced them firsthand, having been sent to the Holy Land by Vatican Radio to report on the pilgrimage. For years to come, he said, Christians would talk to their Muslim friends about the visit of Pope Paul VI to the kingdom of King Hussein, descendant of the Prophet Mohammed.

At the end of the report, Father Farhat made three practical suggestions. First, he recalled that the Pope, in his statement of September 12, 1963, had said that a secretariat for non-Christians would be established at an opportune time, and asked whether that "opportune time" might not be considered as having arrived. In the second place, he suggested that Muslim observers be invited to the third session, a gesture which would deeply touch the hearts of the Muslims. Thirdly, he proposed a plan to counteract the propaganda accusing the Church of evil intentions for introducing the chapter on the Jews. If carried out, he said, it would also prevent governments in Muslim countries from exploiting the chapter on the Jews to the harm of Christendom. His plan was to balance the chapter on Judaism with a chapter on Islam. This new chapter might then serve as a basis for eventual religious dialogue with the Muslims.

Monsignor Carew, like Father Farhat, had been in Jerusalem at the time of the Pope's visit, and had also been struck by the religious awe and reverence manifested by the Muslims. He assured Father Farhat that the report would be laid before the Holy Father without delay. After carefully reading it, the Pope asked that a copy be made for Paolo Cardinal Marella, and another for the Secretariat for Promoting Christian Unity.

On February 27, 1964, the Secretariat for Promoting Christian Unity met in plenary session. At this meeting, all proposals regarding the chapter on the Jews that had been submitted by Council Fathers either in oral or in written interventions were carefully examined. The Secretariat reached the following conclusions: the schema on ecumenism proper would, as was logical, discuss only the question of unity among Christians; the revised chapter on the Jews would be retained because of internal reasons, because of its importance, and because of the universal expectation which it had aroused; because special bonds united the people of the Old Covenant with the Church, the document on the Jews would be retained as an appendix to the text on ecumenism; that appendix would also deal with relations between Christians and non-Christian religions, with special emphasis on Islam.

Three months later, on Pentecost Sunday, May 17, 1964, Pope Paul invited all ecclesiastical students in Rome to attend a special Mass he was celebrating in St. Peter's. At the close of his sermon, he mentioned the great efforts made by the Catholic Church to draw closer to separated Christians and to those belonging to other religions. He then said, "In this connection, we shall make a special announcement for you, hoping that it may draw significance and value from Pentecost. It is this: As we announced some time ago, we shall establish here in Rome, in these very days, a Secretariat for Non-Christians. It will have a structure analogous to the Secretariat for Separated

Christians, but of course will have different functions. We shall entrust it to the Cardinal Archpriest of this Basilica, who, in addition to the wisdom and virtue which endear him to the Church of Rome and win for him its respect, has a rare competence in regard to the religions of the peoples of the world."

The "Cardinal Archpriest" referred to by Pope Paul was Cardinal Marella, Roman by birth and a member of the Roman Curia, who had served as Apostolic Internuncio in Japan during World War II, and currently headed the Sacred Congregation responsible for the maintenance of St. Peter's.

Two days later, on May 19, 1964, Pope Paul VI established the Secretariat for Non-Christians, placing Cardinal Marella in charge.

Two weeks before the opening of the third session, on August 31, 1964, I received a visit from Dr. Joseph Lichten, director of the Intercultural Affairs Department of the Anti-Defamation League of B'nai B'rith. He was deeply concerned over the fact that the phrase exculpating the Jews for the crucifixion of Christ had now been deleted from the Council document, and maintained that the phrase in question was the most important part of the document as far as the Jews were concerned. He had visited various cardinals in Europe on the matter, he told me, and was busy making contacts in Rome. He said further that Cardinal Bea was preparing a special amendment to be presented in the Council hall "on this unfortunate deletion."

At the eighty-eighth General Congregation, on September 25, 1964, Cardinal Bea gave a report on the revised declaration. The problem, he said, was "whether and in what manner the Jewish people, as a people, are to be considered guilty of the condemnation and death of Christ the Lord." He disagreed strongly with those who maintained that the chief cause of anti-Semitism was the aforesaid guilt of the Jewish people. He explained that there were many reasons for anti-Semitism which were not of a religious, but of a national, political, psychological, social, or economic nature.

In his theological exposition, Cardinal Bea said that "the leaders of the Sanhedrin at Jerusalem" had been guilty of the death of Christ, as the efficient cause in the historical order; denied that "the entire Jewish people of that time, as a people," could be declared guilty for what the leaders in Jerusalem had done; and stated that this guiltlessness of the Jews as a people at the time of Christ was all the more true with regard to the Jews of today. The Jewish leaders who condemned Christ to death, he said, were clearly not formally guilty of deicide, since Christ himself (Lk 23:34), St. Peter (Acts 3:17), and St. Paul (Acts 13:27) had all said that those leaders had acted without full knowledge of Christ's divinity. Before concluding his report, Cardinal Bea called attention to the specific reference to Muslims in the new text.

The first of the thirty-four Council Fathers to speak on the revised text was Cardinal Liénart, of France. He said that the Council Fathers from the East were preoccupied with political questions, whereas the matter at hand was an exclusively religious one, to be considered from an ecumenical and pastoral point of view. He was in favor of the text and wanted it to be made even more complete.

Cardinal Tappouni solemnly repeated the grave objections which he and other Eastern patriarchs had raised
during the second session. Their observations were not
to be interpreted as hostility toward the Jewish religion,
he said. Because they foresaw that difficulties would be
placed in the way of their pastoral work, however, and
because they wished to defend the Council against the
unfounded accusation that it was following a particular
political line, they felt it necessary respectfully to call the
attention of the Council Fathers to the inopportuneness
of the declaration. They said that they were fully conscious
of the cause at issue and urged the assembly to set the
matter aside altogether.

Cardinals Frings, Lercaro, Léger, Ritter; Archbishop
Lorenz Jaeger, of Paderborn, Germany; Bishop Pieter
Nierman, of Groningen, who spoke for all the bishops
of the Netherlands; and Bishop Jules Daem, of Antwerp,
Belgium—all urged that the text be retained and improved.

Cardinal König, of Vienna, considered the text good,
but said that more accuracy was needed in certain sections.

Cardinal Ruffini, of Palermo, said that if Jews and Muslims were to be mentioned in the text, then Buddhists and
Hindus should also be mentioned.

Cardinal Meyer, of Chicago, called for the restoration
of the previous year's text, because it was more explicit in
rejecting the accusation of deicide. He also wanted the
declaration to treat of the Jews exclusively. The sections
on the other religions were important, he said, but should
be treated elsewhere.

On the same day, September 28, the bishops of Germany issued a statement through their news agency,

Katholische Nachrichten Agentur, declaring their support of the Council decree on the Jews, "especially because we are aware of the severe injustice committed against the Jews in the name of our people."

On September 26, at a Vatican press conference, Archbishop John Heenan of Westminster, then Vice-President of the Secretariat for Promoting Christian Unity, stated that "the question of the culpability of the Jews for the death of Jesus has been given an altogether exaggerated importance." He did not believe, he said, that most Christians "think of the Jews, when thinking of the passion and death of Our Lord," but rather of their sins since "it is of faith that Christ is the victim of sin and that all sinners—Christians as well as non-Christians—are in this sense responsible for his death."

On the second day of discussion, September 29, José Cardinal Bueno y Monreal, of Seville, recalled that Pope Paul VI, in his first encyclical, *Ecclesiam suam*, had invited Catholics to enter into dialogue with all non-Christians and maintained that the Council could not, therefore, exclude the declaration on the Jews from its acts. However, out of respect for the objections stated on the previous day by the representatives of the Eastern Rite Churches, he said that perhaps all suspicion of politics might be avoided if the title were simply "On Non-Christians," leaving out any mention of the Jews. The declaration could begin with an invitation by the Catholic Church to non-Christians to dialogue. Then mention might be made of the Jews and Muslims. The religions of India, China, and Japan might also be mentioned by name, and all other religions might be mentioned in general. The declaration might then conclude with a condemnation of every kind of discrimination. Such a change in structure might eliminate the difficulties that had been indicated on the Council floor.

These suggestions were to a great extent followed. The declaration was revised in the course of the third session, and given the title "On the Relationship of the Church to Non-Christian Religions." The text dealt first with non-Christian religions in general, then with Hinduism and Buddhism by name, but briefly. Islam was treated next and at greater length because of its absolute monotheism and numerous links with revelation as contained in the Scriptures. The Jews were treated next, at even greater length, because of their singular destiny in the plan of salvation. In conclusion, the text ruled out all discrimination, both in theory and in practice.

On November 20, at the last General Congregation of the third session, a vote was taken on this revised text. There were 1,651 affirmative votes, 99 negative votes, and 242 qualified affirmative votes. Between the third and fourth sessions, the declaration was revised in the light of the suggestions submitted with the affirmative votes.

In mid-October 1965, at the fourth session, 1,763 Council Fathers expressed satisfaction with the way in which the qualifications had been incorporated in the text, and 250 expressed dissatisfaction. The text then went to Pope Paul, who decided that it should be presented for a final formal vote at a public meeting on October 28. The result of this vote was 2,221 in favor, and 88 opposed. The Pope immediately promulgated the declaration.

Cardinal Bea was overjoyed, calling it a "nearly unanimous vote." It was "providential," he said, that, through discussion, the text had come to include reference to all non-Christian religions as well as the Jewish religion.

THE SCHEMA ON DIVINE REVELATION: SOME PAPAL DIRECTIVES

In the preface to its dogmatic Constitution on Divine Revelation, the Second Vatican Council declares that, following in the footsteps of the Council of Trent and the First Vatican Council, it "wishes to set forth authentic teaching about divine revelation and about how it is handed on, so that by hearing the message of salvation the whole world may believe; by believing, it may hope; and by hoping, it may love." In Chapter I, divine revelation is described as an action whereby "the invisible God out of the abundance of his love speaks to men as friends and lives among them, so that he may invite and take them into fellowship with himself. This plan of revelation is realized by deeds and words having an inner unity: The deeds wrought by God in the history of salvation manifest and confirm the teaching and realities signified by the words, while the words proclaim the deeds and clarify the mystery contained in them."

The life span of the schema on divine revelation covered all four sessions.

At the first session, discussion was deadlocked on the crucial matter of a single or twofold source of revelation. Pope John XXIII resolved the deadlock by creating a special joint commission representing both conflicting tendencies and instructing it to draw up a new text. This text was distributed to the Council Fathers in May 1963.

On August 9, 1963, Bishop Schröffer, of Eichstätt, Germany, a liberal member of the Theological Commission, informed the Council Fathers who were preparing to attend the Fulda conference later that month that the revised schema was "the result of a laborious struggle" in the joint commission, and was no more than "a compromise with all the disadvantages that a compromise entails." It had not been possible, he said, to achieve further concessions, and "not much more" was to be hoped for. He enclosed with his letter detailed comments on the schema prepared by Father Rahner, as supported by Fathers Grillmeier, Semmelroth, and Ratzinger, according to which the schema was "a peaceful compromise which avoids many causes of division, but which therefore avoids mentioning many things concerning which additional doctrine would be welcome."

The Fulda conference prepared an official statement on the schema, largely based on Father Rahner's comments, including an "urgent request" that the schema on divine revelation "should not be treated at the very beginning of the second session of the Council, but at a later time." The further request was made that the discussion should start with the schema on the Church. Cardinal Döpfner delivered the statement in person to the Council authorities in Rome and attended the meeting of the Coordinating Commission on August 31, which determined the agenda for the coming session. On his return to Munich, he informed the Council Fathers who had attended the Fulda conference that the schema on the Church was first

on the provisional agenda; the schema on divine revelation was not listed at all.

Although Father Rahner had told the bishops at Fulda
before the second session that there was "virtually no hope
of substituting a new and better schema," this hope was
revived at the end of the second session when the European
alliance succeeded in having four new members elected to
the Theological Commission, which was responsible for
the schema on divine revelation. It was announced at the
same time that further amendments could be submitted
by mail until January 31, 1964.

Three weeks after the close of the second session, the Coordinating Commission instructed the Theological Commission to proceed to a revision of the as-yet-undiscussed
schema. Special subcommissions of the Theological Commission were created to handle the revision; their members included Bishop André Charue, of Namur, Belgium,
chairman; Bishop van Dodewaard, of Haarlem, the Netherlands; Archbishop Ermenegildo Florit, of Florence,
Italy; Auxiliary Bishop Joseph Heuschen, of Liége, Belgium; Abbot Butler, of Downside, superior of the English
Benedictines; Bishop Georges Pelletier, of Trois-Rivières,
Canada; and a large number of *periti*, including Fathers
Grillmeier, Semmelroth, Castellino, Cerfaux, Garofalo,
Turrado, Rigaux, Kerrigan, Gagnebet, Rahner, Congar,
Schauf, Prignon, Moeller, Smulders, Betti, Colombo,
Ramirez, and Van den Eynde.

The bishops and *periti* of these special subcommissions
worked privately before meeting in Rome from April 20
to 24, 1964. Their revised text was sent for approval to the
Secretariat for Promoting Christian Unity, which replied

on May 30 that it was generally satisfied with the text and felt that a joint meeting with the Theological Commission would not be needed.

The text was next taken up at four meetings of the Theological Commission, from June 3 to 5. On June 26, the Coordinating Commission approved the revised text, and on July 3 it was approved by Pope Paul VI as a basis for discussion. On September 30, 1964, two weeks after the opening of the third session, the draft constitution on divine revelation was introduced on the Council floor by Archbishop Florit.

The Archbishop said that many of the written observations submitted by Council Fathers had requested that the schema should include a fuller treatment of tradition. Many had also called for a more profound treatment of revelation itself, asking "that the concept of revelation be further developed, as well as its object, which should include not only truths about God, but God himself; for God reveals himself not only in words but also in deeds carried out by him in the history of salvation."

Another member of the Theological Commission, Bishop Franic´, of Yugoslavia, said that the schema as it stood, while not erroneous, was "notably defective" in its treatment of the fullness of tradition.

Cardinal Döpfner, of Munich, speaking in the name of seventy-eight German-speaking and Scandinavian Council Fathers, commended the text highly, saying that it had successfully skirted the difficult problem of defining whether the whole of revelation was or was not contained in Sacred Scripture.

Cardinal Léger, of Montreal, called the text more than

satisfactory and said a fine balance had been achieved regarding the relation between Sacred Scripture and tradition.

Archbishop Shehan, of Baltimore, called the schema defective because "it does not express what happens to the subject of revelation, that is, to a human mind which receives revelation from God, interprets it, and then transmits it to the People of God."

Bishop Compagnone, of Anagni, Italy, said that there should be no deviation from the doctrine of the Council of Trent and Vatican I, which affirmed that tradition was more extensive than Sacred Scripture, and that revelation was contained not only in Sacred Scripture but also in tradition. Although the majority did not consider it opportune to introduce this teaching in the text, care should be taken to avoid giving the impression that the Council was turning its back on earlier decisions.

Abbot Butler, of Downside, discussed the historicity problem of the Gospels. "In the light of faith," he said, "it is certain that the Gospels, like the other books of the Bible, are inspired, with all the consequences resulting from that dogmatic truth. But it is also certain that the notion of so-called literary types applies to the Gospels as well as to the other books. And it is likewise certain that through this principle many difficulties in the Old Testament have been solved in such a way that no harm was done to faith. At the same time, apparent contradictions between the inspired books and other known truths, whether scientific or historical, have disappeared. . . . There is no reason from faith or from dogma why the same might not happen in the case of the

Gospels." He readily admitted that errors might arise, and that some exegetes might even turn this liberty into license, but this danger must be faced in view of the greater good to be achieved.

The debate was closed on October 6. All suggestions made during the five days of debate, as well as those contained in written interventions, were examined anew. On November 20, at the last General Congregation of the session, the new edition of the schema was given to the Council Fathers, who were told that they might submit further observations up to January 31, 1965.

The International Group of Fathers sent a ten-page criticism of the schema to its mailing list with an accompanying letter stating that one in conscience could give an affirmative vote at the fourth session, if the enclosed amendments were adopted in the schema. The group urged that its amendments be submitted before the January 31 deadline, since experience proved that "suggestions and amendments made to Council Commissions have almost no weight unless they are supported by the largest possible number of signatures."

The effort was wasted, however, because the Theological Commission did not make a revision, in spite of the announcement made in the Council hall.

Voting on the schema took place early in the fourth session, between September 20 and 22, 1965. Contrary to Article 61, Section 3, of the Rules of Procedure, no report was read by a representative of the Theological Commission before the vote. In the course of six ballots, qualifications were submitted with 1,498 affirmative votes. The Theological Commission, however, was not obliged to adopt any of these changes, because each part of the schema had received far more than the required two-thirds majority.

The qualified affirmative votes chiefly concerned the relation between Scripture and tradition, in Article 9; the inerrancy of the Scriptures, in Article 11; and the historicity of the four Gospels, in Article 19. From the outset, these three points had proved particularly difficult, because of different schools of theological thought, because of varied positions dictated by modern biblical studies, and because of ecumenical implications. Practically the same proposal was submitted by 111 Council Fathers in connection with Article 9. They wished to have the following words added to the text: "Consequently, not every Catholic doctrine can be proved from Scripture alone."

To assist the Theological Commission in its deliberations on this point, Pope Paul on September 24 sent it the following quotation from St. Augustine: "There are many things which the entire Church holds, and they are therefore correctly believed to have been taught by the Apostles, even though they are not to be found in written form." For some reason, the quotation was never brought up at any of the meetings of the Commission on October 1, 4, and 6. A long and heated discussion took place on the proposal of the 111 Council Fathers, and the decision was finally reached on October 6 to retain the text unchanged.

In connection with Article 11, on the inerrancy of the Scriptures, 184 Council Fathers asked for the deletion of the phrase "pertaining to salvation" from the statement that "the books of Scripture . . . must be acknowledged as teaching firmly, faithfully, with integrity, and without error, the truth pertaining to salvation." They argued that the phrase seemed to confine the inerrancy of the Scriptures to matters concerning faith and morals. The Commission decided that the schema as it stood did not in fact restrict the inerrancy of Sacred Scripture, and again it decided to make no changes in the text.

The point at issue in Article 19, on the historicity of the Gospels, was the phrase "true and sincere things about Jesus" in the statement, "The sacred authors wrote the four Gospels . . . always in such manner that they told us true and sincere things about Jesus." An amendment prepared by the International Group was submitted by 158 Council Fathers to reword the phrase to read "true and sincere history," or "true historical narrative." The argument was that a writer could be sincere, yet still write only fiction. They also felt that the schema confined the truth of the Gospels to those things which were narrated "about Jesus"; it should be made clear that what was said in the Gospels about other persons was also historically true and sincere. Eighty-five other Council Fathers suggested that the words "true and sincere things about Jesus" should be replaced by the words "objective truths as regards the historical accuracy of the facts."

But again the Theological Commission decided not to change the text. The majority justified their stand on the grounds that the general assembly had already accepted the schema in its existing form by more than the required two-thirds majority, and that the Commission therefore had no authority to alter the text on the basis of suggestions made by a relatively small minority. This position was legally correct, since the vote had in fact proved a great victory for the liberals. Article 9 had been adopted by 83 percent of the assembly; Article 11, by 84 percent; and Article 19, by 85 percent.

Understandably, these decisions occasioned great disappointment in the minority groups concerned, both inside and outside the Commission. Complaints immediately began to reach the Pope through numerous channels. Some *periti* maintained that the schema as it stood contained serious doctrinal error. Bishops pleaded urgently for an authoritative intervention by the Pope. And still others assured the Pope that there was no cause for alarm, and that there was no danger that a false interpretation might be given to the schema. If the Pope was to take any action in the matter, it would have to be prior to the final series of votes on the manner in which the Theological Commission had handled the qualifications.

A solution to the problem of Article 9 was submitted to Pope Paul by Archbishop—now Cardinal—Florit, of Florence, who had helped formulate Article 9 and had supported it in the Theological Commission. He suggested that Pope Paul reconvene the Commission and ask it to reconsider carefully the necessity, or the opportuneness, of stating explicitly in the schema that not every Catholic doctrine could be proved from Scripture alone. The thorny problem of whether tradition contained more revealed truths than Scripture was an altogether different question and would not be touched upon. It was merely a matter of stating more precisely that tradition provided a more explicit and complete expression of divine revelation than Scripture, since tradition could be the determining factor in some cases for arriving at an exact knowledge and understanding of what had been revealed. An affirmation of this sort, said Cardinal Florit, would be fully in harmony with the text. He proposed, therefore, the addition of these words to Article 9: "Consequently, not every Catholic doctrine can be proved from Sacred Scripture alone." This amendment, incidentally, was nearly identical with the one proposed earlier by 111 Council Fathers, and rejected by the Theological Commission.

On October 8, Pope Paul received a memorandum from the International Group of Fathers regarding Article 11. The phrase "truth pertaining to salvation," wrote the authors of the memorandum, had been deliberately introduced in order to confine the inerrancy of Scripture to supernatural matters concerning faith and morals; this was in open conflict with the constant teaching of the Church, they continued, and would encourage exegetes to become increasingly audacious in their demands. Other reactions to this article also reached the Pope, some spontaneously, some solicited by him, and of all shades of opinion.

Complaints were also submitted to Pope Paul concerning Article 19, and it was known that he himself felt the phrase "true and sincere things" to be unconvincing and unsatisfactory. An account that was historically reliable would have a wholly different value from one that was merely sincere, he said. Upon inquiry he learned that Cardinal Bea and the Secretariat for Promoting Christian Unity, together with the Theological Commission, technically made up the joint commission which was competent for revising the schema, but the Theological Commission had drawn up the objectionable passages independently. Pope Paul then conferred with Cardinal Bea.

The Pope gave these questions his most earnest attention, studying the relevant literature and consulting with
competent persons. After discussing the matter with the
four Moderators on October 12, he received from one of
them a memorandum two days later on Article 9, pointing
out that the Theological Commission had been obliged to
act in accordance with the mandate which it had received
from an overwhelming majority of the Council Fathers.
To allay every anxiety, however, the writer suggested, it
might still be stated that not all Catholic doctrine could be
known with certainty from Scripture alone, without the
help of tradition or the teaching authority of the Church.
That solution, he said, would substantially strengthen the
Catholic position in the face of the Protestant position,
without touching upon the question still controverted
among Catholic theologians.

The view of the Moderator coincided with the proposal
made earlier by Cardinal Florit. On October 14, Pope
Paul sent that proposal to the Theological Commission
as his own.

In a letter dated October 18 to Cardinal Ottaviani,
President of the Theological Commission, the Secretary
of State enclosed further observations of Pope Paul on
the three disputed articles, and informed the Cardinal of
the Pope's decision to reconvene the Commission. The
observations, he explained, were not intended "to alter
substantially either the schema itself or the work of the
Commission, but rather to improve it in some points of
great doctrinal importance." The incorporation of these
changes would enable the Holy Father "in all tranquillity" to give the requested approval for the promulgation

of the document which involved "great responsibility for him toward the Church and toward his own conscience." The Secretary of State further gave notice of the Pope's wish that Cardinal Bea, President of the Secretariat for Promoting Christian Unity, who had also served as co-president of the special joint commission established by Pope John XXIII, be invited to attend the meeting of the Commission.

This letter had been dictated by the Pope himself on October 17.

The Commission met on October 19 to hear the contents of the letter. The first of the three papal directives concerned Article 9, and suggested seven possible renderings. Cardinal Bea explained why he preferred the third one. After some discussion and balloting, the Commission decided to add to Article 9 the words: "Consequently, it is not from Sacred Scripture alone that the Church draws its certainty about everything which has been revealed." This had been Cardinal Bea's choice.

In regard to Article 11, the Commission was invited by Cardinal Cicognani, on behalf of Pope Paul, to consider "with new and serious reflection" the advisability of omitting the expression "truth pertaining to salvation" from the text. The Cardinal pointed out that the issue here was a doctrine that was not yet commonly accepted in the theological and Scriptural teaching of the Church; moreover, it did not seem to have been sufficiently discussed in the Council hall. Further, he said, in the judgment of very authoritative persons, the phrase might easily be misinterpreted. The omission of the phrase would not rule out the future study of the problem.

Cardinal Bea also maintained that the phrase was inopportune and open to misinterpretation. He drew attention to the fact that the phrase had not been decided upon at a meeting of the special joint commission, but had been introduced later.

After further discussion and several ballots—there was controversy as to which of these ballots was to be considered valid—the Commission decided to reword the phrase as follows: "The books of Scripture must be acknowledged as teaching firmly, faithfully, and without error that truth which God wanted put into the sacred writings for the sake of our salvation." Almost the same wording had been suggested by 73 of the 260 Council Fathers who had submitted qualifications to Article 11 nearly a month before.

With regard to Article 19, Cardinal Cicognani advised the Commission that Pope Paul regarded the words "true and sincere" as insufficient. That expression, he said, did not seem to guarantee the historical reality of the Gospels, and he added that the Holy Father clearly "could not approve a formulation which leaves in doubt the historicity of these most holy books."

Cardinal Bea subscribed to the views stated by Cardinal Cicognani on behalf of Pope Paul, and supported the alternative formulation suggested by the Pope.

Other Commission members, however, pointed out that not even the suggested formulation would eliminate the difficulty, since many Protestants would place their interpretation upon it. It was then suggested that the historicity of the Gospels should be asserted without equivocation earlier in the same paragraph; this would preclude any ambiguity concerning the words "true and sincere," which could then be retained.

This solution, which achieved the purpose intended by the Pope and also contained the substance of his proposal, was voted upon and adopted. The beginning of Article 19 was thus amended to read as follows: "Holy Mother Church has firmly and with absolute constancy held, and continues to hold, that the four Gospels, . . . whose historical character the Church unhesitatingly asserts, faithfully hand on what Jesus Christ . . . really did and taught for their eternal salvation."

On October 29, Cardinal Florit read a report to the general assembly on the manner in which the Theological Commission had handled the qualifications submitted with the affirmative votes. No mention was made of the special meeting of the Commission or the role of Pope Paul. When the ballot was taken, 2,081 Council Fathers expressed approval of the manner in which the qualifications had been handled, and 27 expressed disapproval.

On November 18, 1965, the Council Fathers, gathered in the presence of Pope Paul VI, voted 2,344 to 6 to accept the Constitution on Divine Revelation. The Constitution was immediately promulgated by the Pope.

While Pope Paul was considering whether to intervene in the matter or not, he received a letter from a leading personality at the Council—not a member of the Theological Commission—who had taken it upon himself to act as the spokesman for some alarmists at the Council. The writer said that if the Pope reconvened the Commission, as it was rumored, he would be guilty of using moral pressure on the Commission and the Council. Such a step, continued the writer, would damage the prestige of the Council and the Church, especially in Anglo-Saxon countries, the United States and Canada, where people were particularly sensitive to any violation of Rules of Procedure.

To this, Pope Paul replied:

> We wish to let you know immediately that it is in fact our intention to invite the Theological Commission of the Council kindly to consider the advisability of improving some points of the schema on divine revelation. We consider it our duty to reach a degree of doctrinal certitude which will allow us to add our approval to that of the Council Fathers.
>
> We believe also that this intervention of ours in the Council Commission is perfectly in order, since it is our responsibility not only to ratify or reject the text in question, but also—like every other Council Father—to collaborate in improving it with opportune suggestions. . . . This also seems the simplest and most courteous way of bringing to the attention of the Commission all those elements which are useful for the work that has been assigned to it. We take the liberty of pointing out, however, that no offense is being committed against the authority of the Council, as you indeed suspect, but rather that a necessary contribution is being made so that it may carry out its functions.

Further, nothing can cause us more pleasure than to see attention called to the liberty of the Council and to the observance of the rules of procedure that have been laid down. These principles are no less dear to the Romans than they are to the Anglo-Saxons.[1] They have been most rigorously observed in the Council.

Father Giovanni Caprile, S.J., who has had access to papal archive material on the Council, has said that the Pope's intervention in this phase of the Council's history "makes us appreciate once more the firm and at the same time gentle moderating action exercised by Paul VI. Together with the Council Fathers, at their side and as their leader, delicately fulfilling the command to strengthen the brethren, he has been the instrument used by the Holy Spirit to assure the Church a flowering of conciliar texts rich in wisdom and safe in doctrine."

WOMEN AT THE COUNCIL

Several months before the opening of the third session, it had been rumored that Pope Paul intended to appoint a number of nuns and laywomen as official auditors—literally, listeners—at the Council. A remote basis for such rumors was Cardinal Suenens' suggestion, on October 22, 1963, during the second session, that "a number of women should be invited to the Council, because women constitute one half of the population of the world." At the

---

1. In Italian usage this term includes German-speaking peoples.

same time, the Cardinal had suggested that the number of male auditors should be increased, that their representation should be on a broader international basis, and that the great congregations of brothers and sisters, "who contribute so signally to the apostolic work of the Church," should also be represented.

It was therefore not too surprising to hear Pope Paul say in his opening address on September 14, 1964, "We are delighted to welcome among the auditors our beloved daughters in Christ, the first women in history to participate in a conciliar assembly." All present were thrilled with the news, and many tried to get a glimpse of these privileged women. But there were none to be seen. Although the Pope had indicated early enough the names of the future women auditors, the invitations had not been sent out.

The only layman invited as an auditor to the first session was Professor Jean Guitton of the University of Paris, a close friend of Pope John, and the rules governing the proceedings of the first session had contained no reference to auditors. But when a revised edition was published on September 13, 1963, immediately before the opening of the second session, it included an article headed "Auditors," which read: "By gracious concession of the Supreme Pontiff, renowned laymen may attend public sessions, general congregations and commission meetings. They may not speak, however, unless they are invited by the Moderator of the assembly or by the president of a commission to express their views, in special circumstances, in the same way as *periti*." Eleven men were invited by Pope Paul to attend the second session as auditors.

On September 20, 1964, the first Sunday of the third session, the Holy Father celebrated a special Mass in St. Peter's for a number of lay Catholic groups engaged in apostolic work. One of the groups represented was the Mouvement International pour l'Apostolat des Milieux Sociaux Indépendants, which was holding its first general assembly in Rome for representatives from twenty-six countries. At the end of the Mass, the Pope addressed this particular group in French, and mentioned its president by name—Mlle. Marie-Louise Monnet, of Cognac, France. He said that the laity's role was to help spread the Council's message throughout the world, "since it is through the common effort of all the baptized that the Council will bear fruit. That is why we insist that the laity should be represented at the Council, and why our choice falls upon men and women completely dedicated to the apostolate. Today we can tell you—in confidence—that your president is on the list of women whom we intend to call to the Council in the role of auditors. May this be an encouragement to you to persevere with renewed ardor in your apostolate for the Church in your own particular walks of life." In this dramatic way, the Pope informed the first woman auditor of her role at the Council. She was then escorted to the papal throne.

On the following day, Miss Rosemary Goldie of Sydney, Australia, Executive Secretary of the Permanent Committee for International Congresses of the Lay Apostolate, received word from the Secretary General of her appointment as an auditor. As the days and weeks passed, more and more women auditors were invited. By the end of the third session, there were forty official auditors at

the Council, seventeen of them women. Among the latter, nine were nuns and eight laywomen. Mr. and Mrs.
José Alvarez Icaza of Mexico City, founders of the Christian Family Movement in Mexico, were the first married
couple to be invited.

Miss Goldie told me at the end of the third session
that all forty auditors had seats reserved for them in St.
Andrew's balcony near the Council Presidents. Each day
they received Holy Communion together at the opening
Mass. There were no rules regarding dress, she said, and
she had worn black only once; the laywomen wore black
veils, however. Translation services were provided by *periti*
seated nearby for those who did not understand Latin. "We
receive all the Latin documents that the Council Fathers
receive," Miss Goldie said, "and we are allowed to keep
them for our files." The auditors also had many opportuni-
ties to discuss Council topics with Council Fathers, *periti*,
and observers from the separated Christian Churches.
Every Monday evening, continued Miss Goldie, and very
often also on Thursday evenings, all the auditors gathered for a two-hour meeting at which a Council Father or
peritus usually gave a short explanatory talk on a schema
currently under discussion. The auditors also drafted proposals which were officially submitted to commissions.
They had been invited, Miss Goldie said, to collaborate
with the Council Commission on the Apostolate of the
Laity, and they had organized themselves in such a way
as to ensure that both men and women would sit on each
of the five subcommissions. When I asked Miss Goldie
whether some women might be given the opportunity to
speak at the Council, she replied, "It seems premature."

The nuns chosen as auditors were all mothers general or heads of large federations of sisters. To their great disappointment, they were at no time invited to attend a meeting of the Commission on Religious. They were perfectly free, however, to submit proposals to the Commission and to speak with its members.

The schema on the apostolate of the laity had been on the agenda of the second session but had not been taken up for discussion. Following the second session, the Coordinating Commission instructed that it be reduced to a few propositions. That order, however, was not carried out. The official reason given by Bishop Hengsbach of Essen, Germany, on behalf of the Commission on the Apostolate of the Laity, was that "such a reduction, in the light of the purpose of the Council, would hardly have satisfied the Council Fathers and the expectations of the laity."

The schema was presented for discussion at the third session, on October 7, 1964, by Bishop Hengsbach, who pointed out that the document insisted on "the vocation of all the faithful to participate in the apostolate of the Church." The aim of the apostolate, he said, was "men's conversion, their progress toward God, the Christian restoration of the temporal order, and the exercise of charity toward one's neighbor." The discussion went on until October 13.

Cardinal Ritter of St. Louis said that the text in general was prolix, diffuse, and often abstract. There was a marked lack of organization in the material, and the whole schema was permeated by an excessively clerical spirit.

Cardinal Browne of the Curia drew attention to the statements in the schema that the vocation to the apostolate was "of the very essence of the Christian vocation," and that "everyone" must receive training in the apostolate. The affirmation of such a universal obligation, he said, was too categorical.

Coadjutor Archbishop Angelo Fernandes of Delhi, speaking on behalf of all the bishops of India, found fault with the schema for reducing the apostolic action of the laity to some sort of "vague philanthropy." The schema, he said, was not sufficiently impregnated with a supernatural spirit, and was in great need of revision.

Bishop Carlo Maccari of Mondovì, Italy, conceded that there were some good points in the schema, but felt that in general it had been hastily pieced together with fragments which did not always fit perfectly. The style and Latin terminology were not accurate enough, and it was hardly satisfactory for a Council document. There was too much repetition, he maintained, and the material had not been developed organically.

Archbishop D'Souza of Bhopal, India, claimed that "a radical reorganization must take place everywhere in the Church" if laymen were to fulfill their proper roles. "My brothers," he asked, "are we—the Catholic clergy—truly prepared to abdicate clericalism? Are we prepared to consider the laity as brothers in the Lord, equal to ourselves in dignity in the Mystical Body, if not in office? Are we prepared no longer to usurp, as formerly we did, the responsibilities which properly belong to them? Or rather—if I may express this a bit more discreetly—are we prepared to leave to them what is more pertinent to them, such as the fields of education, social services, administration of temporal goods, and the like?"

The Archbishop asked why the Church should always have to be represented on international bodies by priests. Why might not laymen take the place of many of the clerics in the Roman Curia? Why might not laymen be admitted to the diplomatic service of the Holy See, and even become nuncios? Numerous possibilities existed, he said, for substitutions of this kind, "on the world level, on the national level, on the diocesan level, and on the parish level." This would make it possible for the clergy "to devote themselves to the exercise of the sacred and sacramental office for which they were ordained." He predicted that such principles in the schema would open up a new era for the Church. The Archbishop's statement was vigorously applauded.

Archbishop Owen McCann of Cape Town, South Africa, said that the schema was poor in inspirational content and did not correspond to the great expectations of bishops, priests and laity throughout the world.

Archbishop Cesar Mosquera Corral of Guayaquil, Ecuador, observed that, while the schema mentioned various types of apostolic work to be performed by laymen, it did not formulate "a true doctrine on the spirituality of the laity, which today constitutes one of the greatest deficiencies in the life of the Church."

On October 13, Mr. Patrick Keegan of London, president of the World Movement of Christian Workers, became the first layman to address the general assembly. He spoke in English and thanked the Cardinal Moderators "for the honor and opportunity of addressing this great assembly." He was very conscious, he said, of his responsibility, "at this historic moment, to try, however inadequately, to voice the sentiments of the faithful laity throughout the world." He called the lay apostolate a part of the new dynamism of the Church which was "seeking new ways to implement the message of the Gospel, seeking new means which are better adapted to the different social, economic and cultural situations of modern man." His eight-minute address was warmly applauded by the Council Fathers.

Even a superficial study of the schema made it clear that it gave preference to the form of apostolate known as Catholic Action, particularly popular in France. It was the only organized form of apostolate mentioned by name, and it was treated at great length. Cardinal Suenens, known as an ardent champion of the Legion of Mary, called this imbalance to the attention of the general assembly. He felt that no form of apostolate should be specifically mentioned in the text, since the apostolate carried out by the laity might be harmed thereby.

Bishop Stefan László of Eisenstadt, Austria, replying to Cardinal Suenens, insisted that Article 16 on Catholic Action be left unchanged. It was impossible, he said, to satisfy everyone; he pointed out that the matter had already been thoroughly discussed in the Council Commission, and that it had not been possible to find a formulation which would take account of all the different opinions.

Many other Council Fathers, however, voiced objections to the singling out of Catholic Action, and proposed that all forms of the apostolate should be treated on the same footing. This never came about.

At the end of the discussion, Bishop Hengsbach promised on behalf of the Commission on the Apostolate of the Laity that the suggestions made would be given careful consideration in a revision of the schema. On May 28, 1965, the revised version was approved by Pope Paul, and on June 12 it was mailed to the Council Fathers. This was now the fourth schema on the apostolate of the laity. It was a large booklet of seventy pages, containing the old and new texts in parallel columns, with detailed reasons for the numerous changes and extensive additions that had been made.

The new schema was voted on at the fourth session, between September 23 and 27, on twenty-two different ballots. There was no further discussion, but Bishop Hengsbach read a short report, pointing out that a new article had been introduced on the spirituality of the laity and another on youth and the apostolate, as many Council Fathers had requested. On every ballot, the necessary two-thirds majority was obtained. On six of the ballots, however, a total of 1,374 qualifications accompanied affirmative votes. These were examined by the Commission, and the text of the schema altered in more than 150 places. At the public session on November 18, 1965, it was officially announced that the Decree on the Apostolate of the Laity had received 2,305 affirmative votes and only two negative votes. Pope Paul then promulgated the decree.

Twelve days later, on November 30, the Secretary General announced that the definitive vote was 2,340 to two. When the ballots had originally been counted, he explained, some of them had been torn by the electronic computer and so were not included in the totals. Notaries, however, had examined the torn ballots and supplied the definitive count.

EXPANDING THE PROPOSITIONS ON PRIESTS AND THE MISSIONS

In the first ten days of the third session, numerous petitions were submitted by Council Fathers and episcopal conferences requesting that a normal discussion period should be granted for all schemas that had been reduced to a series of propositions. On Friday, September 25, 1964, only eleven days after the opening of the third session, the Secretary General announced that the Moderators had agreed to the wishes expressed by the Council Fathers and had decided to allow a short discussion before the votes were taken. He pointed out that the interventions read would not be used for the revision of the propositions, but would serve solely to assist the Council Fathers in deciding how to vote on the propositions. Any proposed changes in the drafts would have to be submitted as qualifications accompanying affirmative votes. He announced further that, by decision of the Moderators, summaries of such interventions must be presented to the General Secretariat by the following dates: on Oriental Churches, by October 10; on the missionary activity of the Church, by October 11; on priests, by October 12; on religious, by October 13; on the sacrament of Matrimony, by October 14; on priestly training, by October 15; and on Catholic education, by October 16.

In the evening of September 25, the bishops representing the world alliance gathered for their weekly meeting at the Domus Mariae and expressed pleasure at this initial victory, but also apprehension lest the "short" discussion should be confined to a single day. They decided that this was not enough, and prepared formal requests, which episcopal conferences would be asked to direct to the Cardinal Moderators, that a fuller discussion of the propositions be authorized.

At their next meeting on October 2 these bishops were asked to promote a "slow down" policy, since the Council had been moving along at great speed until that date. This sudden change in Council policy, which in a matter of days was adopted by nearly all the episcopal conferences, was due to the appearance on September 30 of the Supplement for the schema on the Church in the modern world. Said to be a commentary on the schema, it was rather a collection of liberal teachings which the leaders of the European alliance were anxious to have included in the schema. The technique was to postpone discussion of this topic as long as possible, so that support could meanwhile be won for the Supplement, and then to draw out discussion of the schema so much that completing the revision of it during the third session would be impossible. An aid in achieving this goal was the authorization of a normal period of discussion for all the propositions.

In the morning of October 7, each Council Father received a revised and expanded version of the propositions on priests, differing from the propositions circulated by mail before the third session. The Secretary General announced that the revision had been authorized by the Coordinating Commission, and was based on written interventions that had been officially submitted to the General Secretariat "in the last few months." It was immediately apparent that some 90 percent of the additions and changes resulted from the proposals submitted by the German-speaking and Scandinavian bishops after their conference at Innsbruck in May 1964.

On October 12, the Secretary General announced that, at the decision of the Moderators, the short discussion on the propositions on priests was to begin on the following day, "because the reports for the schema on the Church in the modern world are not yet ready." Psychologically, this was the worst possible moment to launch a short discussion of the 100 lines on priests, since four days had just been devoted to discussing the 476 lines on the apostolate of the laity.

The first speaker on October 13 was Cardinal Meyer of Chicago, who said that the topic of priests merited a proper schema of its own, as well as ample discussion, similar to the discussion devoted to the schema on bishops. His suggestion, he said, was based upon the necessity for giving testimony to the esteem, interest and solicitude which all the bishops in the Council felt for their priests. He found fault with the propositions for speaking exclusively of the obligations of priests, without taking into consideration anything which might comfort or encourage them in fulfilling their difficult role. He was applauded when he stated, in conclusion, that the document should be redrafted.

Speaker after speaker pointed out weaknesses in the schema, calling it shallow, especially in regard to priestly spirituality. Fourteen Council Fathers spoke on that first day.

On the following day, it was announced that the discussion on the propositions on priests would end on the same day. Three cardinals, from Brazil, Italy and Spain, said that the propositions were too much concerned with externals in the life of a priest and too little concerned with his sanctification. Archbishop Salvatore Baldassarri of Ravenna, Italy, stated that it was impossible for the Council to treat of priests, the closest collaborators of bishops, in so offhand a manner. He called for a schema on priests as thorough as the schemas prepared on bishops and the apostolate of the laity.

Archbishop Fernando Gomes dos Santos of Goiânia, Brazil, speaking on behalf of 112 bishops of Brazil and other countries, said: "We are not at all ignorant of the good intentions of those who drafted this text. In fact, we praise their intentions. But it is what they have produced that we deplore!" The text, he said, had proved "a very great disappointment to us . . . and there is no reason why we should not say so." The text of these propositions, he said, was "an insult to those most beloved priests who labor with us in the vineyard of the Lord." If the Second Vatican Council was able to say "so many sublime and beautiful things about bishops and the laity," he asked, "why are so few and such imperfect things now to be said about priests?"

Many things, he said, were urged upon priests in the propositions which the bishops had not dared to prescribe for themselves. He appealed to the general assembly— "and we earnestly beg the most eminent Moderators"— that the matter should be given mature consideration, and that the present text should not yet be submitted to a vote. "Instead, let a new and worthy text be drafted, to be discussed and voted upon at the forthcoming fourth session of the Council. . . . The priesthood is too great and sacred a thing for us to speak hastily about it. We owe at least this testimony of love and veneration to our priests, who have been called to share with us in the work of the Lord."

At the end of the morning, with only nineteen of the twenty-seven speakers on the list of speakers having addressed the assembly, the Moderators sent new instructions to Archbishop Felici, and had him announce that interventions would continue on the following day and that the vote would be postponed until such time as the Moderators saw fit.

On October 15, eight more Council Fathers addressed the assembly. The first speaker was Cardinal Alfrink of Utrecht, Holland, who maintained that it was the conviction of many Council Fathers that the propositions could not be published as they stood without gravely disappointing priests. He therefore suggested that the Commission concerned should be asked to prepare a new text which would better correspond to the expectations of priests and the proposals made by Council Fathers. His suggestion was greeted with applause.

After the eighth speaker, the Moderator announced that the vote would be taken at some as yet unspecified future date. The "short" discussion had extended over three days.

On the following day, the Secretary General read out the following notification: "Many Fathers have requested the most eminent Moderators that all the schemas reduced to propositions, or at least some of them, should be sent back to the Commissions concerned after a short discussion, to be redrafted on the basis of the observations made by the Fathers. The Moderators therefore considered it opportune to refer this matter to the Coordinating Commission, which in turn has carefully examined the requests of the Fathers. Keeping in mind the principles laid down in the Rules of Procedure, this Commission has decided that, after a short discussion of each set of propositions, the views of the Fathers should be requested on the following statement, 'Would it please the Fathers to proceed with the vote now that the discussion is over?' If an absolute majority of the Council Fathers (50 percent plus 1) should reply in the affirmative, then the votes on the individual points in the propositions will be taken immediately in accordance with the threefold formula, 'Yes,' 'No,' and 'Yes, with qualifications.' If on the other hand the reply should be negative, then the entire matter will be referred back to the Commission with instructions to revise the schema speedily in accordance with the observations made by the Fathers."

The Secretary General then announced that the vote on the propositions on priests would be taken at the next meeting, on Monday, October 19. On that day, by a vote of 1,199 to 930, the propositions were referred back to the Commission concerned for revision in accordance with the observations made in the oral interventions. Notice was also given that additional suggestions might be made in writing within three days. The strategy of first expurgating undesirable elements from the text and then expanding it again by new proposals had been successful.

The reaction to the propositions on the missions was no less heated than the reaction to the propositions on priests. The propositions on the missions had been approved by Pope Paul on July 3, 1964, for distribution to the Council

Fathers. Almost immediately thereafter there appeared a counter schema called *Documentum nostrum I* ("Our document No. 1"), followed in quick succession by revised editions entitled *Documentum nostrum II* and *Documentum nostrum III*. All three were in circulation by August 3.

The leader of the group supporting the counter schema was Bishop van Valenberg, who had been connected with the efforts of the Dutch hierarchy early in the first session to secure the rejection of certain schemas. Others in the same group were the superiors general of the White Fathers, the Montfort Fathers, the Society of African Missions, the Picpus Fathers, the Missionaries of the Sacred Heart, the Holy Cross Fathers and the Assumptionists. The group claimed to have found considerable support among bishops and superiors general, and submitted *Documentum nostrum III* to the General Secretariat with the request that it be officially printed as a commentary on the existing propositions, to assist the Council Fathers "in properly and fully understanding the propositions which are to be voted on." But the General Secretariat did not react favorably to the suggestion.

When bishops from mission lands began to arrive in Rome for the third session, it was evident that they were very displeased with the propositions on the missions. This was especially true of the bishops of Africa. The Commission on the Missions had in fact voted unanimously in favor of the propositions at its plenary session from May 4 to 13, 1964. Knowing this, and seeing the dissatisfaction of the missionary bishops, I asked Father Schütte, Superior General of the Divine Word Missionaries, how this could be explained. "Not one of us on the Missions

Commission was satisfied with the propositions," he said. "We voted unanimously in favor of them, however, because the Coordinating Commission had ordered drastic cuts, and we believed that the six pages were the best that could be produced in the circumstances." He had foretold, at that meeting, that the missionary bishops were unlikely to accept the propositions, "since many of them had come to the Council precisely because a full-size schema was dedicated to the missions."

On Wednesday afternoon, September 30, the general secretariat of the Pan-African Episcopal Conference assembled to discuss the announcement made on September 25 that there would be a "short" discussion of all propositions before the voting. This general secretariat consisted of the presidents of the eleven national and regional episcopal conferences of Africa and Madagascar. Archbishop Zoa of Yaoundé, vice-president of the organization and a member of the Commission on the Missions, announced that, at a recent meeting of the Commission, he had suggested that the propositions on the missions should be discussed in the same way as any other schema. The other members on the Commission had also favored the idea, he said, and Cardinal Agagianian, President of the Commission, was to present the proposal in writing to the Council Presidency and the Cardinal Moderators.

As a practical resolution of this meeting, it was decided that each of the eleven national and regional episcopal conferences should directly petition the Council Presidency, the Cardinal Moderators and the Coordinating Commission for a normal discussion of all the propositions. A form letter was drawn up in Latin containing the points to be included, and each conference was to make its own translation and desired changes.

On October 6, the Missions Commission met in plenary session and voted 20 to 4 in favor of asking all episcopal conferences to make a formal request of Pope Paul VI that *Documentum nostrum III* should be printed by the General Secretariat of the Council as an official document and brought up for discussion on the Council floor. At the weekly meeting of the general secretariat of the Pan-African Episcopal Conference on the following day, Archbishop Zoa informed the members of the decision of the Missions Commission, and invited them to send formal requests to the Pope in the name of their episcopal conferences for the official printing and distribution of *Documentum nostrum III*.

At the meeting of the West African Episcopal Conference, held on October 8 at the Residenza Adele di Trenquellion, a hotel at which some sixty African bishops were staying, Archbishop John Amissah of Cape Coast, Ghana, announced that a tactful letter had already been sent to the Holy Father on behalf of many episcopal conferences—including the West African Episcopal Conference—to ask for "sufficient time" to discuss all the propositions on the Council floor.

On October 21, the report on the propositions on the missions was distributed, and it was announced that this topic would be taken up after the discussion on the Church in the modern world. By this time, more than 100 Council Fathers had notified the Secretary General that they wished to speak on the propositions on the missions.

Among the Fathers who had requested to speak were outstanding figures such as Cardinal Bea; Cardinal Frings; Cardinal Alfrink; Laurean Cardinal Rugambwa, of Bukoba, Tanzania; Cardinal Silva Henríquez; Cardinal Suenens; and Bishop De Smedt. Each had been requested to speak by a small group of superiors general headed by Father Leo Volker, Superior General of the White Fathers. The complete texts of their interventions were printed in large quantities for advance circulation among the Council Fathers.

On Thursday morning, November 5, the Secretary General announced that the discussion of the schema on the Church in the modern world would be interrupted on the following day, and discussion of the propositions on the missions would begin in the presence of Pope Paul VI. That afternoon the Roman Union of Superiors General met to listen to a report on the propositions on the missions prepared by Father Schütte.

"For most of us superiors general gathered here," he said, "hardly any schema apart from the one on religious concerns us as much as do the propositions on the missions." He gave a brief history of the process whereby the original schema had been reduced to a series of propositions, and then commented point by point on the thirteen articles included in the propositions. Many improvements, he said, could be made in the propositions, but even if all were adopted, many missionary bishops would remain skeptical and hesitant, because they would feel that the worldwide missionary activity of the Church had not received from the Council the treatment which its significance and urgency demanded.

Father Schütte suggested that the Council Fathers should be allowed to indicate by a vote whether they were satisfied with the propositions, or whether they wished to have a proper schema on the missions. "If the vote should be in favor of a real schema on the missions—and I have no doubt that this will be the case—the new schema should be drawn up by the competent Commission, making use of the former schemas on the missions." The superiors general decided to do everything in their power to secure the rejection of the propositions and the drafting of a new schema.

The same evening, Father Schütte approached Cardinal Frings to ask him to speak in favor of a genuine schema on the missions on the following day, Friday. Cardinal Frings agreed to do so the day after, since he was already scheduled to give a conference on Friday. Still the same evening, Father Schütte set to work with Father Karl Müller, one of his *periti*, to compose a letter to the Cardinal Moderators, stating that the short propositions were utterly unacceptable because the missionary aspect of the Church was far too important. Numerous copies of the letter were made so that signatures might be collected on the following day.

The next day, Friday, November 6, Pope Paul addressed the general assembly. He said that he had chosen to be present on a day when the attention of the Council was centered on the schema on the missions, "because of the grave and singular importance of the topic." He said that he had examined the text which was in the Council Fathers' hands, and had "found many things in it deserving of our praise, both as regards content and as regards orderly explanation. We believe, therefore, that the text will be approved by you without difficulty, after you have pointed out where further improvement is needed."

These words of the Pope were immediately construed as a "qualified affirmative vote" for the propositions. Nevertheless, Father Schütte went on collecting signatures, convinced that the Pope's statement had been based on misinformation regarding the feeling of the Council Fathers on the propositions.

After the Pope's address, Cardinal Agagianian, as president of the Commission on the Missions, read his introductory report, and then the Pope left. All of the remaining speakers that morning suggested major changes in the text.

That afternoon and evening, Father Schütte sent priests of his order to the residences of bishops for additional signatures, and in this way obtained several hundred more, all of which he turned over to the Cardinal Moderators.

The first speaker on Saturday, November 7, was Cardinal Frings of Cologne, who said that the missionary role of the Church was of such importance, especially in present-day circumstances, that the matter could not be disposed of in a few propositions. Instead, he argued, a complete schema on the missions should be prepared and submitted at the fourth session of the Council. This, he said, was not only his opinion, "but also the fervent desire of the superiors general, of many bishops of Africa and of other missions. I humbly ask that this desire may yet be fulfilled." His proposal that the text should be referred back to the Commission on the Missions for complete revision was greeted with two distinct waves of applause, reaching from end to end of the Council hall.

Cardinal Alfrink of Utrecht agreed that it was impossible to give adequate treatment to the missions "in a set of simple propositions." Cardinal Suenens, speaking on behalf of all the bishops of Africa, asserted that the text required major amendments.

Bishop Donal Lamont of Umtali, Southern Rhodesia, speaking on behalf of many bishops of Africa, said: "The presence of the Supreme Pontiff yesterday in the Council hall was a consolation far beyond anything that we had hoped for. We missionaries were all thrilled to see His Holiness, the first missionary, sitting amongst us, and for this we offer him our most profound thanks from our hearts." Then he went on to compare the propositions to the "dry bones without flesh, without sinew," in Ezekiel's vision.

Six more speakers addressed the assembly before the debate was closed on Monday, November 9. The Council Fathers were then asked, "Is it agreed that the schema of propositions on the missionary activity of the Church should be revised once again by the competent Commission?" In reply, 1,601 Council Fathers said "yes" (83 percent), and 311 said "no." This meant that the propositions were rejected and that a proper schema would now have to be prepared by the Commission on the Missions for presentation at the fourth session.

How explain Pope Paul's words? Did he not know of the great dissatisfaction with the propositions on the missions which had been manifested as soon as they were distributed by the General Secretariat? Did he not know of the objections repeatedly voiced by the bishops of Africa and other missionary countries, and by the superiors general of missionary orders? Had none of the petitions directed to him personally reached him? Did Cardinal Agagianian, President of the Missions Commission, fail to inform him of the great dissatisfaction manifested in the Commission itself? Did the other three Cardinal Moderators fail to inform the Pope of the dissatisfaction which they had witnessed and—in part—promoted? Was the Cardinal Secretary of State unaware of the state of affairs?

It is difficult to understand how the Pope could have spoken so optimistically about the propositions in the Council hall had he truly realized the position. The reports which subsequently appeared in the press, stating that the Council Fathers had contradicted the view expressed by the Pope, necessitate a closer examination of what the Pope really said. He did not say that *everything* in the propositions was deserving of praise, but that he had found "many" things "deserving of our praise." Even Bishop Lamont, who spoke more strongly than anyone else, stated that the propositions had much to recommend them, that they were positive in their approach, and that they were useful and necessary. Thus the Pope's judgment on the propositions did not conflict with that of the Council Fathers. He erred, however, in thinking that the propositions would be approved without difficulty, after further improvements had been indicated. In depicting the incident as defiance by the Council Fathers of the Pope, the press was perhaps not aware that the interventions read on the Council floor had been prepared long in advance and would have been delivered had the Pope made his address or not.

There were those who charged that Cardinal Agagianian had invited the Pope to attend the session, hoping thus to win the Council's support for the propositions which he was known to favor. The Cardinal, however, most emphatically denied this, stating that the Pope had spontaneously decided to attend the meeting.

SEATING THE PATRIARCHS

No other Council document had so short a conciliar life span, from the time it was first discussed on the Council floor to its solemn promulgation, as the Decree on Eastern Catholic Churches. The general assembly discussed the schema at the third session, from October 15 to 20, 1964. Votes were taken on individual parts of the schema on October 21 and 22. The schema was then returned to the Commission for revision, and submitted to the general assembly for a further vote on November 20. On the following day, it was solemnly promulgated by Pope Paul VI, at the public session which concluded the third session. Thus its conciliar life span had been five weeks and two days.

The position of the Eastern Rite Churches to the Latin Rite Church was bluntly stated early in the second session by Coptic Archbishop Isaac Ghattas of Thebes, in Egypt, in connection with the schema on the Church. "It would seem," he said, "that for many Council Fathers the Universal Church is the Latin Church, which through a separate schema concedes so-called privileges to a minority group, the Eastern Churches." Many churchmen of the Latin Church, he said, looked upon the Eastern Churches, both Catholic and Orthodox, "as ecclesiastical oddities or exotic creations," instead of "as sister Churches which together with the Latin Rite Church make up the Universal Church." This attitude of the Latin Rite Church was resented, he said, and neither the Catholic nor the Orthodox Eastern Churches would or could accept the Latin Church's tendency to act as though it alone were the Universal Church, dispensing privileges. In the course of his intervention, he pointed out that the schema on the Church made no mention of the different rites within the Church, or of the patriarchs.

Archbishop Ghattas spoke on Thursday, October 10, 1963. On the following Monday, October 14, a visible change was evident in the seating arrangements in the Council hall. Six patriarchs of the Eastern Rite Churches, who had formerly occupied places immediately after the cardinals, were now seated at a table of their own, directly across from the cardinals. Their table, like those of the Moderators and Presidents, was covered with a green cloth and draped in red. It was on a platform one step high. (That of the Moderators was two steps high and that of the Presidents three.) In the official announcements that day, the Secretary General drew attention to the fact that the patriarchs of the Eastern Rites had been assigned new places in the Council hall.

The casual observer might have thought that this greater attention and eminence bestowed upon the patriarchs was a direct result of the fiery intervention of Archbishop Ghattas four days earlier. But the Church of Rome moves much too slowly for the cause to have been as recent as that. The cause went back not four days but four years, to a letter written to Pope John XXIII by Patriarch Maximos IV Saigh, Melchite Patriarch of Antioch, Lebanon.

In that letter, written on October 8, 1959, the Patriarch expressed his joy, and that of the Greek Melchite Catholic Church as a whole, at the Pope's announcement of an Ecumenical Council. Despite his advanced age (he was eighty-one at the time of writing), he said that he wished to take part in the Council in person, because the Eastern Catholic Church represented the hope existing for reunion between the large numbers of Orthodox Christians and the Holy See in Rome. However, he said, there was "one preliminary difficulty" in the way of his personal and fruitful participation in the work of the Council, which he wished to explain "with simplicity and confidence." It concerned the rank of the patriarchs in the Catholic hierarchy and at the Ecumenical Council.

He explained that this question had "occupied much of the attention of the bishops and superiors general of our Churches gathered for their annual synod, over which we presided, at Ain-Traz, in the second half of August 1959." To that synod, he said, it had seemed illogical that the Council, while striving to break down the barriers between the Catholic and Orthodox Churches, should at the same time seat the patriarchs of the Eastern Catholic Churches after the cardinals. One of the most cherished rights which the patriarchs had always enjoyed was their precedence in rank. In earlier centuries, the patriarchs had always followed immediately after the Pope, who himself was still called Patriarch of the West.

"In fact," the letter continued, "ecclesiastical tradition from the earliest centuries consistently lists the rank of the sees in the Universal Church in the following order: Rome, Constantinople, Alexandria, Antioch and Jerusalem. Ecclesiastical tradition is likewise unanimous in recognizing that those in office in those five patriarchal sees take precedence, in accordance with the rank of their respective sees, over all other ecclesiastical dignitaries. In conformity, then, with this ancient and unanimous tradition, the Sovereign Pontiff of Rome is followed immediately in the hierarchy of the Church by those who head these four other patriarchal apostolic sees."

Patriarch Maximos explained that the cardinals gathered around the Pope were really his auxiliaries in so far as he was Bishop of Rome. Their dignity sprang from their participation in the dignity of the first see, which was Rome. But since this dignity was theirs only by participation, it was not logical that they should take precedence over the patriarchs of other patriarchal sees.

At the First Vatican Council, the patriarchs had been seated after the cardinals. This was the first time in history that such a thing had happened, and Patriarch Maximos described it as the result of "a regrettable anti-Eastern mentality which at the time dominated certain elements of the Roman Curia, a mentality comprehensible during a period of history when the West did not know the Eastern Church as it does in our day, and when the Eastern Catholics themselves . . . had a certain inferiority complex toward Europe, which was then at the height of its colonial power. But Your Holiness would certainly not approve of such a mentality."

The members of the Orthodox Churches, he went on, "wish to see from our example what place the Roman Church would give to their patriarchs in case of reunion." He closed the letter with an expression of confidence that Pope John would take the necessary steps to provide the "only just solution which our proposal merits."

Patriarch Maximos never received a reply to this letter.

Undaunted, he wrote another letter in the same vein on September 20, 1962, three weeks before the opening of the Council. He addressed it to Archbishop Felici and explained that the annual synod of the Greek Melchite Catholic Church had begged him to make a further attempt to reach Pope John, and also the Council Presidency, through the Secretary General. The request was the same: that the patriarchs of the East should have reserved for them at the Council "the rank assigned to them by the canons of the earliest ecumenical councils, that is, the first place immediately after the Supreme Pontiff." He pointed out that the decisions of the earliest ecumenical councils in this matter had been respected at the Council of Florence in 1439, where, by order of Pope Eugene IV, the Patriarch of Constantinople, Joseph II, had occupied the first place after the Pope and preceded the cardinals."

Patriarch Maximos was making this appeal, he explained, because the patriarchs of the East knew that those responsible for protocol at the Vatican were preparing to give precedence to the cardinals over the patriarchs at the forthcoming Council. "The question is a grave one," he warned, "and may constitute a nearly insurmountable obstacle to future union between the Orthodox Churches and the Catholic Church." But for the fact that he might give scandal to his own people, he would prefer "not to appear at the forthcoming Council so as to avoid a diminution, in our person, of the honor due to the patriarchal sees of the East." A week later he sent Archbishop Felici six copies of a memorandum "on the rank of the Eastern patriarchs in the Catholic Church."

On October 4, Archbishop Felici acknowledged the receipt of the letter and memorandum. "I have attentively read the considerations presented on the question," he wrote, "and shall submit them to the Holy Father." But again there was no reply from Pope John. And when the Council opened ten days later, the patriarchs of the East were seated after the cardinals, just as they had been at Vatican I.

After the first session, another synod was held at the residence of Patriarch Maximos IV at Ain-Traz. Since no action had been taken by the Vatican on their previous requests, the patriarch and synod now decided to publish the entire correspondence on this matter as an open letter to the Council Fathers. This drastic measure seemed, however, to have no more effect than previous measures, since, at the opening of the second session, under Pope Paul VI, the patriarchs were still seated after the cardinals.

Ten days after the opening of the session, Archpriest Borovoy, one of the two observer delegates from the Moscow Patriarchate of the Russian Orthodox Church, told a reporter, "When I return to Russia, no one is going to ask me what the theologians said. But they will ask, 'Were some of the Eastern patriarchs there, and what places did they occupy?'" Then he added, "I must tell you that the places which they occupy in St. Peter's are not in fact conducive to ecumenical dialogue." These remarks were published in the Paris *Figaro* of October 12, 1963.

When the patriarchs of the Eastern Catholic Churches walked into the Council hall on Monday, October 14, they found waiting for them new places of honor opposite the cardinals. The significant gesture had been ordered by Pope Paul VI. But did it mean that they were above the cardinals in rank? Most people thought so.

A year later, at the third session, the schema on the Eastern Catholic Churches came up for discussion.

Archbishop Ghattas proposed on October 16, 1964, that the schema should be suppressed and its contents inserted in other schemas, where the treatment of the subject more properly belonged. Since the Eastern Catholic Churches were parts of the one Catholic Church, he said, there should not be a separate schema on them.

Patriarch Maximos said that the weakest chapter of the schema was "indubitably the one devoted to the patriarchs." He called it "inadmissible" in its existing form. "In the first place, it is false to present the patriarchate as an institution proper to the East," he said. "The first patriarch in the Catholic Church is the Pope, the Bishop of Rome, who is described in the *Annuario Pontificio* itself as 'Patriarch of the West'." He also objected to the "infinite number of times" that patriarchs were obliged to have recourse to the Sacred Congregations of the Roman Curia. The patriarch and his synod, he said, "without prejudicing the prerogatives of the successor of Peter," should normally be the highest authority for all affairs concerning the patriarchate.

Maronite Bishop Doumith of Sarba, Lebanon, told the assembly that the great hopes stirred in the Eastern Churches by the Second Vatican Council had "almost completely vanished after an examination of this schema." Apart from the praise which was usually given the Eastern Churches in any discussion of the subject, he said, "there is nothing of momentous importance in the schema: prejudices are not corrected, useless things are repeated, special problems are not always resolved in the best manner and, finally, the more serious matters which ought to be treated are avoided."

The most serious problem of all, he said, that of having bishops of different Eastern Catholic rites in the same see, with jurisdiction over the same territory, was passed over. In so doing, he maintained, "the Council seems to be neglecting forever a unique occasion for bringing about a necessary reform. At least it should be stated that reform is necessary, even if it cannot be carried out at once." After pointing out that little would remain if matters which were better handled in other schemas were omitted, he requested the assembly to "reject the entire schema in all tranquillity, inserting certain points in other schemas, and referring other points to the code of canon law."

Auxiliary Bishop Gerald McDevitt of Philadelphia pointed out that the schema obliged converts throughout the world to retain their rite on becoming Catholics. This was contrary to the entire spirit of the Second Vatican Council, he said, which had so much to say on liberty of conscience and the pastoral and ecumenical spirit. Recalling his ten years of service in the apostolic delegation in Washington, D.C., he said, "I worked almost daily on petitions requesting transferal to another rite, and I know well how much time is required to prepare these petitions for the Holy See. . . . Ordinarily six months and often a full year are required before such petitions are processed and a decision reached." In his opinion it was "quite surprising, not to say cruel," to make it compulsory for persons who became Catholics to apply to the Holy See for permission to transfer from one rite to another.

Discussion of the text on the Eastern Catholic Churches ended on October 20. Since 88 percent of the assembly asked for an immediate vote, the voting took place on October 21 and 22. On each of the seven ballots, an average of 91 negative votes and 235 qualified affirmative votes were cast. On the second ballot, on the section covering the point stressed by Bishop McDevitt, there were 719 qualified affirmative votes and 73 negative votes. This meant that only 63 percent of the assembly was satisfied with the text as it stood, and that the text must therefore be revised.

A total of 607 Council Fathers had submitted qualifications which in substance favored the proposal made by Bishop McDevitt. The Commission on the Eastern Churches, however, divided up the qualifications on the basis of wording and not of meaning, and then reported back to the assembly that a majority in the Commission had decided against the adoption of the suggested changes. This meant that less than thirty Council Fathers on the Commission on the Eastern Churches were powerful enough to overrule the wishes expressed by ballots of 607 Council Fathers.

In the amended text which the Commission presented

for a vote on November 20, 1964, merely a word here and a phrase there had been changed. That was the only evidence of four days of debate on the Council floor and of 1,920 qualifications submitted. When the Council Fathers were asked to signify their approval or disapproval of the manner in which the Commission had handled the qualifications, a total of 471 negative votes were cast on two separate ballots. But when the schema was voted upon as a whole, the negative votes dropped to 135. And on November 21, when a vote was taken in public session in the presence of Pope Paul VI, 2,110 affirmative votes were cast and 39 negative votes. The Pope then promulgated the Decree on Eastern Catholic Churches.

The official recognition which Pope Paul had given to the rank of patriarchs at the Council removed one of the obstacles to unity with the Orthodox Churches, those Eastern Rite Churches which do not accept the principle of the primacy of Rome. Several schisms between those churches and the Church of Rome had led to a final break in 1054, when Patriarch Michael Caerularius of Constantinople and his adherents were excommunicated by a legation of the Roman see under the leadership of Cardinal Humbertus. The Patriarch and Synod of Constantinople thereupon pronounced excommunication of the legates, and the Patriarchs of Antioch, Alexandria and Jerusalem followed the Patriarch of Constantinople into schism. Temporary reunions were effected by the second Ecumenical Council at Lyons in 1274, and the Ecumenical Council of Florence in 1439. But in 1472 all union was repudiated by a Synod called by Patriarch Dionysius I of Constantinople.

In an effort to remove these and other obstacles to union, Pope Paul VI at the beginning of 1964 personally visited Patriarch Athenagoras I of Constantinople, successor to Patriarch Michael Caerularius, to exchange a fraternal embrace and to discuss inter-Church relations. The resulting improvement was so great that, on December 7, 1965, the day before the closing of Vatican II, the Pope and the Patriarch simultaneously lifted the excommunications dating back to 1054.

On that same December 7, the recently consecrated Bishop Willebrands of the Secretariat for Promoting Christian Unity read a declaration in the presence of the Pope and the Council Fathers. He said that, after their meeting in the Holy Land, Pope Paul VI and Patriarch Athenagoras I had determined to omit nothing "which charity might inspire and which might facilitate the development of the fraternal relations thus initiated between the Roman Catholic and the Orthodox Church of Constantinople. They are persuaded that, by this action, they are responding to the call of that divine grace which today is leading the Roman Catholic Church and the Orthodox Church, as well as all Christians, to overcome their differences in order to be again 'one,' as the Lord Jesus asked of his Father for them." The reading of the declaration drew thunderous applause from the Council Fathers.

While this statement was being read in the Vatican, it was also being issued by the Patriarch of Constantinople at Istanbul, where Cardinal Shehan of Baltimore had been sent by Pope Paul as leader of a special mission. The ceremony took place in the patriarchal cathedral of Fanaro. After the excommunications had been mutually lifted, Patriarch Athenagoras I and Cardinal Shehan embraced, while the bells of the cathedral rang out. News of this act of charity, which brought the two Churches closer together, was then formally communicated by the Patriarch of Constantinople to the Orthodox Patriarchs of Alexandria, Antioch, Jerusalem, Moscow, Belgrade, Bucharest and Sofia, and to the Orthodox Churches of Greece, Poland, Czechoslovakia, Azerbaijan and Cyprus.

Pope Paul VI and Patriarch Athenagoras I, with his Synod, said in their joint declaration that they hoped that "the whole Christian world, especially the entire Roman Catholic Church and the Orthodox Church, will appreciate this gesture." It was intended "as an expression of a common and sincere desire for reconciliation." It was also to be considered "as an invitation to continue in a spirit of trust, esteem and mutual charity the dialogue which, with God's help, will lead, for the greater good of souls and the coming of the Kingdom of God, to that living together again in the full communion of faith, fraternal accord and sacramental life which existed during the first thousand years of the life of the Church."

The apparent precedence enjoyed by the patriarchs during the Council was short-lived, because the *Annuario Pontificio* (Pontifical Yearbook) for 1966 once again listed them behind the cardinals, unless they happened to be cardinals themselves.

THE CHURCH IN THE MODERN WORLD

No schema was more talked about at the Council than that on the Church in the modern world. The inspiration for it came from Pope John XXIII, who unwittingly outlined it in a radio-television address on September 11, 1962, exactly one month before the opening of the Council. The Pope's mind and heart were filled with the great things which he wished the Council to accomplish. The theme of his address was that Christ had illuminated the Church, and that it was the Church's mission to illumine the nations.

In his practical and down-to-earth manner, he used a globe, four feet in diameter, as a stage property, to show that he was talking about a very real world. And to make sure that no one would miss his point, he had the Vatican photographer take his picture with the globe at his side, and on the picture he wrote four words, in Latin, summarizing his address, *Ecclesia Christi lumen gentium* ("Christ's Church is the light of the nations").

The Council's task, Pope John said, was to concern itself with the twofold vitality of the Church. There was first the Church's vitality *ad intra*, relating to the internal structure of the Church and, principally, to "the treasures of illuminating faith and sanctifying grace." Very little of his address, however, was devoted to this aspect of the Church's vitality. Secondly, there was the Church's vitality *ad extra*, relating to situations outside itself, such as the wants and needs of Christians and non-Christians "in the modern world." The Church, he asserted, had responsibilities and obligations bearing on every phase of modern life: man's need for daily bread; the administration and distribution of the world's goods; underdeveloped nations; civil society and a new political order; war—which was to be detested; peace—which was to be sought after; private property; a more profound application of the principles of brotherhood and love among men and nations; killing; adultery and fornication; the sacred nature of matrimony; the religious and moral aspects of procreation; indifferentism in religion; the use of science and technology to raise the economic and spiritual standards of nations; etc.

This was virtually a complete outline of a schema on the Church in the modern world. What Pope John had done in effect was to touch upon a number of suggestions submitted by Council Fathers during the preparatory stages of the Council.

On December 4, 1962, near the end of the first session, Leo Jozef Cardinal Suenens of Mechelen, Belgium, used many of Pope John's ideas and some of the same words in proposing to the general assembly that the Church should consider its relations with the world at large—*ad extra*—"since this Council should aim to make the Church the real light of the nations." On the following day, Pope John created the Coordinating Commission and appointed Cardinal Suenens to it, giving him the task of drawing up a new schema containing those teachings of the Church that touched directly on the problems of the modern world.

At its first meeting in January, 1963, the Coordinating Commission ruled that the new schema should be called "The effective presence of the Church in the world today," and that it should have six chapters: on the admirable vocation of man; on the human person in society; on marriage and the family; on the proper promotion of cultural development; on economics and social order; and on the community of nations and peace. It was also decided that some elements for the new schema should be taken from three of the dogmatic constitutions prepared by the Theological Preparatory Commission and rejected during the first session. These dealt with the Christian order; with chastity, matrimony, family and virginity; and with the preservation of the deposit of faith.

Cardinal Suenens, as the promoter of the schema, proposed that the task of drawing it up should be entrusted to a special joint commission composed of all the members of the Theological Commission and the Commission on the Apostolate of the Laity, with Cardinals Ottaviani and Fernando Cento of the Roman Curia as co-presidents. The proposal was adopted. It was further suggested that other elements for the new schema should be drawn from the schema "on social action in the lay apostolate" prepared by the Commission on the Apostolate of the Laity, and from two doctrinal schemas of the Theological Preparatory Commission, "on social order" and "on the community of nations."

Work on the new schema began in February 1963. Between April 24 and 26, a special session was held to which twenty-three highly qualified laymen were invited, only fifteen of whom were able to attend. The schema was ready before the end of May for presentation at the next meeting of the Coordinating Commission, scheduled for June 4. However, owing to Pope John's death on June 3, the meeting was postponed for one month.

On July 4, after Cardinal Suenens had pointed out both the positive and the negative aspects of the schema in the Coordinating Commission, the Commission decided that the schema was unsatisfactory. The Cardinal was given another mandate to produce a new text which would elaborate on the doctrinal points contained in Chapter 1. The remaining five chapters were to form a supplement. This, of course, would greatly reduce the authority of the teaching contained in those chapters.

Cardinal Suenens proceeded to call some *periti* to Belgium to prepare a new draft. Strangely enough, during the second session no action was taken by the joint commission responsible for the schema until November 29, 1963, the day on which eight liberal candidates proposed by the world alliance were added to the commission, making the liberals eight votes stronger. The new draft and the original draft were discussed at length on this day, but inconclusively. Finally, Bishop Pelletier of Trois-Rivières, Canada, suggested that a central subcommission should be created to coordinate the work of five other subcommissions, which were to prepare further revisions of the five chapters of the supplement. This proposal was unanimously adopted.

The joint commission then elected the following six members for the central subcommission by secret ballot: Bishops Schröffer and Hengsbach of Eichstätt and Essen in Germany, Bishops Jacques Ménager and Ancel of Meaux and Lyons in France, Auxiliary Bishop Mark McGrath of Panama City and Bishop Emilio Guano of Livorno, Italy. These six members were then authorized to add two others, and they chose Bishop Wright of Pittsburgh and Bishop Blomjous of Mwanza, Tanzania. Of these eight, all but Bishop McGrath had originally been elected to Commission seats as European alliance candidates; he had been associated with the alliance, however, from the very first days of the Council.

As a result of this meeting, the new schema was now completely in the hands of the European alliance policy-makers. And since the central subcommission wanted as little resistance as possible from conservative members of the Italian and Spanish hierarchies, it elected Italian-born Bishop Guano to serve as chairman and later to introduce the schema in the Council hall. The eight bishops then indicated the general lines of the new draft. A few days later, the session closed, and the bishops returned to their dioceses.

The bishops had chosen the liberal moral theologian, Father Bernard Häring, C.SS.R., as secretary. Under the chairmanship of Bishop Guano, Father Häring, Monsignor Achille Glorieux, Father Raymond Sigmond, O.P., and Father Roberto Tucci, S.J., met several times during the month of December and in the first part of January, 1964. They determined more exactly the spirit of the schema, the general lines which it should follow, its content, its purpose and the persons to whom it was to be directed. They decided that the first draft should be written in French by Father Sigmond.

In February, the central subcommission met for three days in Zurich, Switzerland. Further changes were suggested. On March 4 and 9, two plenary meetings took place of the joint commission, but the schema and supplement were not approved, and the central subcommission had to start work on them again. The joint commission met again between June 4 and 6, and still further corrections and changes were suggested. It began to look as though the schema and supplement would not be ready by the third session. Finally, it was decided to print the schema despite its imperfections, and circulate it to the Council Fathers. Pope Paul gave his approval on July 3. Because of its position on the official list, it came to be called "the thirteenth schema." The supplement was still not ready. The liberal element was not yet strong enough to insert in the schema the teachings contained in the supplement, so it planned to have them inserted through speeches from the Council floor. Meanwhile, the *periti* began to work overtime on the supplement.

They worked so fast and so well that the 57-page supplement to the 29-page schema was ready for distribution to the Council Fathers on September 30, 1964, two weeks after the opening of the third session.

Queries were at once directed to Council authorities on the significance of the supplement and its origin. Since the front cover bore the official heading of Vatican II documents, and since inside was the statement that "the supplement is not to be discussed in the Council hall," some explanation was called for. The Secretary General, upon instructions from the Council Presidency or the Moderators, announced that the supplement had been drawn up by the joint commission and "sent to the Secretariat for distribution as a purely private document, having no official status whatsoever." It had been drawn up "to make known the mind of the commission." In response to further queries, the Secretary General made a second announcement shortly after, which showed that the supplement had more authority than his initial announcement had indicated. "The supplement was drawn up by the joint commission," he said, "at the request of the Coordinating Commission. . . . However, it is not a Council document and therefore will not be discussed in the hall."

When the press accused the Secretary General of conservative "intrigue" and "maneuvering" in making the first announcement, and stated that he had been obliged by the Cardinal Moderators to make the second one, he issued a communiqué calling these reports "inexact and tendentious." As Secretary General he never spoke in his own name, he said, "but always in the name of the Moderators or of the Presidency." In fact, the second announcement had been made on his initiative, after he had received the necessary "authorization of the Moderators."

Three weeks later, on October 20, the schema finally came up for discussion. By that time, five weeks of the session had passed. The Moderators had postponed the discussion until that date, announcing on October 12 and again on October 13 that the "introductory reports" were not yet ready. The fourth speaker on that first day of discussion was Cardinal Lercaro of Bologna, one of the Moderators. "It seems difficult or well-nigh impossible," he said, "for a new revision of this schema and its final approval to take place during this session." Large numbers of Council Fathers had given notice of their wish to speak, he said, and it was also most important and necessary that this schema, on the Church in the modern world, should be discussed in detail on the Council floor. "It is even doubtful that there will be sufficient time for the task if the fourth session takes place next year," he said.

The enthusiastic applause which greeted this statement must have been most pleasing to Cardinal Suenens, to the eight bishops of the central subcommission and to their *periti*, for it meant that the Council Fathers were prepared to postpone final deliberation on the schema until the fourth session, an absolute necessity if the teachings contained in the supplement were to be incorporated in the schema itself.

Cardinal Döpfner of Munich spoke next on behalf of eighty-three German-speaking and Scandinavian Council Fathers, expressing wholehearted agreement with Cardinal Lercaro. The Council Fathers, he said, should have all the time they needed to study the text with calm, "so that they might truly make it the crowning achievement of the Council." These words sounded strange coming from a man who up till this point had been driving the Council Fathers at breakneck speed.

A third Moderator, Cardinal Suenens, spoke on the following day. The schema in general was satisfactory, he said, "for the reasons stated yesterday by the two Moderators." He then went on to say that it would be fitting "to include in the schema various topics contained in the supplement," such as the section on matrimony and the family.

Archbishop Heenan of Westminster, England, who by this time had founded the opposition group known as St. Paul's Conference, called the schema "unworthy of an Ecumenical Council of the Church." He proposed that it should be taken away from the commission which was now handling it and referred to another commission, to be set up forthwith. "Then, after three or four years, let the fourth and final session of the Council be convened to discuss all the social problems," he said. The Council, he predicted, which had spent so much time on "theological niceties," would become "a laughingstock in the eyes of the world if it now rushed breathlessly through a debate on world hunger, nuclear war and family life."

He also pointed out that, according to instructions, the schema was to be debated, while the supplement was to be passed over without comment in the Council hall. "But if we fail to scrutinize both documents with great care," he said, "the mind of the Council will have to be interpreted to the world by the *periti* who helped the Fathers of the commission to draw up the documents. God forbid that this should happen! I fear *periti* when they are left to explain what the bishops meant. . . . It is of no avail to talk about a College of Bishops if *periti* in articles, books and speeches contradict and pour scorn on what a body of bishops teaches." He warned that "the theories of one or two theologians must not be mistaken for a general agreement among theologians." Only this "general agreement" enjoyed special authority, he said.

Father Benedict Reetz, Superior General of the Benedictines of Beuron, Germany, answered Archbishop Heenan the next day and defended the *periti*, saying that they had "labored and sweated over the schema," and that they "need not be feared but rather loved and praised, especially for the supplement, from which very much should be taken and added to the schema itself." His only criticism was of the Latin, which he called "disgraceful."

Bishop Charue of Namur, Belgium, said that the world was waiting for this schema, and that therefore "we cannot wait four years." It should be published the following year, even if the supplement had to be completed later.

Cardinal Meyer of Chicago and Cardinal Bea of the Curia both had general praise for the schema, but said that it was too naturalistic and needed a more profound theological and scriptural basis. Cardinal Léger of Montreal and Cardinal Liénart of Lille said much the same.

Maronite Patriarch Paul Meouchi of Lebanon felt that the structure of the schema was not logical, its style uncertain and its content repetitive. It gave the impression, he said, that the Church had been founded to conduct charitable works and busy itself with social, economic and political affairs. And it seemed to presuppose a conception of history in which Providence played no part. He insisted on a radical revision of the text.

Archbishop Raymond-Marie Tchidimbo of Conakry, Guinea, considered the schema "mediocre" and "directed exclusively to the peoples of Europe and the Americas." It contained no reference at all to the problems of Africa, such as those resulting from colonialism and racial discrimination.

Archbishop William Conway of Armagh, Ireland, said that the schema contained "only a fraction of what the Church has to say to the modern world." This fact, he said, should be clearly stated at the very beginning of the schema, for otherwise people would ask, "Do you have nothing else to tell us? Is this all?" He expressed great surprise that the schema should have "so little to say about conditions in areas where the Church lies in chains and lives in silence." He was also surprised that the document should say nothing about the commercialization of sex and the desecration of human love in so many of the communications media.

Archbishop Morcillo González of Madrid wondered why the schema was silent on problems such as those of "human labor, the elevation of the whole man to his natural and supernatural perfection, the right of migration, the flood of sensuality and sexuality, atheism . . . , the progress of new nations toward liberty . . . , the extreme poverty and famine which now afflict great multitudes of men." The schema "either says nothing about them, or speaks of them only in a whisper, as if they were far removed from the modern world." He, too, called for a complete revision of the schema.

Archbishop Patrick O'Boyle of Washington, D.C., speaking on behalf of the United States bishops, said that it was necessary to devote a paragraph to the problem of racial discrimination. He wanted precise theological reasons given, constituting an open condemnation of racial discrimination, which he called "one of the most deplorable and repugnant crimes of mankind today."

Discussion of the schema ended on November 10, eleven days before the end of the session. When the assembly was asked whether the schema was suitable as a basis for further discussion, the vote was 1,579 to 296 in favor. On December 30, the Coordinating Commission ruled that the supplement, at least in substance, should be included in the schema. This decision was formally conveyed to Cardinals Ottaviani and Cento, co-presidents of the joint commission, by a letter dated January 2, 1965, and signed by Cardinal Cicognani, president of the Coordinating Commission.

When the Council Fathers received the latest revision of the schema during the summer, it consisted of 79 pages instead of 29, as previously. Explaining the great difference in size, the central subcommission stated that the new draft consisted basically of three elements. First there was the original draft. Then there were the oral and written interventions, totalling 830 pages, which had been very carefully examined. And finally, "in accordance with the wishes expressed by many Council Fathers, the supplement accompanying the previous text has been inserted in the new text, at least in substance."

It had been a long, hard battle, but once again the liberals, aided by the Moderators, had succeeded in getting their way.

Defeat for the Moderators

In the past decades, a startling phenomenon has been taking place in the United States and Europe: The percentage of young men choosing to become secular, or diocesan, priests has been decreasing, while the percentage of those choosing to become priests as members of religious orders has been increasing. In the United States, the percentage of secular priests dropped from 73 percent of the national total in 1925 to 61 percent in 1965. The percentage of religious order priests rose in the same period from 27 to 39 percent. In some areas, priests who are members of religious orders outnumber secular priests. In the archdiocese of Chicago, for example, the percentage of secular priests dropped from 59 percent in 1925 to 46 percent in 1965, while that of religious order priests rose from 41 to 54 percent in the same period. In Germany, similarly, the percentage of secular priests dropped from 92 percent in

1915 to 78 percent in 1960, while during the same period the percentage of priests belonging to religious orders rose from 8 to 22 percent.

Bishop Karl Leiprecht of Rottenburg, Germany, a member of the Council's Commission on Religious, called attention to this trend at the Fulda conference in August, 1963, observing that it would oblige bishops to make greater demands than ever before on religious orders for pastoral work.

The problem, however, was how to obtain greater control over the members of religious orders. The solution proposed by adherents of the European alliance was to stress the importance of apostolic work, calling it a necessity for all religious orders of men and women, even for contemplative orders. The alliance also insisted on basic changes in the structure of religious orders, calling this an "adaptation to modern times." But the emphasis on apostolic work was such that, in the eyes of the religious orders, the goal in view appeared almost purely utilitarian, without regard for the spiritual life of the individual. And some of the changes suggested made it appear that the aim was to standardize the religious orders, that is, recast them in the same or similar molds. Superiors general naturally considered this as the death knell to their institutes, and so began a struggle for survival.

A severe blow came on January 30, 1963, when the Coordinating Commission delivered instructions to the Commission on Religious drastically to reduce its schema and to make certain changes. The instructions had been prepared by Cardinal Döpfner, who was responsible to the Coordinating Commission for the schema on the religious life, as Cardinal Suenens was responsible to it for the schema on the Church in the modern world. The original schema had been drafted by the Preparatory Commission on Religious and contained thirty-two chapters, including 201 articles and covering 110 pages. It was very thorough and detailed, dealing with all questions pertaining to the religious life. The Commission on Religious in plenary session reduced this schema to nine chapters within two months of receiving the aforesaid instructions, and referred it back to the Coordinating Commission for approval.

On March 27, 1963, Cardinal Döpfner in his report to the Coordinating Commission said that he was satisfied with the great reduction in size, but not with the title "On Religious," or with the frequent use of the term "states of perfection." He suggested three points that should be taken into consideration in improving the text:

1. The text as it stood was lacking in scriptural and theological depth in its presentation of the religious life and the evangelical counsels. Nor was sufficient stress laid on appropriate renewal. Too little consideration was given to the Christological and ecclesiological aspects of the religious life.

2. The text did not constitute an adequate response to the wish expressed by all Council Fathers for clear and practical directives for the adaptation of religious orders to modern needs. Too little space was given to this topic.

3. Even though withdrawal from the world was a necessary characteristic of religious orders and must be especially stressed today, there should not be so many warnings against the world and the spirit of the world.

An effective apostolate was possible only if those engaged in the apostolate knew the modern world and could reach modern man. There was much complaint about the lack of knowledge of the world among members of religious orders, especially the women's orders. Here there was need for change.

The Coordinating Commission, however, approved the revised schema in substance; whereupon Valerio Cardinal Valeri, president of the Commission on Religious, and a member of the Roman Curia, appointed a committee of five to make the additional changes and additions suggested by Cardinal Döpfner. He cancelled the plenary session of his Commission, originally scheduled for May 1963, considering it unnecessary, and on April 23 presented the revised text to the Secretary General.

Cardinal Döpfner heard of this at once, and was very much annoyed. He again submitted the suggestions that he had originally made, and some new ones besides. This time, however, he and his *periti* worked them out in detail, with exactly the wording which they wished to have incorporated in the schema. Cardinal Döpfner wrote to Cardinal Valeri that he was enclosing, "by way of example," some proposals "which could easily be inserted in the existing schema at the places indicated." His letter arrived after the revised schema had been submitted to the Secretary General, and Cardinal Valeri had to get it back again. The same committee of five was put to work on it, and finally, on May 8, the text was returned to the Secretary General for printing.

Strangely enough, when the printed version appeared, it carried a note to the effect that it had been approved by

Pope John XXIII on April 22, 1963. But it had not been in the hands even of the Secretary General by that date, let alone in those of the Pope. This raises the question whether the Pope ever saw the document.

At the time Cardinal Döpfner sent his proposals to Cardinal Valeri; Bishop Gérard Huyghe of Arras, France, also protested and sent proposals of his own. He was a member of the Commission on Religious and was greatly displeased that the scheduled plenary session for May had been canceled. About half of the proposals submitted by Cardinal Döpfner were incorporated in the text, but none of those submitted by Bishop Huyghe; Cardinal Döpfner's were used because they were considered as elucidating his original report to the Coordinating Commission. Both sets of proposals, however, were mimeographed and sent to all the members of the Commission on Religious. On seeing that his proposals had been ignored, Bishop Huyghe combined them with the unused proposals made by Cardinal Döpfner, as well as with proposals made by two other Commission members (French and Belgian) which had likewise been ignored. He then asked all the bishops of France and all those who attended the Fulda conference to give their support to his combined list.

Bishop Leiprecht, who had been commissioned by Cardinal Döpfner to prepare a written report on the revised schema dated April 22, 1963, for the Fulda conference, maintained that "the Commission members residing in Rome, and also their *periti*, who had edited the shortened draft, had too much control." And he concluded that "the schema in its present form is not yet ready to be taken up by the Council Fathers. It is not sufficiently in step with the needs of modern times and of the Council." The Fulda conference endorsed this view, labeled the schema unsatisfactory, and informed Rome accordingly. The schema did not come up for discussion during the second session.

Toward the end of the second session, on November 29, the Coordinating Commission instructed Ildebrando Cardinal Antoniutti, the new president of the Commission on Religious (Cardinal Valeri had died in July), to shorten the schema still further, and also to prepare an appendix listing "in great detail those observations made by Council Fathers which were not accepted by the Commission, together with the reasons for their rejection."

Further instructions were issued by the Coordinating Commission on December 28, 1963, and January 15, 1964, and these were sent to Cardinal Antoniutti on January 23. The Cardinal was informed that the schema must now be reduced to propositions which would be voted on in the Council hall, but without discussion. Cardinal Döpfner sent still more proposals on January 24. As a result of these instructions, the schema was reduced to 118 lines of propositions.

The third session opened on September 14, 1964, and on September 29 the Roman Union of Superiors General held a meeting to decide what action to take with regard to the propositions. Some 100 superiors general were present. Father Armand Le Bourgeois, Superior General of the Eudists, read a detailed report on the development of the propositions, with an analysis of each of the articles. His conclusion was that the propositions as they stood were unsatisfactory, but could be improved. The matter was then discussed at length, but no decision was reached.

On October 7, the executive committee of the Roman Union met at the generalate of the Oblates of Mary Immaculate. Present were the superiors general of the Franciscans, Dominicans, Carmelites, Benedictines, Oblates of Mary Immaculate, Marists and Eudists. An animated discussion took place on policy, and it was unanimously agreed not to reject the propositions, but rather to improve them by submitting qualifications with affirmative votes. In their written report to all other superiors general, they stated that "a massive negative vote" might have unfortunate consequences, and pointed to four specific points which, in their judgment, required amendment. At the same time, they assured the other superiors general that they were perfectly free to take whatever stand they chose on the issues. They also began to prepare interventions on these points, and to draw up qualifications to be printed and distributed before the voting.

On October 23, the Secretary General announced that the report on the propositions would be distributed on the same day, as well as "an appendix to the schema, which, however, will not be matter for discussion." On receiving the printed copy of the report, the Council Fathers were surprised to find enclosed in the same booklet an amended and lengthened version of the propositions. Some of them asked the Bishops' Secretariat, headed by Archbishop Perantoni, what it thought of the new version. The Archbishop thereupon called together his central committee, whose members decided unanimously that the propositions were acceptable. They prepared a circular letter explaining their views, and on November 8 had it delivered to more than 1,100 Council Fathers.

The letter announced the names of five Council Fathers scheduled to make oral interventions on the propositions, and stated that each one, through the efforts of the Bishops' Secretariat, had obtained several hundred supporting signatures. Attached to the letter were five qualifications recapitulating the five interventions, which the recipients were invited to sign and submit with their affirmative votes.

On November 10, two days after this letter was delivered, the propositions on the religious life came up for discussion. By this time, the propositions on priests and on missions had already been rejected. There was time for only one speaker that morning, Cardinal Spellman of New York, a member of the Coordinating Commission.

Cardinal Spellman expressed general satisfaction with the text. "If some amendments and clarifications on a few fundamental points are introduced in the text," he said, "this schema can be accepted by the Council as a basis for a genuine renewal of religious life in the Church." He pointed out that modernization had "in fact been in progress in religious communities for many years." The issue now was "a secondary and incidental adaptation, not a changing of the very essence of religious life"; much confusion, he said, existed on that point. "Recently," he added, "certain things have been written and said about the religious life and its adaptation to modern conditions which seem to contribute to this confusion. They seem to neglect and almost to deny the special witness given to Christ by the religious life. In a word, these things . . . tend to destroy religious life." In his own archdiocese of New York, he said, there were more than 8,000 women in the religious life, and not a few of them were "uneasy because of these things which are being said so confusedly, incautiously and imprudently regarding the modernization of religious life in the Church." Some Council Fathers and *periti* took these words as intended for Cardinal Suenens, who had published a book on the subject, *The Nun in the World*, and who had recently lectured in the United States on the religious life.

Seventeen speakers took the floor on the following day. The first was Jaime Cardinal de Barros Câmara of Rio de Janeiro, who said on behalf of 103 bishops of Brazil that the schema was on the whole acceptable. He pointed out that the doctrinal aspect of the religious life had already been dealt with in Chapter 4 of the schema on the Church, and that the duties of members of religious orders in the external apostolate had been discussed in the schema on the pastoral office of bishops in the Church. It was therefore unnecessary to treat of religious in the schema at any great length; it was, however, necessary to determine more clearly the competent authority which should promote and guide the desired renewal of the religious life.

The fourth speaker was Cardinal Döpfner, who severely criticized the propositions and asked for a complete revision. They did not adequately touch the central problems of renewal, he said.

Cardinal Suenens also asserted that the schema was unacceptable because it failed to deal adequately with the problems of adaptation and modernization of the religious life. He spoke especially about congregations of sisters "in the so-called active life." They should enjoy the genuine freedom required for apostolic action, he said.

The apostolate itself should be defined in the sense of "evangelization," so that there would be a hierarchy of values in the life of the Sister, each one having some time for such apostolic work. On the practical level, he asked that new rules should be elaborated for convents, so that individual Sisters might cooperate actively and "as adults" for the good of the whole community. This would avoid the concentration of power in a single Mother Superior on the one hand, and an overly passive, infantile obedience on the other. He advocated balanced structures of government, changes in the system of naming superiors, and general chapters which would more faithfully represent the entire congregation. Antiquated customs should be changed, separation from the world should not prevent a religious from engaging in apostolic work, the "distinctive but ridiculous garb of many communities must be changed," practices based on "outdated notions of the inferiority of women" should be abandoned, and no Sister should have to travel with a companion.

On the same day, four of the five speakers announced in the circular letter of the Bishops' Secretariat were given the floor. Father Anastasio del SS. Rosario, Superior General of the Carmelites, and president of the Roman Union of Superiors General, spoke first in the name of 185 Council Fathers, and asserted that the propositions deserved a qualified affirmative vote. Appropriate renewal was definitely needed in the religious life, he said, but it was absolutely necessary to have a clear concept of what this entailed. It entailed, he explained, two essential elements: a return by the members of religious communities to the spirit and fervor which had animated those communities at the time of their foundation; and adaptation to the world and to modern times. Only this twofold norm would provide the necessary "solid and supernatural criteria for the various aspects of renewal," and could prevent "a restless search after novelty which wants to discard everything."

Archbishop Perantoni spoke in the name of 370 Council Fathers. He said that the schema as it stood was "good and should be retained as a basis for discussion, despite the opinion of those who had asked for its complete rejection." He spoke out against the standardization of religious orders, saying that the orders should be regarded "as the expression of diverse charisms in the Church." He requested the Council to state its high esteem for the "lay religious life," since religious communities of Brothers and Sisters made such a useful contribution to the pastoral work of the Church by educating the young, caring for the sick and discharging other services.

The next speaker was a French Jesuit, the retired Archbishop Victor Sartre of Tananarive, Madagascar, who spoke on behalf of 265 Council Fathers and also expressed the views of 250 superiors general of religious congregations of women. The schema, he said, had many good elements, "and we hope that it will be approved." Primacy of place, he said, should clearly be given to the interior and spiritual life of the members, and, in any program of adaptation, the spirit of the founders must be loyally preserved, as well as all the particular goals and sound traditions of each community.

He was followed by another Jesuit, Bishop Guilly of Georgetown, British Guiana, who spoke for 263 Council Fathers. The propositions, said Bishop Guilly, merited approval in substance, although they had many weaknesses. For instance, it was "truly amazing" that so little should be said about the contemplative orders. The propositions, he maintained, depicted the modern apostolate "in a much too restricted sense, as an external apostolate." In the theological and technical terminology of the Church, however, the word "apostolate" designated all activities of Christ's followers which promoted the kingdom of God on earth. He therefore called for the addition of a distinct proposition in which the Council would express its high esteem for the contemplative institutes and declare their life to be "eminently apostolic."

On the following day, Auxiliary Bishop James Carroll of Sydney, Australia, spoke in the name of 440 Council Fathers. He called for a special paragraph on Brothers engaged in teaching work, thus stressing in a practical way the apostolic character of lay religious. It would also be opportune, he said, for the Council to rectify the ideas of numerous priests and laymen "who do not esteem those who embrace the religious life without embracing the priesthood."

Never in the history of the Council had a series of speakers been given so much backing. A reaction was inevitable.

Bishop Charue, of Belgium, announced his complete agreement with the conclusion of Cardinal Döpfner. Father Joseph Buckley, Superior General of the Marists, speaking on behalf of 130 Council Fathers, said that the schema was "simply not satisfactory," and would have to be completely rewritten with the aid of *periti* "of a more modern mentality and broader experience," in line with the renewal promoted by the Council. Bishop Huyghe of Arras, France, expressed his "wholehearted" agreement with everything that had been said by Cardinal Döpfner, Cardinal Suenens, Bishop Charue and Father Buckley. "The propositions are inadequate," he said, "because they lack spirit, are too juridical, too exclusively Western, and contain very little for a true renewal of the religious life. . . . A new schema should be prepared."

On the third day, the debate was closed on a motion proposed by Cardinal Suenens. Twenty-six oral interventions had been made, and thirty-six interventions had been submitted in writing. The Secretary General now asked the assembly to vote on the following question: "Do the Fathers desire to proceed to the vote on the twenty individual propositions which make up the schema 'On the appropriate renewal of the religious life,' now that the discussion has been completed?" If the majority voted "no," a new draft would have to be prepared. If the majority voted "yes," the propositions would be retained, and voting on the individual propositions would follow.

Why did the Roman Union of Superiors General and the Bishops' Secretariat wish to have the propositions retained and amended, while Cardinals Döpfner and Suenens pressed for their rejection? The underlying reason was the vastly different conception, on either side, of the religious life and its function in the Church. The Roman Union and the Bishops' Secretariat realized that, in a complete revision of the schema, the ideas of Cardinals Döpfner and Suenens would gain more ground. They also suspected that the Cardinals might have a substitute schema ready, or nearly ready, to impose upon the Commission on Religious. Thus the retention of the unsatisfactory propositions and their improvement through qualifications became in their eyes the preferred solutions.

As a *peritus* of the Bishops' Secretariat explained to me, it was widely felt that Cardinal Döpfner's conception of the religious life was "lacking in theological depth, clarity and precision." Cardinal Suenens, he said, "who is much less concerned with theological problems, seems to think of religious mainly in so far as they are useful to the external apostolate." It was felt, in other words, that Cardinal Suenens did not give its proper place to the interior life of a religious. It had created an odd impression, the *peritus* added, that Cardinal Döpfner, of all people, should have attacked the propositions so strongly, "after he had himself, in his capacity as official spokesman of the Coordinating Commission, insisted so emphatically that the text be reduced to its present dimensions." And when I asked why the Bishops' Secretariat had collected a total of 1,523 signatures for only five interventions, he reminded me that its founders had been silenced by the closing of the debate during the discussion of the schema on the Church. They had feared that this might happen again, and believed that the hundreds of signatures would force the Moderators to give them the floor, as had in fact happened.

When the ballots were distributed on Thursday, November 12, Cardinals Döpfner and Suenens were confident of victory. For days they had been privately assuring Council Fathers that the propositions would certainly be rejected. But to their great surprise, when the results were announced, 1,155 had voted in favor of retaining them, and only 882 against them. In the face of this defeat, the Moderator for the day, Cardinal Suenens, had no choice but to announce that the voting on the propositions would take place on the following Saturday and Monday.

The German and Belgian *periti*, whose job it was to devise strategy for the two Cardinals, had been caught off guard. Impulsively they suggested that all those who shared the Cardinals' views should now be asked to cast a negative vote on each of the nine proposed ballots, thus in effect rejecting the propositions. But this was only a temporary reaction, for they soon realized that they would never be able to muster sufficient votes to reject the propositions outright. Such tactics would give the Roman Union and the Bishops' Secretariat a free hand.

The *periti* of the two Cardinals then decided to draw up and print a series of qualifications of their own, imitating the action taken four days earlier by the *periti* of the Bishops' Secretariat. They also prepared a covering letter, asking their supporters to cast qualified affirmative votes and submit the qualifications prepared by them. The covering letter was signed by ten Council Fathers, including Cardinal Döpfner, Cardinal Suenens and Bishop Huyghe.

The Bishops' Secretariat was quite pleased with many of the qualifications prepared by the *periti* of Cardinals Döpfner and Suenens; it opposed the two Cardinals not so much for what they wanted included in the schema, but rather for what they wanted excluded from it.

The *periti* of the Bishops' Secretariat, meanwhile, had not been idle. As they explained in a new letter, dated November 13, "many excellent points came up during the discussion in the Council hall, which most certainly can help make the schema more complete." They enclosed in their letter a new set of thirteen qualifications, including the five which they had distributed on November 8. One of the new qualifications called for the preservation of the "authentic concept of religious obedience," described as "that sublime holocaust whereby a person, for the sake of the kingdom of heaven, completely subjects himself and all that he has to the will of Christ, whose place is taken by the superior." In answer to the great emphasis placed by some speakers on dialogue between subjects and superiors, this qualification pointed out that nothing would remain of religious obedience "if it is conceived only as a dialogue in which the superior keeps trying to persuade a subject by explaining to him all the reasons for a given order."

The *periti* of the Bishops' Secretariat distributed their qualifications to more than 1,100 Council Fathers in the afternoon of November 13. Voting was to begin the next day. They had purposely waited until the last minute so that the two Cardinals' *periti* would have no time to prepare counter qualifications.

In the voting on each of the first five ballots, there was an average of 930 affirmative votes, 952 qualified affirmative votes, and 68 negative votes. On the very first ballot, 1,005 qualified affirmative votes were cast, the largest number on any ballot in the history of the Council. From the voting returns it was impossible, of course, to tell whether the qualifications submitted were mainly those of the Bishops' Secretariat or of Cardinals Döpfner and Suenens.

Previously, the rule had always been that qualifications must be submitted at the time of voting. But on this particular day, Saturday, November 14, the Moderators decided that such qualifications might be submitted as late as the following Tuesday, provided that the Council Fathers indicated on their ballots that they were casting qualified affirmative votes. The reason for this sudden change in Council procedure was—to all appearances—a breakdown in Cardinal Döpfner's and Cardinal Suenens' distribution plan. Many of the Council Fathers who were supposed to have received qualifications had heard of them, but did not have them by the time the voting began that Saturday morning.

An examination of the qualifications showed that the five which received the largest backing had all been prepared by the *periti* of the Bishops' Secretariat. For the rest, it was almost a tie, with qualifications from both sides winning extensive support. Most were incorporated in the schema.

The revised and expanded text, now called a decree, returned to the Council floor on October 11, 1965, during the fourth session. The supporters of the views both of the Bishops' Secretariat and of Cardinals Döpfner and Suenens showed their satisfaction with the new text by voting 2,126 to 13 in its favor. In the final vote at the public session on October 28, 1965, the Decree on the Appropriate Renewal of the Religious Life received 2,321 affirmative votes and only 4 negative votes. It was then promulgated by Pope Paul VI.

SEMINARIES AND SCHOOLS

The schema on priestly formation was reduced to propositions by the Coordinating Commission shortly after the end of the second session. By letters of May 11 and July 7, 1964, the Secretary General informed the Council Fathers of the procedure prescribed for the propositions: No proposals were to be submitted for amending the text, but a vote would be taken upon it after the reading of an introductory report.

Nevertheless, the German-speaking and Scandinavian Council Fathers, meeting at Innsbruck in May, 1964, prepared fifteen long pages of commentary. For all practical purposes, this was a substitute schema, since it contained numerous proposals for rearranging the text of the propositions and inserting lengthy additions. The degree of control exercised by this small group of bishops over the Council became evident on the following October 14, during the third session, when each Council Father received a revised edition of the propositions. They were twice as long as before, many had been changed, and lengthy additions had been made. A careful comparison of these revised propositions made it perfectly clear that some 90 percent of the changes and additions had come from the fifteen-page commentary prepared by the Innsbruck conference. This was proof enough that one of the purposes of reducing schemas to short propositions had been to render possible the introduction of more of the ideas of the bishops and *periti* of the European alliance.

The revised propositions came up for discussion on November 12, 1964. Auxiliary Bishop Jozef Drzazga of Gniezno, Poland, speaking on behalf of the bishops of Poland, praised the text, but observed that its principles on priestly formation were too vaguely stated. "It is not enough to say that priestly training may be adapted to local circumstances by the competent territorial authority," he said, "because such authorities expect to receive from the Council norms which are valid for the entire world."

Archbishop Giovanni Colombo of Milan, Italy, who had been rector of the archdiocesan major seminary of Milan from 1954 to 1963, said that a great defect in seminary training was the lack of organic unity. It was due, he said, to the fact that the "programs of spiritual, intellectual, pastoral and disciplinary formation were independent of one another, so that each went its own way without a common meeting point, without any unifying and dynamic idea." This fault was remedied in the schema, he said, because it set up Jesus Christ as the unifying, focal point. "And because it is so excellently stated in these propositions that the renovation of seminaries depends more on qualified men than on good precepts," he added, "we should brook no delay and spare no sacrifice in securing such men, who are truly specialists and animated with the spirit of this Council." He also called for new textbooks for seminaries. "Without qualified teachers and suitable books, there is a danger that the wisest prescriptions of this Holy Synod may remain a dead letter."

Cardinal Léger wanted the text to cite St. Thomas Aquinas as a master and model for all those studying theology. "In this way," he said, "the doctrine of St. Thomas will not be imposed, but rather the scientific and spiritual approach will be extolled whereby he creatively utilized the knowledge of his day in the service of the Gospel."

Cardinal Döpfner expressed great satisfaction with the amended propositions, which, he said, followed a middle road in the very difficult question of priestly formation "by retaining rules proved by the experience of centuries and introducing new ones more appropriate in changed circumstances."

Cardinal Suenens called the schema "generally satisfactory," but suggested the addition of a new proposition providing for the establishment of a special commission to study the question of seminary renewal. A published text was not sufficient to bring about the renewal intended by the Council, he maintained.

Bishop Sani of Den Pasar, Bali, said that the Council should not place too much emphasis on the negative aspect of separation from the world. "It has the positive effect of freeing the student from distractions in his studies," he said. Sufficient pastoral and practical experience could be gained during vacation time, he suggested, and this could be supplemented in the seminary itself through frequent conferences by clerical and lay experts.

Archbishop Denis Hurley of Durban, South Africa, said that the apostolic character of seminary formation should in no way detract from the importance of study or the value of scholasticism. He agreed with Cardinal Suenens that existing methods of teaching philosophy should be re-examined, but felt that scholastic teachings should not be brushed aside. Some of its themes were essential to a Catholic philosophical approach, he said; without them, philosophy and theology might come to be regarded as incompatible. If philosophy demanded unlimited freedom of inquiry, then "we concede that Catholics cannot be philosophers." Only in the light of divine faith and scholastic principles, he said, was the Catholic free to embark on a philosophic investigation of God, man and the universe.

Archbishop Jean Weber of Strasbourg, France, speaking from twenty-five years' experience in a Paris seminary, called the propositions fair and full of wisdom, even though short. He hoped, however, that two extremes would be avoided: on the one hand the "determination to tear down everything that has been set up by holy men since the Council of Trent," and, on the other, "opposition to any change whatsoever, even when this is demanded by changing times and attitudes." He hedged somewhat in his comments on the principle in the schema that episcopal conferences and diocesan bishops should be the competent authorities in regulating seminary training. "For Italy or France this is good today," he said, "but it may not be good elsewhere, and it is not something eternal." Seminary authorities, he said, should form among themselves a true "college," since the greatest difficulties in seminaries arose from disagreement among the authorities and from the absence of dialogue between them and students.

One of the last speakers was Archbishop Garrone of Toulouse, France, who praised the schema highly and called Article I most opportune for stating that programs of priestly formation should be drawn up in each country by the episcopal conferences concerned, to be revised at stated intervals and approved by the Apostolic See. This would ensure the adaptation of universal laws to special circumstances of time and place, so that priestly formation would always answer the pastoral needs of the area where the ministry was to be exercised. Such decentralization, the Archbishop said, would alter and increase the duties of the Sacred Congregation of Seminaries, which would now have to acquaint itself with the needs and problems of the different countries, and to take note of progress and change in the disciplines pertaining to seminary training. To achieve the first goal, the Sacred Congregation must no longer remain behind the times, or be negative in its approach. "It would also be necessary that this Congregation have as members men from all over the world, so that it might better know the conditions of priestly life." The second goal could be achieved if the Sacred Congregation were to use men who were true experts in the sacred and social sciences, and who likewise represented all regions of the world.

Probably unwittingly, Archbishop Garrone was outlining a task which he himself would be asked to carry out. Less than two months after the end of the Council, Pope Paul named him pro-prefect of the Sacred Congregation of Seminaries and Universities. This meant that he would automatically head the Sacred Congregation on the retirement of Giuseppe Cardinal Pizzardo, the existing incumbent, who was eighty-eight years old when the appointment was announced.

The discussion was concluded on November 17, 1964. In the voting, only 41 called for the rejection of the propositions, but numerous qualifications were submitted on each of the seven ballots. These, together with ninety-nine oral and written interventions, were used to revise and lengthen the text, which was officially designated as the Decree on Priestly Formation. The new text was formally adopted by a vote of 2,318 to 3 on October 28, 1965, and immediately promulgated by Pope Paul VI.

The Commission responsible for the schema on priestly formation was also responsible for the schema on Christian education, and discussion on the latter text began on the day on which discussion of the former ended.

Once again, the Council Fathers were surprised at the distribution of a revised set of propositions. This time, however, the text had been shortened instead of expanded. The propositions distributed before the opening of the third session had contained seventeen articles and covered 165 lines. The revised version contained 11 articles and covered 106 lines. This extremely brief text was the seventh revision of the schema.

One of the speakers on the first day of debate was Cardinal Spellman of New York, who directed his attention to Article 4, on the rights of children and parents. He said that parents should be free to choose the schools they wished for their children. They should not, therefore, be subject to unjust economic burdens which infringed upon this freedom of choice. Since it was the function of the State to promote civil liberties, justice and equity demanded that a due measure of public aid be available to parents in support of the schools they selected for their children. Moreover, if those schools served the public purpose of popular education, the fact that they might be religious in their orientation should not exclude them from a rightful measure of public support.

Coadjutor Bishop Elchinger of Strasbourg, France, said that it was unfortunate that the schema should have been drafted before account could be taken of the other important schemas discussed during the third session. The existing text, he said, needed complete revision. The purpose behind Christian education should be the development of what he called a missionary spirit, so that young persons thus educated would not hide their faith, but would base their personal and social lives in the modern pluralistic and ecumenically minded society in which they lived on their Christian faith.

Cardinal Léger suggested that the schema should be referred back to the Commission together with the comments of the Council Fathers, so that it might undergo a thorough revision, prior to presentation at the fourth session. "At the present time," he said, "we do not seem to have sufficient time, or sufficient strength, for a fitting examination of this schema and the preparation of adequate amendments." He asked the Council Fathers not to approve too hastily what would become a *Magna Carta* of Christian education and higher studies for years to come. He found fault with the schema for not giving sufficient attention to scientific investigation and for its lack of inspiration. He asked specifically for practical proposals on coordination and cooperation among Catholic universities, especially with regard to theological, scriptural, philosophical and sociological studies. The promotion of such coordination and cooperation by modern means should be the chief task of the Sacred Congregation for Seminaries and Universities.

Auxiliary Bishop Luiz Henriquez Jimenez of Caracas, Venezuela, criticized the schema for placing too much stress on Catholic schools, which he called "lovely and enclosed gardens cultivated with much love, but whose fruits for the evangelization of the world seem to diminish with each passing day." In the Middle Ages, when the

State was helpless in educational matters, the Church had assumed the whole field of education as a supplementary role. But now that the State had taken up this task, with technical and financial resources far beyond the Church's means, it was high time for the Church to determine whether its schools really served the cause of evangelizing modern youth as a whole, especially the poor, who were often unable to attend Catholic schools because they could not pay the tuition.

The bishop pointed out that the Catholic Church was virtually absent from the public school. "We have lacked the interest to train Catholic teachers who might transform those schools from within," he said. "Those who already work in public schools have been, as it were, abandoned by us and sometimes have been made to feel like traitors to Catholic education." In the name of 120 Council Fathers, he then asked that the schema be thoroughly revised, and Catholic education subjected to critical analysis, so that it might become an efficacious instrument for preaching the Gospel. He also suggested that youth should be fully prepared to assume teaching positions in public schools and universities, and that, if necessary, special institutes should be established for their training.

Bishop Simon Nguyen-van Hien of Dalat, Vietnam, said that in mission lands the Catholic schools served as a most efficacious means of the apostolate. Many non-Christian parents in Asia, where Christian morals were respected, preferred to send their children to Catholic schools, especially when these were directed by priests and religious.

The discussion of the text on Christian education ended

on November 19. The vote was 1,457 to 419 to proceed to a vote on the text, without referring it back for revision. Nevertheless, there was still much dissatisfaction with the text, since on each of the four ballots an average of 161 negative votes and 168 qualified affirmative votes were cast.

After the close of the third session, the text was revised, and presented during the fourth session for further voting. On the last ballot before it was sent to the Pope, there were 183 negative votes—an extraordinarily large number. At the final vote, however, on October 28, 1965, in the presence of the Pope, the vote on the Declaration on Christian Education was 2,290 to 35; those Council Fathers who were dissatisfied with it felt that they had sufficiently indicated their displeasure at the previous vote. The document was then promulgated.

THE PRELIMINARY EXPLANATORY NOTE

The most important and dramatic battle which took place at the Second Vatican Council was not the widely publicized controversy over religious liberty, but the one over collegiality, which happened mostly behind the scenes. The drama was caused by controversy over the true and proper way in which collegiality was to be understood in Chapter 3 of the Dogmatic Constitution on the Church. There were three interpretations of collegiality.

According to the first, the college of bishops did not exercise supreme power by divine right, but only by human right. That meant that it rested with the Pope to make the episcopal college the subject of supreme power, for example by convening an ecumenical council. According to this explanation, the Pope alone enjoyed supreme power, by divine right. That was the conservative stand.

2. According to the second, or extreme, interpretation, which was defended and promoted by some liberals, the only subject of supreme power was the college of bishops together with its head, the Pope. The Pope could exercise supreme power; but in so doing, he would be acting only as head of the college, or, in other words, only in so far as he represented the college. He would be bound in conscience to request the opinion of the college of bishops before making a pronouncement because, as representative of the college, he was obliged to express the thinking of the college.

3. According to the third, or moderate, interpretation, which was held by Pope Paul and other liberal Council Fathers, the Pope personally was the subject of supreme power in the Church, and also the college of bishops when united to its head, the Pope. In this hypothesis, the consent of the Pope was necessary as an essential constituent element of the supreme power of the college. In other words, the Pope possessed supreme power by divine right and was always free to use it; while the episcopal college possessed supreme power by divine right but was not always free to use it. Since the college was obliged to act with and under its head, the Pope, it was dependent upon the Pope in using its supreme power. In this way, the unity of the supreme authority in the Church was not impaired.

Pope Paul, first as a priest and later as Cardinal-Archbishop of Milan, had thoroughly studied the hierarchical structure of the Church and also the problem of collegiality. As Pope, he kept abreast of the latest theological literature and developments in this field. In the official archives for the preparatory period of the Council, his name can be found on documents requesting a determination of the powers and charisms proper to bishops in the government of the Church, according to the will of Christ. After he became Pope, he informed the Theological Commission of his views and got the impression that it shared them.

Collegiality was discussed in the Council hall at great length during the second session, in 1963. The Theological Commission established a subcommission on collegiality which worked so rapidly that, by March 6, 1964, the revised text on collegiality was ready. It was later submitted to Pope Paul, but he was not satisfied with it, and, on May 19, 1964, had the Secretary General forward some suggestions which he wished the Theological Commission to take into consideration, stating that it was free to adopt them or not at its next plenary session, scheduled for June 5.

On May 27, the Secretary General wrote to Father Benjamin Wambacq, Secretary of the Pontifical Commission on Biblical Studies, on behalf of Pope Paul, asking for urgent replies to two questions.

The first was whether, according to the Pontifical Commission, the following text in the schema could be proved from Scripture: "Just as, by the Lord's will, St. Peter and the other apostles constituted one apostolic college, so in a similar way the Roman Pontiff, as the successor of Peter, and the bishops, as the successors of the apostles, are joined together." In reply, the Pontifical Commission ruled, at a meeting of May 31, that, whereas the first part of the statement (up to the word "college") could be proved from Scripture, the rest could not be proved from Scripture alone.

The second was whether it could be said, from the Scriptural passages indicated in the following statement, that the office of binding and loosing, granted to Peter alone, belonged also to the college of apostles, in the sense defined in the schema: "The power of binding and loosing, which was given to Peter (Mt 16:19), was granted also to the college of apostles, joined with their head (Mt 18:18)." The Pontifical Commission replied that the power of binding and loosing referred to in both passages seemed to be the same, but that it did not follow that this power was "supreme and full over the entire Church" as the schema indicated.

These replies were referred to the Theological Commission for consideration at its meeting on June 5. The Commission also discussed Pope Paul's eleven suggestions, seven of which referred to collegiality. The Commission incorporated eight of the suggestions and a part of another in its text. With regard to the decisions of the Pontifical Commission on Biblical Studies, the Theological Commission ruled that they did not necessitate any alteration in the two passages of the schema concerned. The revised text was approved by Pope Paul on July 3 as a basis for further discussion, and mailed to the Council Fathers.

By July 28, Archbishop Staffa, of the Curia, had ready a lengthy study on the two newly revised schemas on the Church and on bishops, which he circulated to the

Council Fathers. Referring to the sections on collegiality in both schemas, he expressed the deep conviction "that these propositions are opposed to the more common teaching of the saintly Fathers, of the Roman Pontiffs, of provincial synods, of the holy Doctors of the Universal Church, of theologians and of canonists. They are also contrary to century-old norms of ecclesiastical discipline." The Archbishop quoted from the theological works of an Italian Jesuit, Father Giovanni Bolgeni (1733-1811) and commented that "the fundamental positions of Bolgeni and those of the schema on the Church are substantially identical." He considered it extraordinary that, after 140 years, Bolgeni's principles, which theologians and canonists had long been "unanimous in rejecting as unacceptable and foreign to the sound tradition of the Church," should now suddenly be accepted as the foundations of a Council schema. He maintained that the schema deprived the Pope of his personal supreme power, and limited his primacy to serving as moderator for the bishops, in whom, according to the schema, the supreme power was vested.

The day after the opening of the third session, Archbishop Staffa had a list of more than seventy names which he submitted to the Cardinal Moderators with the request to be allowed to address the general assembly before the voting began on the important Chapter 3, on collegiality. He appealed to Article 57, Section 6, of the Rules of Procedure, under which, even after discussion had ended on a specific topic, the minority view was entitled to "designate three speakers . . . who would also be given the privilege of exceeding ten minutes," provided the request was made in the name of at least seventy other Council Fathers. Archbishop Staffa's petition was not granted.

The voting on the third chapter took place from September 21 to 29. Eight of the ballots concerned Article 22, on collegiality, and on three separate ballots over 300 negative votes were cast. In an overall vote on collegiality, the result was 1,624 affirmative votes, 572 qualified affirmative votes and 42 negative votes. Many of the qualifications submitted on this ballot had been prepared by the International Group of Fathers, which numbered Archbishop Staffa among its collaborators.

The subcommission on collegiality of the Theological Commission worked hard comparing these qualifications with one another and with the text of the schema. The work was completed in about a month because of the very large number of *periti*. The membership was as follows: Archbishop Parente of the Curia, Archbishop Florit of Florence, Bishop Schröffer of Eichstätt, Bishop Hermann Volk of Mainz, Auxiliary Bishop Heuschen of Liège and Auxiliary Bishop Henriquez Jimenez of Caracas. The *periti* were Fathers Rahner, Ratzinger, Salaverri, Schauf, Smulders, Thils, Betti, Dhanis, D'Ercole, Gagnebet, Lambruschini, Maccarrone and Moeller.

Before the work was completed, Archbishop Staffa and the leaders of the International Group of Fathers heard that their qualifications were being ignored by the subcommission on collegiality, whereas others, which were believed to be "less important," were being incorporated in the text. Whereupon Archbishop Staffa composed a lengthy letter to Pope Paul, dated November 7, 1964, copies of which were given to twelve active members of his group, each of whom passed the text on to twelve other Council Fathers, inviting them to read and sign it. This project became known as "Operation Staffa."

Because it was rumored that the Theological Commission's report on the revision of the schema was already in the press, the canvassing of signatures had to be cut short. The letter informed the Pope that all who had signed it were convinced that an extreme form of collegiality was contained in the schema, and that they would feel bound in conscience to vote against it. Archbishop Staffa charged that he had been illegally refused permission to speak on the subject by the Moderators.

On receiving the letter, Pope Paul called for an official investigation of this and other alleged violations of Council procedure, and he passed on the theological views stated in the letter to the Theological Commission, for its consideration.

Meanwhile, thirty-five cardinals and the superiors general of five very large religious orders had written to the Pope stating that, while the text on collegiality in the schema had the appearance of presenting the moderate liberal view, it was in fact ambiguous, and might, after the close of the Council, be interpreted according to the extreme liberal view.

The Pope found it difficult to believe this, and sent a reply to the cardinal whose name headed the list, attacking the arguments given in the letter. Whereupon the Cardinal went to see the Pope, on behalf of the others in his group, and explained the grounds for their suspicions. But the Pope took no action.

The Cardinal then suggested that the theologians of his

group be allowed to debate the issue in the Holy Father's presence with his theologians, but the Holy Father did not agree to this plan. He asked the Cardinal, however, to name the theologians of his group, and when he named three, the Pope at once became visibly disturbed, since they were well known and he esteemed them highly. Again he took no action, recalling that the text on collegiality had been accepted by far more than the required majority. Before casting their votes, he said, the Council Fathers had certainly given the matter deep study and devoted much prayer to it. The Cardinal excused himself for remarking that he could not wholeheartedly share these sentiments. But the Pope still took no action because of his great faith in the Theological Commission.

Then one of the extreme liberals made the mistake of referring, in writing, to some of these ambiguous passages, and indicating how they would be interpreted after the Council. This paper fell into the hands of the aforesaid group of cardinals and superiors general, whose representative took it to the Pope. Pope Paul, realizing finally that he had been deceived, broke down and wept.

What was the remedy? Since the text of the schema did not positively make any false assertion, but merely used ambiguous terms, the ambiguity could be clarified by joining to the text a carefully phrased explanation. This was the origin of the Preliminary Explanatory Note appended to the schema.

On November 10, 1964, Pope Paul without delay instructed his Secretary of State to write to Cardinal Ottaviani, stating that there were still some points in the schema which ought to be more precisely phrased. In particular, he wished it to be expressly stated that a necessary and essential constituent of the collegial authority of the bishops was the consent of the Roman Pontiff. Enclosed in the letter were further specific proposals for changes which would make the text clearer and which, the Pope insisted, must be incorporated in the text before he could give it his support and promulgate it. And in order to make absolutely sure that, after the Council, no one could possibly place the extreme liberal interpretation upon the concept of collegiality, the Theological Commission must prepare a Preliminary Explanatory Note to precede this particular chapter. The note and the suggested changes, the letter said, would reassure many Council Fathers and make possible a more extensive acceptance of the text. A special study on collegiality by Father Wilhelm Bertrams, S.J., was also enclosed in the letter.

The amendments called for by the Pope had already been requested by large numbers of Council Fathers who had submitted qualifications with their affirmative votes. Previously, however, the Theological Commission had always overruled them, stating that the qualifications were contrary to the wishes of the majority. Now, at the insistence of Pope Paul, some of the suggested changes were incorporated in the body of the schema. The Theological Commission also drafted the prescribed note, and sent it to the Pope, who made some revisions in it before giving it his approval.

On Saturday, November 14, the booklet containing the qualifications submitted by Council Fathers on Chapter 3, together with the replies of the Theological Commission, as well as the Explanatory Note, was distributed in the Council hall. The note was believed to be an addition spontaneously made by the Commission, since it began, "The Commission decrees that the following general observations should precede the evaluation of the qualifications."

In the forty-eight hours that followed, there was much discussion among Council Fathers and *periti* as to the significance of this note. Some maintained that it changed the teaching contained in the schema. Others maintained that, because the explanations were contained in a note and not in the text, they did not change the schema.

On Monday, November 16, the Secretary General made three important announcements addressed to all the Council Fathers, including the Council Presidency and the Cardinal Moderators. The first two—although this was not stated—referred to the letter of November 7 prepared by Archbishop Staffa. The third referred to the Explanatory Note. The Secretary General, using Curial terminology, referred to the Pope as the "Superior Authority."

In the first announcement, he said that some Fathers had complained to the Superior Authority that, in the discussion and voting on Chapter 3 of the schema on the Church, the regulations governing procedure had not been observed; the same Fathers were filled with anxiety and had raised certain doubts about the doctrine expounded in that chapter. The matter had been carefully examined, he said, and the Council Fathers concerned might rest assured that there had been no violation of the Rules of Procedure. As for doubts concerning the doctrine contained in Chapter 3, these had been referred to the Theological Commission, and duly examined.

The second announcement concerned the assent which all members of the Church were expected to give to the teaching contained in this chapter. The teaching, according to this announcement, was not to be considered an infallible definition or dogma, but to be accepted on the supreme teaching authority of the Church.

The third announcement was as follows: "Finally, the Fathers are hereby informed by the Superior Authority of a Preliminary Explanatory Note to the qualifications on Chapter 3 of the schema on the Church. The doctrine contained in this chapter must be explained and understood according to the meaning and tenor of this note." He then read the complete text as it had appeared in the booklet containing the qualifications to Chapter 3 which had been distributed on Saturday, but with one major difference: this time, the note was called to the Council Fathers' attention by the Pope, rather than by the Theological Commission itself. The Pope also explicitly extended the interpretation of the note to the whole of Chapter 3, and not only to the qualifications.

The precise theological terminology of the Explanatory Note made it clear beyond all doubt that the interpretation to be placed on the concept of collegiality as taught by the schema was the moderate liberal one. (The ambiguity, now removed, had been recognized by Cardinal Ottaviani as early as the second session, when he so strenuously objected to the phraseology of the four points presented for the vote by the Cardinal Moderators on October 30, 1963.)

On Tuesday, November 17, each Council Father received a personal printed copy of the Preliminary

Explanatory Note, and afterwards the Council voted 2,099 to 46 in favor of the manner in which the Theological Commission had handled the qualifications for Chapter 3.

On November 19, in announcing that the vote on the schema as a whole would take place that morning, the Secretary General explained that this vote, as well as the vote which was to take place two days later at a public session, must be understood in accordance with the announcements which he had previously made upon instructions from the Superior Authority. Those announcements, he added, would be inserted in the official record of the Council.

The result of the vote that morning was 2,134 to 10 in favor of the schema. It was greeted with enthusiastic applause.

BLACK WEEK

The liberals had four major reasons for dissatisfaction with Pope Paul VI during the final week of the third session. First, there was his insistence on a Preliminary Explanatory Note on collegiality, which was officially communicated to the general assembly on Monday, November 16, 1964. Then there was his decision regarding the vote on religious liberty, scheduled for the Thursday of that week. A third reason was his last-minute action on the schema on ecumenism. And finally there was his unexpected announcement on Saturday, November 21, the closing day of the third session, on the application of the title "Mother of the Church" to the Virgin Mary. The

Dutch quickly invented a graphic term for this period of the Council's history: "Black Week."

The story of the Explanatory Note has already been told. To understand the conflict about the schema on religious liberty it is necessary to go back to September 23, 1964, when discussion on the topic began. The discussion continued for three full meetings and part of a fourth, and then the Secretariat for Promoting Christian Unity set to work revising the text. It completed its work by the end of October, and then passed the text on to the Theological Commission, which examined and approved it on November 9. The conservative elements on the Theological Commission were accused of having deliberately dragged their feet, so that there would be no time left for a vote before the end of the third session. The text was printed and distributed to the Council Fathers on Tuesday, November 17. The vote was announced for Thursday.

The revised schema was contained in a booklet together with a report by Bishop De Smedt of Bruges, scheduled to be read on Thursday, which began, "The text which we present for your vote today differs greatly from the text which was discussed in the hall." The International Group of Fathers, gathered for their regular weekly meeting, studied the revised schema and came to a number of startling conclusions: First, the former text of 271 lines had been expanded to cover 556 lines. Secondly, only 75 of the 556 lines had been taken from the former text. Thirdly, the structure of the argumentation was different; the presentation of the question was different; the basic principles had been altered; and major paragraphs in Articles 2, 3, 8, 12 and 14 were completely new.

For these reasons, the International Group considered the text equivalent to a new schema, and believed that the procedure to be followed was that contained in Article 30, Section 2, of the Council's Rules of Procedure, which provided that schemas "must be distributed in such a way that Council Fathers have a suitable period of time to take counsel, to come to a mature judgment and to determine how they will vote." Since there was to be another General Congregation on Wednesday morning and the voting was to take place on Thursday, there was not really sufficient time available for a responsible and thorough examination of a schema which was practically new. Moreover, the Council Fathers were already overloaded during this particular week, since they were discussing schemas on seminary training, Christian education and matrimony, and had to cast ten important ballots on schemas on the Church, the Eastern Catholic Churches and ecumenism.

The group therefore decided to draw up a letter to the Council Presidency, calling attention to Article 30, Section 2, of the Rules of Procedure, and asking for a delay in the vote. Over one hundred signatures were collected. The letter was dated Wednesday, November 18, and was delivered to the Council Presidency early that morning. Similar petitions were submitted by other groups. Cardinal Tisserant, Dean of the Cardinal Presidents, took up the matter with the Cardinal Moderators, who requested the Secretary General to read out one of the appeals and to announce that the matter would be settled by a vote of the general assembly. The Secretary General said that a preliminary vote would be taken the following day to decide whether to proceed to a vote on the schema. "This has been decided by the Dean of the Cardinal Presidents and by the Cardinal Moderators," he explained.

Bishop Carli, of Segni, Italy, one of those who had signed the International Group's letter requesting more time for study of the schema, appealed to Francesco Cardinal Roberti, Chairman of the Administrative Tribunal, against the decision of Cardinal Tisserant and the four Moderators. That decision, he wrote, "appears illegal to the undersigned because of lack of form and lack of substance. 1. It is lacking in form because the decision was not taken collegially by the Council Presidency, but only by the Cardinal President together with the Moderators. 2. It is lacking in substance, because the assembly cannot be asked to decide whether or not specific articles in the Rules of Procedure issued by the Supreme Pontiff should or should not be observed. Either the petition of the more than 100 Fathers was unfounded, in which case the Council Presidency should declare it unacceptable, giving its reasons; or it was well founded, in which case no one, except the Supreme Pontiff, is entitled to ignore it."

In conclusion, Bishop Carli asserted his view that the reasons given in the original petition were still valid, since Council Fathers were entitled not to proceed to a vote on a text which was substantially new without first discussing it in the Council hall and having enough time to determine how to vote. "Therefore the undersigned requests that this Most Excellent Tribunal intervene to ensure observance of the Rules of Procedure."

Bishop Carli handed this letter to Cardinal Roberti early on Thursday morning, November 19. A short while

359

later, Cardinal Tisserant rose in his place and read out the following statement on behalf of the Council Presidency. "After giving the matter mature consideration, it appears to the Council Presidency that this matter, which touches the Rules of Procedure of the Council, cannot be decided by a vote of the general assembly. Therefore the same Council Presidency has decided that the report [on the schema] is to be read, but that the votes will not be taken during this session of the Council. Those Fathers who wish to present their views in writing may do so up to January 31, 1965."

Cardinal Meyer, one of the twelve Council Presidents, made no attempt to hide his great surprise and deep displeasure at the announcement. Had he been unaware that it was to be made? He had been one of the greatest protagonists of the declaration on religious freedom, and had eagerly looked forward to its adoption. Bishop Francis Reh, Rector of the North American College in Rome, and two *periti*, Monsignor John Quinn of Chicago and Father Frederick McManus of Washington, D.C., hurried over to confer with him. After a brief consultation, they decided upon the wording of a special petition to be circulated immediately. It was the famous "*Instanter, instantius, instantissime*" petition to the Holy Father consisting of only one sentence: "Reverently but insistently, more insistently, most insistently, we request that the vote on the declaration on religious freedom be allowed to take place before the end of this Council session, lest the confidence of the Christian and non-Christian world be lost." Angry bishops meanwhile poured from their stalls and formed excited groups. Copies of the petition passed rapidly from hand to hand. Never had there been such a furious signing of names, such confusion, such agitation. Never had there been such wild and harsh words as in this moment of panic when it seemed that a cherished Council document might be tabled forever.

The signed petitions were quickly collected and given to Cardinal Meyer, who had meanwhile been joined by Cardinals Ritter and Léger. Together they left the Council hall while the meeting was still in progress, and went to see the Pope, begging him to overrule the decision announced by Cardinal Tisserant, so that the long awaited vote might still take place that morning.

Meanwhile, Cardinal Döpfner, the Moderator for the day, followed the directive announced by Cardinal Tisserant and called upon Bishop De Smedt to read his report. The bishop admitted that the structure of the schema had been changed, and that in general it was much different from what it had been before. "All this, however, has not changed the substance of our exposition," he said. "Therefore we offer you today the same doctrine but, as we hope, expressed more concisely, clearly, accurately and prudently." He pointed out that the text had been unanimously approved by the members of the Secretariat for Promoting Christian Unity, and that more than two thirds of the Theological Commission had also given their approval.

Bishop De Smedt succeeded in stirring his audience. He was wildly applauded five times during his speech, and for several minutes afterwards. The thunderous applause at the end rose and fell in three distinct waves. Never had a speaker in the Council hall received such enthusiastic applause. Cardinal Döpfner understandably protracted the meeting beyond the usual time, but when, by 12:44 P.M., no word had come from the Pope, he brought the meeting to a close.

The press carried stories about a "massive revolt" led by American bishops; and various figures were cited—from 500 to 1,500—for the signatures to the petition addressed to the Pope. NCWC News Service, the U.S. Bishops' news agency, quoted an unnamed American bishop as stating that "perhaps 1,000 signatures from bishops from all over the world had been collected." When an exact count was made for publication after the close of the session, the number was found to be actually 441.

On Friday, November 20, at the last business meeting of the third session, Cardinal Tisserant once again addressed the general assembly: "Venerable Fathers," he said, "many Fathers were greatly distressed because the voting on the schema of the declaration on religious freedom did not take place, and they earnestly requested the Supreme Pontiff to provide that the voting might somehow take place before the end of this session." The Cardinal then explained that the rest of his statement was being made on the Pope's authority. "Let these Fathers know that the postponement of the vote was granted by the Council Presidency because this was required by the Rules of Procedure governing the Council. An additional reason for the postponement was a certain respect for the liberty of other Council Fathers who have very much at heart a proper, profound and careful examination of a schema of such great importance. Therefore the schema of the declaration on religious freedom will be treated at

362

the next session of the Council and, if possible, before all other schemas."

Unfortunately Cardinal Meyer, who had championed the schema so ardently, would not be present at the next session; he died from a brain tumor five months before the fourth session began.

Another way in which Pope Paul became unpopular with the liberals during Black Week was through his last-minute action on the schema on ecumenism. Although a total of 421 different qualifications had been submitted by the Council Fathers in the balloting, only 26 of these had been incorporated in the schema by the Secretariat for Promoting Christian Unity. Council Fathers whose qualifications had not been adopted appealed to the Pope, presenting forty further amendments, and stating that they would be unable to support the document unless those amendments were accepted.

Since Pope Paul was particularly interested in having as few negative votes as possible cast in the vote on ecumenism, he asked Cardinal Bea to examine the proposed changes together with other qualified representatives of his Secretariat, and suggested that it would be well if some of those changes were adopted, since that would probably win greater support for the schema.

Among the amendments were many which, if adopted, would have altered the orientation and even the substance of the schema. These Cardinal Bea and his associates ignored. They adopted only nineteen, which were reproduced and distributed to the Council Fathers on November 19. That day the Secretary General announced that the vote on the schema on ecumenism as a whole would take place the following day. Then he continued: "In addition to the amendments already introduced in the text in accordance with qualifications made by Council Fathers, the following amendments have been introduced to give the text greater clarity. This was done by the Secretariat for Promoting Christian Unity, which in this way adopted the kind suggestions that had been authoritatively presented." He then read the text of the nineteen amendments.

The announcement could not have come at a more inopportune time. The atmosphere in the Council hall was already tense as a result of the postponement of the vote on religious freedom. The new announcement aroused tempers again. The liberals correctly interpreted both measures as victories for the conservatives, and resented the fact that the Pope had apparently become their patron. This attitude was reflected by the press, which blackened the public image of the Pope. Nevertheless, the schema on ecumenism, as amended at the Pope's request, was approved by a vote of 2,054 to 64.

On Saturday morning, November 21, 1964, the closing day of the third session, the Council Fathers took their places in the Council hall in a none-too-happy frame of mind. "Evidence of the tension and frustration was most dramatically obvious," wrote Mr. Donald Quinn in a front-page story in the *St. Louis Review*. "As Pope Paul was carried into St. Peter's on his *sedia gestatoria* [portable throne], he passed between the two rows of 2,100 stonily silent bishops. No applause from the bishops' stalls greeted him. Even as the Pope made a simple blessing sign, only one in ten of the bishops crossed themselves.

Newsmen witnessing the scene double-checked with each other about what they were seeing."

A solemn Mass of concelebration was offered by the Pope and twenty-four Council Fathers representing sees with national shrines in honor of the Blessed Virgin Mary. Then the voting took place. The Dogmatic Constitution on the Church, containing the much-discussed chapter on collegiality, was adopted by 2,151 votes to 5. The Decree on Eastern Catholic Churches was adopted by 2,110 votes to 39. And the Decree on Ecumenism, with the last-minute changes referred to above, was adopted by 2,137 votes to 11. After the results of each ballot were announced, there was sustained applause. And after each document was promulgated by the Pope, there was again enthusiastic applause.

But the enthusiasm was to be chilled for some Council Fathers by an unexpected announcement in the Pope's closing address.

The year before, at the close of the second session, Pope Paul had told the Council Fathers that he hoped for the "unanimous and loving acknowledgment of the place, privileged above all others, which the Mother of God occupies in the Holy Church. . . . After Christ, her place in the Church is the most exalted, and also the one closest to us, and so we can honor her with the title 'Mother of the Church' to her glory and to our benefit." But the bestowal of this title had met with opposition. Some episcopal conferences, such as those from German-speaking and Scandinavian countries, had objected to the title, and Bishop Méndez Arceo of Mexico had spoken out against it on the Council floor. Cardinal Wyszynski of Poland, however, had announced that he and all the bishops of Poland had sent the Pope a special request for this title. And the International Group of Fathers had collected signatures for a petition to the Pope which read, "At the forthcoming third session, may the Blessed Virgin Mary be proclaimed Mother of the Church by the Council, that is, by Your Holiness, as head, together with the Fathers, as members." There had been other petitions to the same effect.

The Theological Commission, however, without ever putting the matter to a vote, on its own authority had removed the title from the chapter on the Blessed Virgin in the schema on the Church. The title had previously been inserted on instructions from the Coordinating Commission. (Those instructions, according to one competent authority, Father Balić, might well have been issued at the desire of Pope John XXIII.)

On Wednesday, November 18, 1964, in the midst of Black Week, Pope Paul made a statement at a public audience which went largely unnoticed. "We are happy to announce to you," he said, "that we shall close this session of the Ecumenical Council . . . by joyfully bestowing on Our Lady the title due to her, Mother of the Church."

At the public meeting on Saturday, November 21, the last day of the session, Pope Paul said in his concluding address that the close relations existing between Mary and the Church, "so clearly established in today's Conciliar Constitution," caused him to feel that this was "the most solemn and appropriate moment to fulfill a wish to which we referred at the end of the preceding session. . . . Very many Council Fathers," continued Pope Paul, "have made this wish their own, pressing for an explicit declaration during this Council of the role as Mother which the Virgin exercises over the Christian people. To achieve this aim, we have considered it opportune to consecrate, at this public meeting itself, a title in honor of the Virgin which has been suggested by various parts of the Catholic world. It is particularly dear to us because it sums up, in an admirable synthesis, the privileged position recognized by this Council for the Virgin in the Holy Church. Therefore, for the glory of the Virgin Mary and for our own consolation, we proclaim the Most Holy Mary as Mother of the Church, that is to say, of all the People of God, of the faithful as well as the pastors [bishops], who call her their most loving Mother. And we wish that from now on the Virgin should be still more honored and invoked by the entire Christian people by this most dear title."

The standing ovation which greeted this announcement signified the warm assent of the Council Fathers. The Pope was interrupted seven times by applause during his address; the applause increased in intensity as the address continued. He announced that he would make use of the long-discussed episcopal synod, and that the reorganization of the Roman Curia was undergoing careful study. He also announced his intention of sending a special mission in the near future to Fátima, in Portugal, to carry a golden rose to the shrine of Our Lady of Fátima. "In this manner," he said, "we intend to entrust to the care of this Heavenly Mother the entire human family, with its problems and worries, with its lawful aspirations and ardent hopes." This gesture was considered a partial reply to 510 heads of dioceses, archdioceses and patriarchates from seventy-six countries who had petitioned Pope Paul to consecrate the entire world during the Council to the Immaculate Heart of Mary, as requested by Our Lady of Fátima. The signatures of these prelates had been delivered to the Holy Father on February 3, 1964, by Archbishop Sigaud of Diamantina, Brazil. But the bishops of Germany and France, as well as Cardinal Bea, were known to be opposed to such a consecration, and it did not take place.

While many Council Fathers were reassured by the proceedings of the public meeting, for others the last week of the third session remained Black Week. When the leading *peritus* of the Dutch hierarchy, Father Schillebeeckx, returned to Holland after the Council, he was appalled to find the press and the country so antagonistic to the Pope because of the events of Black Week. He immediately published an article in defense of the Pope in *De Bazuin*, a religious weekly published in Amsterdam. As a result, the antagonism was directed toward him. He retorted with another article in *De Bazuin* (January 23, 1965), giving the background of the Preliminary Explanatory Note appended to the chapter on collegiality in the schema on the Church.

As early as the second session, wrote Father Schillebeeckx, he had told a *peritus* on the Theological Commission that he was sorry to see in the schema what appeared to be the moderate liberal view on collegiality; he personally was in favor of the extreme liberal view. The *peritus* had replied, "We are stating this in a diplomatic manner, but after the Council we shall draw the conclusions implicit in it." Father Schillebeeckx had called such tactics "unfair." During the last month of the third session, he wrote, bishops and theologians had continued to speak of collegiality "in a sense which was not expressed anywhere in the schema." He pointed out that the minority had understood well that the vague phraseology of the schema would be interpreted after the Council in the strongest sense. The minority, he explained, had not been against collegiality as literally formulated in the text, but had been opposed "to that orientation full of hope which the majority of the Theological Commission wished to convey through the text." The majority, he said, had resorted to a deliberately vague and excessively diplomatic parlance, and he recalled that even Father Congar had much earlier objected to a conciliar text's being deliberately ambiguous.

Father Schillebeeckx maintained that a conciliar text on collegiality must be unequivocal, expressing clearly either the moderate or the extreme liberal view. Pope Paul had therefore had no alternative but to issue a Preliminary Explanatory Note. Without it, Father Schillebeeckx insisted, an ambiguous text would have been approved. With this exposé, he destroyed the basis for the greatest grievance against the Pope.

Another liberal theologian at the Council, Father John Courtney Murray, S.J., the leading American *peritus* on religious freedom, told a vast audience at Georgetown University, in Washington, D.C., shortly after the end of the third session, that the postponement of the vote on religious freedom had been a "wise" decision. He also admitted that the action taken by the Council Presidency had been technically correct, since extensive revision had actually turned the document into a "substantially new text." Again a liberal had vindicated the Pope of charges leveled against him during Black Week.

As for the nineteen changes introduced in the schema on ecumenism at the Pope's request, Cardinal Bea wrote later that, on calm consideration, they revealed no grounds for alarm. He pointed out that the original panic had resulted from an incorrect translation of the Latin text of one of the nineteen amendments. The incorrect translation had read that the separated brethren, in reading the Bible, sought God "as though he were speaking to them in Christ." Understandably, it caused surprise in Catholic circles and widespread alarm among the separated brethren. But when the matter was clarified by Cardinal Bea, who insisted that the only correct translation was that the separated brethren "seek God as he speaks to them in Christ," the grounds for alarm were removed. Once more, Pope Paul was justified.

The *St. Louis Review* voiced the complaints of certain bishops and *periti* in telling its readers that "the granting of the title, Mother of the Church, to Mary by the Pope's words on Saturday was in direct contradiction to the will of the majority of the Fathers." Cardinal Bea, commenting on charges like this, simply pointed out that the question as to whether Our Lady should be given this title had never been voted on in the Council. "By what right, then," he asked, "can one pretend to know something about the presumed majority opinion of the Council?" Although some had spoken against this title on the Council floor, he explained, the positions taken in Council interventions, being limited in number, were "not a reliable indication at all for knowing the majority opinion of the Council Fathers."

In taking this action, the Pope did not even contradict the will of the majority in the Theological Commission. To do so, he would have had to place the title back into the schema after the Theological Commission had removed it. This he did not do. What took place that closing day of the third session was a twofold exercise of supreme authority in the Catholic Church. In the first exercise of this authority, Pope Paul conformed himself to his College of Bishops and promulgated the Dogmatic Constitution on the Church, which included the new title for Our Lady in an "equivalent" manner. When this action was completed, the Pope used his own supreme personal authority to state in an explicit manner what he, together with his College of Bishops, had a few minutes earlier stated in an implicit or "equivalent" manner.

So perhaps Black Week had not been so black after all.

371

THE FOURTH SESSION

September 14 – December 8, 1965

ALIGNMENTS ON THE SCHEMA
ON RELIGIOUS FREEDOM

The four setbacks which the liberals had suffered during Black Week made them realize that their control over the Council was not so absolute as they had imagined. And the conservatives, for their part, drew fresh courage from the liberals' perplexity. Bishop Carli of Segni, of the International Group of Fathers, quickly published a lengthy article on Black Week in which he quoted from the article of Father Schillebeeckx and from the remarks made by Father John Courtney Murray, S.J. Had the minority not taken action on the text on religious freedom, he said, that schema, "so full of serious defects, would no doubt have been approved by a very large majority." Every commission, and even the general assembly itself, he said, should always be prepared to reconsider its stand right up to the very last.

In a letter dated December 18, 1964, the International Group sent fifteen pages of suggested amendments to the schema on religious freedom to all Council Fathers on their mailing list, reminding them that the deadline for submitting amendments was January 31. When a fourth edition of the schema was published in June, 1965, the group circulated another letter with twenty additional pages of amendments. And on August 13, Archbishop Sigaud of Diamantina, Brazil; Archbishop Lefebvre, Superior General of the Holy Ghost Fathers; and Abbot Jean Prou, Superior General of the Benedictines of Solesmes, France, met at Solesmes to prepare additional strategy. They determined topics and selected speakers for five interventions on the schema, and they decided to send the gist of their proposals to the Pope should those proposals not be incorporated in the schema as a result of the discussion and voting.

Certainly no Council Fathers were harder to please than the leaders of the International Group. Bishop Carli alone, for example, had submitted fifty-two amendments on an early draft of the schema on ecumenism. It was difficult, therefore, for those revising the schema on religious freedom to determine what points the Bishop considered of major or of minor importance. The same was true of all other amendments regularly prepared and circularized by the International Group.

The three aforementioned prelates sent Pope Paul a letter dated July 25, 1965. They drew attention to the fact that the Rules of Procedure provided that reports might be read to the general assembly before the vote by Council Fathers representing both the majority view and the minority view in Council commissions. But it was not regular Council practice, they said, for the minority view in commissions to be heard. They requested that this rule be enforced in particular for the schemas on religious freedom, divine revelation, the Church in the modern world and the relationship of the Church to non-Christian religions. They also made the following requests: that such speakers be given sufficient time to prepare their main arguments; that the spokesman for the minority view be selected by the minority; that the names of the majority and minority speakers be published long enough in advance for objections and supporting arguments to be directed to them; that their reports be printed and distributed to the Council Fathers; and that each speaker be given a short time for rebuttal.

Cardinal Cicognani, Vatican Secretary of State, replied to Bishop Carli on August 11, stating that Pope Paul had given careful attention to the proposals. "I must inform Your Excellency, however," he went on, "that some surprise was occasioned by the fact that the request had been presented on behalf of an 'International Group of Fathers, with similar views on theological and pastoral matters,' that is, by a particular group within the Council. This initiative might be deemed to authorize the official foundation of other 'alliances,' to the detriment of the Council assembly. As Your Excellency can well understand, this would in fact take from Council Fathers that freedom of judgment and of choice which must be ensured over and above every particular interest. It would also lead to the accentuation of tendencies and divisions among the Council Fathers themselves, whereas everything possible should be done to minimize them for the sake of serenity, concord, the happy outcome of the Council and the honor of the Church. The enterprise, therefore, cannot in itself be approved, and it would be well for this 'Group' not to function as an organ representing the positions of the Council Fathers belonging to it."

It should be recalled, in connection with this letter, that the Rules of Procedure of the Council as revised and approved by Pope Paul actually encouraged the formation of groups with similar views on theological and pastoral matters. Thus Article 57, Section 3, provided: "It is most desirable that Council Fathers who intend to present similar arguments should join together and choose one or several of their number to speak on behalf of all." As far back as August 5, 1964, Archbishop Sigaud had pointed out that the new ruling requiring a speaker to have collected seventy signatures in order to be permitted to speak after closure of debate forced the minority to organize itself, and he had cited Article 57, Section 3, as justifying such action.

Bishop Carli forwarded Cardinal Cicognani's letter to Archbishop Lefebvre in Paris, who in turn forwarded it to Archbishop Sigaud on August 20 with these comments:

"It seems that the Holy Father or the Cardinal Secretary of State has been frightened by a title which appears to them to designate an association which is highly organized and may easily cause divisions.

"We have never attached any importance to this title, and it makes little difference to us whether we have it or not. What really matters is the desire of a certain number of Council Fathers to give one another mutual support and help in their defense and explanation of the truth. There is nothing about this which is not most legitimate. We can very well eliminate the name. Personally, I see nothing against this. It will not change the reality in any way.

"As far as the freedom of the Council Fathers is concerned, I truly believe that we have never offended against it in the slightest. God knows that we have exerted no moral pressure." He closed his letter by saying that those who exerted intolerable moral pressure, and who "suffocated" the minority, were rather the national episcopal conferences.

The International Group of Fathers was not the only opposition group under attack. Cardinals Döpfner and

Suenens went directly to the Pope to complain about the Bishops' Secretariat. When that group's president, Archbishop Perantoni, learned of this, he explained to the Holy Father that his organization had come into being only to ensure a hearing for a minority which the powerfully organized European alliance, protected and promoted by the two Cardinal Moderators, was ignoring. As long as the pressure group of Cardinals Döpfner and Suenens continued, he said, the Bishops' Secretariat would also be forced to remain in existence.

At a press conference held in Rome on September 13, the day before the opening of the fourth session, Cardinal Döpfner said that the Pope and a large majority of Council Fathers wanted the forthcoming session to be the last one. The work on the remaining schemas was so far advanced, he said, that the session could easily be closed before Christmas "without restricting the liberty of the Council Fathers and without strangulating the Council itself." He also stressed that the Rules of Procedure would be observed "in their entirety."

But despite Cardinal Döpfner's assurances, the Council during the fourth session was in fact "strangulated" more than ever before. This was because the cardinals nearly monopolized prime time. So many of them spoke each day that the interventions of bishops were often read only at a late hour when Council Fathers were either tired or missing from their places. And bishops were repeatedly silenced by closure of debate. Fifty-one cardinals, making up only 2 percent of the general assembly, delivered 33 percent of the oral interventions made during the fourth session.

On September 14, 1965, the opening day of the fourth session, the Holy Father announced that, "in accordance with the wishes of the Council," he intended to establish an episcopal synod composed of bishops to be chosen "for the greater part by conferences of bishops, and approved by us." The synod, he said, would be convened "by the Roman Pontiff, for consultation and collaboration, when this seems opportune to us for the general good of the Church." He made it clear, however, that this synod would not supplant the Roman Curia. Just as diocesan bishops needed a chancery office to run their dioceses, he said, "so we too always need the Curia to carry out our Apostolic responsibilities."

On the following day, Pope Paul formally constituted the Synod of Bishops, thereby fully complying with the wishes of the Council Fathers even before they had given formal approval to their own suggestion.

As the Pope had promised, the fourth session began with the discussion of the revised schema on religious freedom. A total of sixty-six speakers addressed the assembly on this subject between September 15 and 22, 1965.

Because no apparent action had been taken on its letter of July 25 to Pope Paul, the International Group of Fathers drew up a new letter dated September 18, addressed to the Cardinal Moderators. Referring to Article 33, Section 7, of the Rules of Procedure, which provided that a substitute schema or an organic list of amendments might be submitted by fifty Council Fathers at any time, the signers asked for authorization for the reading of a second report on religious freedom to the general assembly, a report "which would completely and systematically explain and defend another manner of conceiving of and declaring this doctrine." The letter was reproduced and signatures collected, but the Moderators seem to have ignored it.

The general assembly subsequently accepted the fourth edition of the schema "as a basis for the definitive declaration" by a vote of 1,997 to 224. When the fifth edition came back to the Council hall for a vote on October 26 and 27, hundreds of qualifications were submitted with affirmative votes. Once again the schema was revised, and on Wednesday, November 17, the sixth edition was distributed to the Council Fathers. They were informed at the same time that they would be asked to vote two days later on whether they were satisfied with the way in which the qualifications had been handled by the Secretariat for Promoting Christian Unity.

The sixth edition did not completely satisfy the International Group. In a new letter dated November 18, distributed to 800 Council Fathers, the group acknowledged that notable improvements had been made in Article 1 regarding true religion. It argued, however, that the criterion determining the limits of religious freedom should be the common good, and not the preservation of law and order. The State, it maintained, must safeguard the common good as a whole, and not only in part, and the preservation of law and order was only "a part of the common good, as is expressly stated in the schema." If this "correction" were made in two places in the text, and if in one of those two places the pertinent words of Pope John XXIII's *Pacem in Terris* were quoted, then the text would be satisfactory, and the International Group would give it an affirmative vote. The desired changes, however, were not made.

According to the letter, the fundamental thesis of the Secretariat for Promoting Christian Unity was that state neutrality should be considered as the normal condition, and that there should be cooperation between state and Church only "in particular circumstances." This principle the International Group could not in conscience accept. To justify its stand, the group cited Pope Pius XII's statement that the Church considered the principle of collaboration between Church and State as "normal," and that it considered "as an ideal the unity of people in the true religion, and unanimity of action" between Church and State.

In the balloting which took place on the following day, 246 negative votes were cast on the first ballot, 237 on the second, and 217 on both the third and fourth. In the overall vote, 1,954 voted in favor and 249 cast negative votes. This meant that far more than the required two-thirds majority was in favor of the text as it stood.

On December 3, Monsignor Giuseppe di Meglio, an Italian specialist on international law, circulated a letter stating that the voting figures indicated "that for a notable number of Council Fathers the teaching and practical applications of the schema are not acceptable in conscience. In fact, the fundamental principle of the schema has remained unchanged despite the amendments that have been introduced: that is, the right of error. . . . Since the declaration on religious freedom has no dogmatic value, the negative votes of the Council Fathers will constitute a factor of great importance for the future studies of the declaration itself, and particularly for the interpretation to be placed upon it."

Father Courtney Murray described Monsignor di Meglio's position as the "tolerance" theory, based on the principle that "truth has exclusive rights and error no rights." Those who held this position, he said, were of the opinion that Catholicism should be the State religion wherever possible. Where this was not possible, non-Catholic religions were merely to be tolerated as the "lesser evil." By contrast, the supporters of what Father Courtney Murray called "the more contemporary theory of religious freedom" were convinced that this freedom was "an exigency of the dignity of the human person." They favored religious freedom not for opportunistic reasons, but because it was sound doctrine.

The sixth edition of the schema received the support of Pope Paul despite the large number of negative votes that had been cast against it. The final and formal vote took place at the public session of December 7. On this ballot, the negative votes dropped to 70, and 2,308 Council Fathers voted in favor of the text. It was then promulgated by Pope Paul VI to the accompaniment of great applause. Nearly all of the 70 negative votes had been cast by the hard core of the International Group of Fathers. And yet, after the voting was done, they were as ready as the next man to accept the promulgated decree. Basically, this was the attitude of all Council Fathers, whether they belonged to the liberal or to the conservative camp; each was convinced that his position on a given topic was the correct one, the one which would bring greater blessing upon the Church and mankind. But these men, trained in Church law, also realized that both sides could not be right. And ultimately they went along with the majority view, when this finally became clear and was promulgated by the

Pope as the common doctrine taught by the Second Vatican Council.

Solving the World's Problems

At Ariccia, a suburb of Rome, the schema on the Church in the modern world was subjected to thorough revision during a week of meetings in early February, 1965. Present were twenty-nine Council Fathers, thirty-eight *periti* and some twenty laymen, in addition to men and women auditors. The central subcommission then worked on the revision for another week, and in early April the text was approved by the Joint Commission (Theological Commission and Commission on the Apostolate of the Laity). The Coordinating Commission approved the new schema on May II and Pope Paul gave it his approval on May 28.

In the process, the schema had been expanded from forty-five to 122 pages. Since the supplement had been incorporated in the text, the entire schema had to be discussed once more on the Council floor. The discussion continued from September 21 to October 8. Archbishop Garrone of Toulouse, in presenting the schema to the general assembly, said that it had been so extensively altered in size and content because the Joint Commission had been anxious "scrupulously to satisfy the wishes expressed by the Council Fathers."

Cardinal Bea called the Latin of the schema "frequently unintelligible" and "unworthy of the Council." Although the text was to be issued in several modern languages, the Latin version, he insisted, was the only official one.

A fundamental revision of the Latin was therefore necessary; otherwise there would be "endless discussions as to its meaning, and the doctrinal authority of the document would suffer by reason of the uncertainty of the text."

Cardinal König of Vienna asked for the introduction of more fundamental principles in the schema which would show that the Church "always had the task of diagnosing the signs of the times, and that new attempts must continually be made to achieve such analyses." Like Cardinal Siri of Genoa, who spoke immediately after him, Cardinal König called for the inclusion of concepts that had been omitted by those who had prepared the schema, concepts such as "sin, the truth of the Cross, the need for repentance and the hope of resurrection with Christ." Only thus could the danger be averted of "promising a paradise on earth and a solution to all problems, something that cannot be realized save in the world to come."

In the name of ninety-one Scandinavian and German-speaking Council Fathers, Cardinal Döpfner of Munich said that the schema had made much progress. It presented the problems more clearly, set forth more profound doctrine, and used a language which was better suited to modern man. At the same time, he said, it did not clearly distinguish the natural and supernatural orders, nor did it adequately describe the deep consequences of the state of sin. He also wanted the text to state more precisely how faith could illumine and strengthen the world.

Speaking for a group of Italian bishops, Archbishop Giuseppe Amici of Modena said that the entire text needed revision, since it was "only a first step toward dialogue with the world." In form and substance it was unsatisfactory, because it only affirmed "in simple propositions of common sense what everyone regarded as obvious." Since the text said little to men who desired to know the "authentic Christian concept of life," it would not succeed in establishing dialogue with all men.

Bishop Russell McVinney of Providence, Rhode Island, asked that the schema reassert the necessity of obedience to lawful authority, especially since the decline of public authority, both civil and religious, was "one of the chief causes of the constant decay of moral standards in our world."

Bishop Paulus Rusch of Innsbruck, Austria, said that philosophical considerations prevailed over theological considerations in the schema, that the text was static in its approach rather than dynamic, and that it was more abstract than practical.

Coadjutor Archbishop Simon Lourdusamy of Bangalore supported the text on behalf of sixty-two bishops of India, but indicated that certain improvements were desirable. The description of man in the schema applied to industrialized areas of the world, he said, "but what about the greater part of humanity, in Africa, Asia and Latin America?" He asked that the reasoning of the schema should be based on theology, rather than on natural philosophy.

Bishop Mason of El Obeid, Sudan, said that the text was so long that modern men would hesitate to read it. He suggested that the schema should confine itself to the present generation, since future generations would have their own bishops to look after them. He also asked that debate on the schema should be prudently limited so that sufficient time might remain for other topics which, he felt, pertained more closely to the renewal of the Church.

Cardinal Frings of Cologne called for a substantial reorganization of the entire text because of a dangerous confusion between human progress, resulting from dialogue, and supernatural salvation, wrought by Christ's mission.

Coadjutor Bishop Elchinger of Strasbourg said that the schema did not strictly follow the plan which it had laid down for itself of showing how the Church understood its presence and activity in the modern world. It was not enough for the Council to repeat generalities already known to all. The schema should deal, he said, not with the modern world, but with the Church in the modern world, that is, in its new relationships to the world.

Cardinal Gracias of Bombay announced that five laymen in India had made a study of an English translation of the schema and had given it unanimous praise, saying that in this document the Church really did have something to say which was relevant to modern problems.

Bishop Hadrianus Ddungu of Masaka, Uganda, speaking on behalf of ninety-four bishops, said that the subject of racial discrimination was treated much too lightly and too confusedly in the schema, since only four lines were devoted to the problem and its solution. The problem should be treated forcefully, at greater length, and without ambiguity.

Archbishop Émile Blanchet, Rector of the Institut Catholique of Paris, said that the schema's description of contemporary culture was inadequate, since it said nothing about history and philosophy. The style, too, was faulty, he said. In his view, everything was treated with "undue optimism, as though all differences could be composed by good will."

Cardinal Bueno y Monreal of Seville found fault with the text for omitting any reference to the organization of collective production, "although many await the Church's judgment on this aspect of present-day economic life." He wished to have the text revised so that it might include references to the "possible common ownership of land." The schema should mention the more human and Christian concept of such enterprises as communities of persons bringing their materials, technical skill and labor to the common task of production, and then sharing the profits in accordance with their contributions.

Auxiliary Bishop Edward Swanstrom of New York City, Director of the National Catholic Welfare Conference Relief Services, praised the schema for treating "in an admirable manner the searing issue of hunger, disease, ignorance and overall misery within our human family." He proposed, practically, "that the Church launch a deep and long-term campaign of education, inspiration and moral influence to promote among Christians and all men of good will a vital understanding and concern for world poverty," and he suggested that a Secretariat should be established for this purpose.

Coadjutor Archbishop Fernandes of Delhi, speaking in the name of all the bishops of India and more than 100 other Council Fathers from Asia, Africa, Europe, Latin America and Canada, called for a permanent post-conciliar commission "for the promotion of international justice and the integrated development of all peoples." Through such an organization, the Church could use its influence and moral authority "so that gradually the political, social and economic structures of all nations will be oriented, not toward war, not even defensive war, but toward the establishment of true and lasting peace."

Bishop Joseph Höffner of Münster, speaking on behalf of eighty German-speaking bishops, said that Chapter 3, on the social and economic life of man, should be completely recast. The text was too optimistic, he said, giving the impression that the sincere cooperation of men was the only thing needed for a just social order. The idea was false because "social injustice will disappear only when sin disappears."

Bishop Mariano Gaviola, of Cabanatuan City, Philippines, said that the schema seemed to endorse the theory that the overpopulation of the earth in the near future was a certainty. The Commission responsible for the schema, he said, should also consider the opposite scientific theories, which dismissed the theory of overpopulation "as something not even probable, at least if considered in relation to the land of the whole earth which has been given to man to inhabit."

Bishop Alexandre Renard of Versailles said that the first half of the schema, on "The Church and Man's Calling," was worthy of the Council, but that the second half, on "Some Problems of Special Urgency" seemed weak, and should be more modestly entitled "Notes for the Solution of Certain Difficulties," or something along those lines. The schema, moreover, appeared to display excessive optimism. The emphasis on "basic human values" gave the impression that these were hardly contaminated by original sin, and that they would lead to Christ. "Metaphysically this is not far from the truth," he added, "but psychologically these values can either open or close the door to faith."

When the discussion ended, Archbishop Garrone said that the sharp criticisms voiced by the Council Fathers had been expected. The Joint Commission would try to shorten the text, he said, and in the major revision now required, it would attempt to consider all the views presented, even though many conflicted with one another.

On October 4, while the Council Fathers were discussing the manner of the Church's dialogue with the modern world, Pope Paul was flying across the Atlantic to do the very thing that they were talking about. Immediately upon landing on American soil, he carved a cross in the sky, saying, "May the cross of blessing which we now trace over your skies and your land preserve those gifts which Christ gave you and guaranteed to you: peace, concord, freedom, justice, and above all the vision of life in the hope of immortality. God bless this land of yours!"

Some hours later, he addressed the United Nations General Assembly, and said, "We bring to this organization the suffrage of our recent predecessors, that of the entire Catholic episcopate and our own, convinced as we are that this organization represents the obligatory path of modern civilization and world peace."

The Holy Father's fearless step had the immediate effect of giving the Council Fathers in Rome renewed confidence in him. On the following day, they extended their meeting in St. Peter's so that they might be able to greet and cheer him on his return to the Vatican, and to hear an immediate report on his visit to the United Nations.

THE CHURCH'S MISSIONARY ACTIVITY

After the rejection of the propositions on the missions at the third session, the task of preparing a new schema was assigned to a five-man sub-commission of the Missions Commission, chosen by secret ballot. Father John Schütte, Superior General of the Divine Word Missionaries, who had received the most votes, was named chairman. The subcommission selected their own *periti*: Father Ratzinger, personal theologian to Cardinal Frings of Cologne, and Father Yves Congar, who were to prepare the theological groundwork of the schema.

The subcommission met from January 12 to 28, 1965, in the newly built house of the Divine Word Society overlooking Lake Nemi, south of Rome, and completed a fresh draft which was circulated to all the members and *periti* of the Commission on the Missions. Copies were also sent to Cardinals Döpfner and König for their comments, because of their great influence on the Coordinating and Theological Commissions.

A plenary session of the Commission on the Missions was held, again at Nemi, during the week beginning Monday, March 29. In the interval, a total of 131 pages of comment on the new schema had been submitted to the Commission's secretariat, including four pages each from Cardinals Döpfner and König. There was also a page of comment from Pope Paul VI, who pointed out that every conceivable requirement of a missionary had been indicated save that of obedience. The daily meetings lasted from 9:00 until 1:00, and again from 4:15 until 7:30.

According to the schedule of work for the fourth

session, the schema on the missions was to be treated in the third place, after the schemas on religious freedom and the Church in the modern world. That meant that little time would be left for the Commission to put its text into final form before the end of the Council. Consequently the aim at Nemi was to produce a schema which would prove readily acceptable to the Council Fathers. Such excellent accord was reached by the Commission that, before the week was over, each of the five chapters and the schema as a whole were approved unanimously by secret ballot.

Father Schütte requested Bishop Adolf Bolte of Fulda, one of the Commission members, to win Cardinal Döpfner's support for the new schema. This he did, and the schema passed through the Coordinating Commission without difficulty. By mid-June 1965, it was on its way to the Council Fathers around the world. Cardinal Döpfner remarked later that even a man "as critical as Father Rahner" had expressed himself emphatically as in favor of the text.

Bishop Bolte had become a member of the Commission on the Missions in an unusual way. This Commission was the only one to which no German Council Father had been elected or appointed in the first days of the Council. Archbishop Corrado Bafile, Apostolic Nuncio to Germany, expressed his disappointment, stating that representation on this Commission was owed to the German hierarchy in recognition for all that it had done for the missionary work of the Church through its charitable agencies, *Misereor* and *Adveniat*. Then in June 1963, before the second session, Archbishop Luciano Perez Platero of Burgos, Spain, died and his seat on the Commission was quietly given to Bishop Bolte. It almost seemed that Council leadership was being forced on Cardinal Frings, whose archdiocese was on the banks of the Rhine.

Pope Paul in making this appointment went counter to the usual procedure, because the replacement for Archbishop Pérez Platero, an elected member, should have been the Council Father next in line, according to the highest number of votes received in the original election. Bishop Bolte, however, had been on no list of candidates and had received no votes. In this way the first German member was added to the Commission on the Missions; the second was Father Schütte, elected to office at the end of the second session.

When the schema came up for discussion in the Council hall on October 7, 1965, the introductory report was read by Father Schütte, who called attention to the chapter on the planning of missionary activity. Here it was stated that the Sacred Congregation for the Propagation of the Faith, which was a Curial office to direct and coordinate missionary work throughout the world, must no longer be merely an administrative agency, but also an agency of dynamic direction, using scientific methods and means suited to the conditions of modern times. The future members of this Curial office, said Father Schütte, should be drawn from those who actually took part in missionary work: cardinals, patriarchs, bishops, heads of missionary orders and directors of pontifical mission aid societies. According to the schema, "these representatives will be called together at fixed times and collegially will exercise supreme control of all mission work, under the authority of the Supreme Pontiff." Father Schütte stressed the fact that each chapter of the schema had been unanimously approved by the Commission on the Missions.

At the end of his printed report, however, there appeared an amendment which was said to have originated with the Missions Commission, but which had in fact been forced upon the Commission by the Pontifical Commission for the Reorganization of the Roman Curia. According to this amendment, the aforementioned representatives would not be members of the dynamic directive body governing all missionary activity, but would instead "participate" in its deliberations. Since participation could mean giving advice without voting, this amendment represented a drastic weakening of the original text.

Surprisingly enough, the amendment imposed by the Curia went unchallenged on the Council floor. Many Council Fathers were apparently deceived into thinking that the amendment had originated with the Commission on the Missions, and therefore raised no objections. Archbishop D'Souza of Bhopal, India, said privately, however, that the whole force of the schema hinged on the paragraph which was attacked by the amendment; "if that paragraph falls," he said, "the entire schema will disappear into thin air as so many pious exhortations."

The debate was closed on October 12. On the following day, however, ten additional speakers who had obtained seventy signatures apiece addressed the assembly. Bishop Herman Westermann of Sambalpur had decided to speak strongly against the weakening amendment, but his list of signatures was presented too late, and he had to submit his paper in writing.

By a vote of 2,070 to 15, the Council Fathers showed their satisfaction with the schema as a working basis for the final document. Once again the five-man subcommission, assisted this time by ten *periti*, met at Nemi to study the 193 oral and written interventions and revise the text. Their revision was then examined by the Commission on the Missions in Rome on October 27, and again unanimously approved.

When the new version was distributed, it became evident that over 300 Council Fathers had opposed the Curia's amendment in writing, and that the Commission had therefore been in a strong enough position virtually to ignore it. While the text did not use the explicit term "members" in referring to the representatives to be added to the directive body, it stated that they would exercise "an active and decisive role in the direction" of the Curial office for the Propagation of the Faith, "in ways and under conditions to be determined by the Roman Pontiff." There was thus no longer any doubt as to the kind of authority which these "representatives" were to enjoy, and the revision was regarded as a defeat for the Pontifical Commission for the Reorganization of the Roman Curia, headed by Cardinal Roberti.

Twenty ballots were taken on the new schema between November 10 and 12, and the negative votes on the individual chapters ranged only from 6 to 13. However, a vast number of qualifications were submitted with affirmative votes, with the result that considerable revision was apparently again required. Chapter 5 on the planning of missionary activity alone received 712 qualified affirmative votes, which meant that it fell 8 votes short of the necessary two-thirds majority required for adoption. An examination of the qualifications showed that the task of revision would not be so difficult as the total number of qualifications had seemed to indicate, since hundreds of them were identical printed copies submitted by large numbers of Council Fathers.

On November 30, further balloting took place on the manner of the Commission's handling of the qualifications submitted, and the vote was favorable, 2,162 to 18. The text was then forwarded to His Holiness for his private study, and presented by him for the final formal vote at the public session of December 7, where it was adopted by 2,394 votes to 5. This was the largest number of affirmative votes ever to be cast on a Council document.

AUTHORITY OF BISHOPS OVER SCHOOLS

The schema on the pastoral office of bishops in the Church was discussed at the second session, revised in the months that followed, and was scheduled to be voted upon at the third session on November 5, 1964. In Article 35 on the relationships of bishops with religious orders, it was stated that the local bishop should have control over "the general management of Catholic schools." The official report prepared by the commission pointed out that the interpretation of these words was to be found on page 96, Number 10, in the fifth appendix of the schema "On the Care of Souls."

Those Council Fathers who took the trouble to check what Number 10 of the fifth appendix had to say saw that it gave diocesan bishops the right to inspect—besides the usual things like divine services, care of souls, preaching, religious and moral instruction, and catechetical and liturgical training—also every other possible aspect of education, like student life, discipline, studies, personnel, and even the tuition fee.

Section 2 of Number 10 extended the powers of the bishops even further, since it authorized them, either directly or through a delegate, to check whether or not "the just civil laws concerning pedagogy, hygiene, and insurance were being observed in all schools, hospitals, orphanages, and similar institutes, as well as in all religious, charitable, spiritual and temporal activities of all religious, even those who are exempt, regardless of whether these institutions are their own, or have been entrusted to them."

In short, the religious orders could continue to supply manpower and funds to their institutions, but the bishops would be the principals, supervisors, managers and directors.

To combat this legislation the Bishops' Secretariat issued a letter on November 3, 1964, signed by its Franciscan president and Jesuit vice-president, and by the Carmelite president of the Roman Union of Superiors General. This letter invited the Council Fathers to cast a negative vote on the single ballot covering Articles 33 to 35, and to sign and submit a special qualification for Article 35. Largely as a result of this letter, 172 Council Fathers cast negative votes against Articles 33 to 35, and 889 submitted qualifications on the chapter as a whole. Since the straight affirmative votes amounted only to 57 percent, the necessary two-thirds majority was not reached, and the commission had to revise the entire chapter.

The qualification on schools, prepared by the Bishops' Secretariat, was submitted by 273 Council Fathers, and had to be taken into consideration by the commission. The amendment called for the addition of the following phrase to Article 35: "The legitimate autonomy of these schools, however, should remain intact." As the text of the schema stood, these Council Fathers argued, legitimate autonomy was diminished, and this was contrary to the principle of subsidiarity, which was "necessary for the normal conduct and healthy development of Catholic schools." The qualification also asked for the deletion of the reference to Number 10 in the fifth appendix of the schema "On the Care of Souls," because here the commission was asking the Council to approve a doctrine "in a certain appendix to a certain schema which had never come up for discussion."

A long list of supporting reasons was appended to the qualification: The fine detail regarding tuition fees and insurance policies was said to be contrary to the otherwise general tenor of the decree. The Roman Curia had repeatedly been criticized for violating the principle of decentralization, and now the schema was guilty of the same violation, by indicating that everything connected with schools was to be under the bishop's control. The long pedagogical experience of religious orders was not sufficiently esteemed, and the individual character proper to each school was threatened. Finally, the principles laid down for religious in this schema were substantially different from those which the Council had laid down in the schema on the apostolate of the laity, when treating of the responsibilities and rights of adults.

When the schema was once again presented to the Council Fathers for a vote on October 6, 1965, during the fourth session, the proposed addition on legitimate autonomy had been made, and the objectionable reference to the fifth appendix had been deleted. The handling of the qualifications was then judged acceptable by a vote of 2,167 to 15, and at the public session of October 28, 1965, the Decree on the Pastoral Office of Bishops in the Church was accepted by a vote of 2,319 to 2. It was then promulgated by Pope Paul VI.

The Post-Conciliar Commission on Bishops and the Government of Dioceses, made up of the same members as the corresponding Council commission which was responsible for this decree, incorporated verbatim in its "Instruction" the text of Number 10 in the fifth appendix of the schema "On the Care of Souls," in spite of its having been defeated by ballot during the Council. The ruse was discovered shortly before the "Instruction" was to be published, and by order of Pope Paul VI publication was delayed so that the citation could be removed and a new text, in full conformity with the document as accepted by the Council, could be substituted.

PRIESTLY CELIBACY

The sensational and unfounded news reports that the Council might decide to allow Catholic priests to marry caused large sections of the world to believe that the Council would in fact make such a decision. The press and the public apparently did not realize that the Council Fathers took celibacy so much for granted that they did not even intend to deal with the subject in any of their decrees. And precisely because the press sensationalized the matter and spread so much confusion about it, the Council found itself forced to come out more strongly on celibacy than ever before in the history of the Church. The Council stressed the importance, necessity and obligation of permanent celibacy for priests of the Latin Rite, and exhorted the married Eastern Rite clergy to live model lives.

The episcopal conference of France was the first to react to the spreading confusion by issuing the following statement to the press on November 15, 1963: "Since some bishops are in favor of conferring the diaconate on married men, the public has been assured by fantastic stories that the Church is progressively moving toward a married priesthood. Realizing the confusion which such news can create in people's minds, the French episcopate declares unanimously that these assertions are completely false. Among the hundreds of interventions made at the Council, none has envisaged the possibility of any change whatsoever in the law of priestly celibacy as practiced in the Latin Church. In spite of unfortunate cases which might result, the Latin Church has no intention whatsoever of setting aside a law which, while having its origin in the Church, has its primary source in the Gospels and in the priest's complete gift of himself to Christ and the Church."

An even stronger reaction came between the second and third sessions from the bishops of Germany, Austria, Switzerland, Luxembourg and Scandinavia. At Innsbruck, in May 1964, they prepared their official comments on the propositions on priests. Since the propositions contained nothing on the law of celibacy, and since it was being called into question "by public opinion and by certain Catholics," they decided that a sound explanation of its significance should be given in order to clarify the issue for the public, and they prepared an appropriate text. At the same meeting, these Council Fathers examined the propositions on seminary training. The original schema on this subject had contained a paragraph on training for celibacy, but in the shortening process this paragraph had been dropped. The Innsbruck conference called attention to this omission and requested that the subject should be reintroduced in the form of a statement on the kind of training needed by those who were to bind themselves by the law of celibacy. This suggestion was acted upon.

The propositions on priests were on the agenda of the third session and were scheduled to come up on Tuesday, October 13, 1964. Two days earlier, the following "Declaration" appeared in *L'Osservatore Romano*:

"Stories, interviews and fantastic comments regarding the law of ecclesiastical celibacy have lately been multiplying in the press.

"We are authorized to make the following clarifications: The law is to remain intact and in full force. As for cases where sacred ordinations and their resultant obligations have been declared null and void, or where dispensations have been granted, all this has been done in conformity with canonical practice and Church discipline. There exist regular established processes which the Church is accustomed to use in examining and judging such cases. The Church determines whether certain reasons exist which prove or disprove the validity of the obligations assumed

401

by those who have approached Holy Orders. It also determines the obligations of validly ordained priests who have become unworthy to belong to the clergy.

"A judgment of nullity or an eventual dispensation from obligations, issued after rigorous examination of motives, far from weakening the law of sacred celibacy serves rather to guarantee its integrity and safeguard its prestige."

Such a statement could not, of course, have appeared in the semiofficial Vatican newspaper at that time without the knowledge and approval of Pope Paul VI.

Archbishop François Marty of Rheims, France, presented the propositions on the priesthood to the general assembly on behalf of the Commission on the Discipline of the Clergy and Faithful. Explaining why the Council Fathers had received a revised text of the propositions, the Archbishop said: "Because so many confused voices are making themselves heard today in an attack upon sacred celibacy, it has seemed most opportune expressly to confirm celibacy and to explain its exalted significance in the life and ministry of a priest."

Article 2 of the newly revised propositions exhorted "those who have promised to observe sacred celibacy, trusting in God's grace," to hold fast to it magnanimously and wholeheartedly. They should persevere faithfully in that state, rejoicing that through celibacy they were inseparably united to Christ (see 1 Cor 7:32-34), and more free to render service to the family of God.

After discussion in the Council hall, the propositions were revised by the competent Commission and returned to the Council Fathers on November 20, the day before the third session ended. The ten lines on celibacy and "perfect chastity" had been expanded to eighty, and a spirituality proper to priests was gradually being developed around this section of the schema. This might never have happened had it not been for the great confusion spread by the press and by the anti-celibacy campaigns. Yet another revision was made between the third and fourth sessions, and the schema was now so changed that it had to be discussed all over again.

Although it was clear that the Council would not seriously consider allowing priests to marry, a new suggestion was now proposed that married men might be permitted to become priests. The advocates of this proposal drew their arguments from the circumstance that the Council, at the end of the third session, had decreed that the diaconate might be conferred, with the consent of the Roman Pontiff, "upon men of more mature age, even upon those living in the married state." If married men of mature age might become deacons, they argued, why might they not also become priests?

One Council Father publicly took action in the matter early in the fourth session. He was Dutch-born Bishop Pedro Koop of Lins, Brazil, who gave wide distribution to an intervention on the subject which he planned to read in the Council hall. This intervention began: "If the Church is to be saved in our regions of Latin America, then there must be introduced among us as soon as possible a married clergy, formed from our best married men, but without introducing any change in the existing law of celibacy."

To show the need for priests, he used the same statistical argument as Bishop Kémérer of Posadas, Argentina, had used during the second session in connection with a married diaconate. He also said that the Church was obliged by divine command to evangelize and sanctify the world, and that the People of God had "a strict right to receive the Gospel and to lead a sacramental life. This is a true right, which no human law can obliterate. The Church in justice must respect it." In conclusion, he made the dire prophecy that the Church in Latin America would collapse if the Council did not "throw open the door to the possibility of conferring the sacred priesthood upon suitable laymen who have been married for at least five years."

There were recent precedents, of a sort, for the proposal, since Pope Pius XII had allowed married German Lutheran pastors who became Catholics to become priests and retain the use of their marriage rights. This practice had been continued by Pope John XXIII and Pope Paul VI.

A group of eighty-one professional men and women from around the world lent indirect support to the proposal by circulating among the Council Fathers a letter strongly advocating that married men should be allowed to become priests, and that priests should be allowed to marry. Their reasons against celibacy were the shortage of priests, their own dissatisfaction with "the manner in which priests are coming to terms with their vow of celibacy," and their claim that "priests are finding it increasingly difficult to radiate the new glory of the Church in a state of celibacy."

On October 11, two days before the new schema on the priesthood was to come up for discussion, the Secretary General interrupted the proceedings to announce that he had a special letter from Pope Paul to Cardinal Tisserant,

404

to be read to the Council Fathers. The Pope said, in his letter, that it had come to his attention that some Council Fathers intended to bring up the question of the celibacy of the clergy of the Latin Rite for discussion on the Council floor, and that he therefore wished to make known his own views in the matter, without at all limiting thereby the freedom of the individual Council Fathers.

To treat the subject in the Council hall, wrote the Pope, was equivalent to treating it in full view of the general public. This, he felt, was inexpedient, since celibacy called for such delicacy of treatment and was of such far-reaching importance for the Church. He personally was resolved that celibacy should not only be preserved in the Latin Church, but that its observance should be reinforced, since through it "priests can consecrate all their love to Christ alone and dedicate themselves totally and generously to the service of the Church and the care of souls." Here the Council Fathers interrupted the reading with warm and prolonged applause.

The Pope concluded by requesting any Council Fathers who had something special to say on the subject to do so in writing, and to submit their views to the Council Presidency. These observations would then be forwarded to him, and he promised "to examine them attentively before God." Once again there was a burst of applause throughout the Council hall.

After more discussion on the Council floor, the schema on the priesthood was referred back to the appropriate commission for revision. The voting took place on November 12 and 13. The sections on celibacy, humility, and obedience were accepted by a vote of 2,005 to 65. On the twelfth ballot, when qualified affirmative votes on this section were permitted, 123 Council Fathers asked for a modification of the text in Article 16 where the schema stated that the present Council "again approves and confirms" the law of celibacy for priests. They wanted the document to be changed to read that the Council "makes no change" in the law. Their argument was that altered conditions might prompt a future Pope to abolish celibacy. If, therefore, the Second Vatican Council reinforced the law, such a decision would have to go counter to the present Council.

This qualification might well have been prepared by Father Stanislaus Lyonnet, S.J., dean of the faculty of the Biblical Institute in Rome, who five months earlier had issued a six-page study warning that the wording of the schema would "forever close the door" to a married priesthood. His study had included all the arguments contained in the qualification, which were much like those used by Bishop Koop as well.

The Commission's reply to this qualification was very blunt: To alter the wording as requested would be "a substantial alteration of a text already approved by the Council"; moreover, it said, the reasons given in favor of such an amendment were not valid.

The Commission did, however, accept two other qualifications prepared by the Bishops' Secretariat and submitted by 332 and 289 Council Fathers respectively. According to these Council Fathers, the schema implied that "the sole or principal theological reason for celibacy" was its value as a symbol and a witness. They called this a contradiction of the Dogmatic Constitution on the Church and of the Decree on the Appropriate Renewal of the Religious Life, both of which had already been approved and promulgated. According to these two documents, they argued, the more basic reason for the observance of celibacy was that it made possible a more intimate consecration to Christ. The "symbolism" theory advanced by Cardinals Döpfner and Suenens, which had already been demoted in the scale of values set forth in those two documents as a result of previous campaigns by the Bishops' Secretariat, was also demoted in the schema on the life of priests as a result of this campaign. The Commission admitted the contradiction, and modified the text.

In its final form, the schema on the ministry and life of priests stated that "through virginity or celibacy observed for the sake of the kingdom of heaven, priests . . . profess before men that they desire to dedicate themselves in an undivided way to the task assigned to them." The schema said further that "many men today call perfect continence impossible. The more they do so, the more humbly and perseveringly priests should join with the Church in praying for the grace of fidelity. It is never denied to those who ask. . . . This most holy Synod beseeches not only priests, but all the faithful to have at heart this precious gift of priestly celibacy. Let all beg of God that he may always lavish this gift on his Church abundantly."

On December 2, the Council approved the manner in which the Commission had handled the qualifications by 2,243 votes to 11. On the final ballot in the presence of Pope Paul, at the public meeting of December 7, the result was 2,390 votes to 4. Pope Paul then promulgated the Decree on the Ministry and Life of Priests.

MARRIAGE AND BIRTH CONTROL

One of the tasks before the Council was to re-examine Church legislation on mixed marriages and the prescribed form of marriage. Cardinal Döpfner of Munich called for major changes, but was opposed by Cardinal Spellman of New York, who was supported by over 100 United States bishops; by Archbishop Heenan, supported by all the bishops of England and Wales; by Archbishop Conway of Armagh, Ireland, who spoke for more than eighty bishops of various countries; and by Cardinal Gilroy of Sydney, Australia. All these prelates stressed the benefits derived from the existing legislation, and the harm that might result from the legislation favored by Cardinal Döpfner. Seeing his measure defeated on the Council floor, the Cardinal Moderator after one day's debate called upon the Council to renounce its right to treat the matter any further, and instead to transmit it immediately to the Pope for appropriate action. The proposal was adopted, at the last business meeting of the third session (November 20, 1964), by a vote of 1,592 to 427.

The desired decree, however, did not appear until after the Council, on March 18, 1966, and it was signed by Cardinal Ottaviani. It altered the legislation but not substantially, as Cardinal Döpfner had wished, and it was clearly a victory for the English-speaking bishops. Had they been as well organized throughout the Council as they were on this issue, the Second Vatican Council might have taken an altogether different course.

The doctrinal aspect of marriage was dealt with in the schema on the Church in the modern world, and came

up for discussion during the third session. The Moderator, Cardinal Agagianian, announced on October 28,
1964, that "some points" had been reserved for the Pope's
special commission on birth control. Those points were,
in particular, the progesterone pill, as Archbishop John
Dearden of Detroit officially announced on the following day and, in general, "the problem of birth control,"
as Cardinal Suenens put it in an intervention a year later.
The Council Fathers were free to submit observations on
these "points" in writing, and were given the assurance
that the Pope's special commission would give them serious consideration.

On October 29, 1964, the debate opened on Article
21, "The Sanctity of Marriage and the Family." Cardinal
Léger of Montreal said that many theologians believed
that the difficulties regarding the doctrine of marriage
had their origin in an inadequate exposition of the purposes of marriage. He advocated that fecundity should be
called a duty pertaining to the state of matrimony as a
whole, rather than to an individual act. "It is altogether
necessary," he said, "for human conjugal love—I speak of
human love, which therefore involves soul and body—
to be presented as constituting a true purpose of marriage, as something good in itself, having its own needs
and laws."

He was pleased that the schema avoided applying the
expressions "primary purpose" to procreation and "secondary purpose" to conjugal love. But the avoidance of words
was of little use, he said, if afterwards the schema did not
refer to conjugal love except as related to fecundity. The
schema should affirm, he maintained, that the intimate

marital union also had conjugal love as its true purpose, and that consequently the marriage act was "legitimate even when not directed toward procreation."

17. B

Cardinal Suenens also spoke on the first day of debate, and outlined the doctrinal, ethical and scientific norms which, he said, should be kept in mind by the Pope's special commission on birth control. That commission, he said, would have to "examine whether we have kept in perfect balance the various aspects of the Church's doctrine on marriage." Perhaps, he suggested, so much stress had been placed on the words of Scripture, "Be fruitful and multiply," that gradually another phrase, which was also the word of God—"and the two become one flesh"—had been disregarded. Each was a central truth, said the Cardinal, and each was contained in Scripture. They should therefore serve to clarify one another. One of the Cardinal's many proposals was that Pope Paul should reveal the names of the members of his special commission, so that the entire People of God might be able to send them their views on marriage and birth control.

Cardinal Ottaviani spoke on the following day. "I am not pleased," he said, "with the statement in the text that married couples may determine the number of children they are to have. Never has this been heard of in the Church." He was the eleventh son in a family of twelve children, he said. "My father was a laborer, and the fear of having many children never entered my parents' minds, because they trusted in Providence." He concluded his brief statement by expressing his amazement "that yesterday in the Council it should have been said that there was doubt whether a correct stand had been taken hitherto on the principles governing marriage. Does this mean that the inerrancy of the Church will be called into question? Or was not the Holy Spirit with his Church in past centuries to illumine minds on this point of doctrine?"

Bishop Hervás y Benet of Ciudad Real, Spain, said that the schema spoke "little and much too timidly about supernatural faith and confidence in Divine Providence, about love and acceptance of the Cross, which ought to illumine Christian prudence. We are not here to compose a philosophical and hedonistic document, or one that is merely technical or scientific, but one that is Christian." He said that the parents of large Christian families should be held in honor, and asked that those who had drafted the schema should keep this in mind in their revision. Nor should they pass over in silence "what the modern sciences of psychology and pedagogy had to say in praise and in favor of large families." He received a warm round of applause.

Pope Paul VI was so distressed by Cardinal Suenens' intervention of October 29 that he requested the Cardinal to come to see him. Some days later, on November 7, Cardinal Suenens interrupted the debate on the schema on the missions to deny publicly that he had questioned authentic Church teaching on marriage, and to state that all matters pertaining to the study conducted by the Pope's special commission on birth control clearly "depended solely upon his supreme authority."

Archbishop Adrianus Djajasepoetra of Djakarta, Indonesia, speaking on behalf of bishops from many nations, said in the Council hall on November 20, 1964, that the Council did not take adequate account of different cultures. Marriage, he felt, should be described as a sacred and human community of life instituted by God for the founding of a family. Conjugal love should not be given undue primacy, he said, because marriages often took place between persons who hardly knew each other, at the bidding of parents or relatives. In those cases, love was a gradual fruit of the marriage. It should be remembered, he said, that the founding of a new family and the continuation of a particular group was sometimes the primary intention in marriage.

After the third session, the schema was so thoroughly revised that it had to be debated once again. Auxiliary Bishop Kazimierz Majdanski of Wloclawek, speaking on September 29, 1965, at the fourth session, on behalf of the bishops of Poland, said that the modern world "abhors the bloodshed of war, but looks with indifference on the destruction of unborn human life." Pointing out that the number of abortions annually exceeded the total number of persons killed in World War II, he called for a solemn declaration by the Council on the absolute inviolability of all innocent human life, asking that those practicing abortion be denounced as guilty of homicide.

Another revision was prepared as soon as the debate ended, and was distributed on November 12. This new version could be interpreted as leaving it to the spouses to decide whether or not to use artificial contraceptives to limit the size of their families, provided their ultimate aim was the fostering of conjugal love.

The schema containing this doctrine now totaled 152 pages, and was distributed to the Council Fathers in two sections on Friday and Saturday, November 12 and 13.

Thirty-three ballots were to be taken the following Monday, Tuesday, and Wednesday. With so many momentous issues at stake in this schema, the Council Fathers perhaps should have spent the weekend examining the revised text. Instead, 500 of them left for Florence on chartered buses shortly after midday on Saturday, November 13, for an all-expenses-paid weekend to celebrate the Seventh Centenary of the Birth of Dante, Italy's renowned poet. Late Sunday night, they returned to Rome and early Monday morning they began voting, some of them frankly admitting that they had had no time to examine the text.

The chapter on marriage as a whole was approved by the general assembly by 1,596 votes to 72, and 484 affirmative votes with qualifications. The subcommission which processed the qualifications on this chapter ignored any major amendments, stating that these would substantially alter a text which had already received more than the required two-thirds majority.

On November 25, Pope Paul took action and through his Secretary of State sent four special amendments on the marriage section to the joint commission. Each commission member was given a copy, but beforehand the *periti* were asked to leave the room. Tension immediately mounted and Cardinal Léger sprang to his feet in angry protest. When some doubt arose as to the binding character of the amendments, the members were informed by another letter on the following day that they were not free to reject the amendments, but only to determine their phrasing. That day the tension was somewhat relieved when the *periti* were once again allowed to attend the meeting.

The first of these amendments called for the insertion of the two words "artificial contraceptives" among the "deformations" detracting from the dignity of conjugal love and family life, such as polygamy, divorce, and free love. At the same time, the Pope called for a precise footnote reference to the two pages in Pope Pius XI's encyclical *Casti Connubii*, where the use of artificial contraceptives was condemned. The commission excused itself from introducing "artificial contraceptives," used instead "illicit practices against human generation," and omitted the reference to *Casti Connubii*.

The second called for the deletion of the word "also" from the statement that the procreation of children was "also" a purpose of marriage, because in the context this word made it appear that procreation was a secondary purpose of marriage, and conjugal love a primary purpose. This was the opposite of the Church's traditional teaching, and the Council had pledged itself to avoid this controversy. The amendment also called for the insertion of the following sentence: "Children are the supreme gift of marriage and contribute very substantially to the welfare of their parents." The commission adopted both suggestions.

The third called for the substitution of the words "it is not lawful" for the words "should not" in the prohibition to "sons of the Church" to use methods of regulating procreation "which have been or may be found blameworthy by the teaching authority of the Church." A footnote was to be added here, calling attention both to *Casti Connubii* and to Pius XII's allocution to midwives, which reiterated the teaching of that encyclical, stating that the prescription against artificial contraceptives was derived from "natural and divine law."

The joint commission adopted this third amendment in substance, but failed to refer to the statements of Popes Pius XI and XII as the "two most outstanding documents on this subject," as Pope Paul wished. It further added a reference of its own, the allocution of Pope Paul VI to the College of Cardinals on June 23, 1964, in which he had given the cardinals a progress report on the work of his special commission on birth control. "Let us now state with all frankness," he had said at the time, "that we do not yet have a sufficient motive for considering as outdated—and therefore as not binding—the norms laid down by Pope Pius XII in this matter; therefore they must be considered as binding, at least as long as we do not feel obliged in conscience to modify them. . . . And it seems opportune to recommend that no one, for the present, should take it upon himself to make any pronouncement at variance with the norm in force." By citing this allocution of Pope Paul, the joint commission—and subsequently the entire Council—implicitly confirmed the traditional teaching of the Church in this matter.

The fourth and final amendment proposed by Pope Paul referred to the temptation to married couples to use artificial contraceptives, and even abortion. It called for the insertion of a sentence to the effect that, in order that the spouses might overcome such temptations, it was "altogether necessary that they sincerely practice conjugal chastity." This amendment was retained in substance, but was inserted in another part of the text.

According to the Pope's directives, the amended text was submitted to him before being sent to the printer.

On December 3, 1965, the final revision of the schema was distributed to the Council Fathers. At once there was much agitation behind the scenes because the joint commission, contrary to Pope Paul's wish, had failed to indicate in a footnote the specific pages of *Casti Connubii* where artificial contraceptives were condemned. Before the voting started on December 4, a special announcement was made on instructions from the Pope. The Council Fathers were asked to note that the page references in one of the footnotes had been omitted, and that, in voting on the text, they must understand that they were voting on that footnote as well, together with the specific page references. They were also informed that the page references would be indicated in the official text which would be presented for the final and formal vote on December 7.

The chapter on marriage and the family was adopted by 2,047 votes to 155 on December 4, and the schema as a whole was formally adopted at the public session on December 7 by a vote of 2,309 to 75. It was then promulgated by Pope Paul VI.

ATHEISM AND COMMUNISM

On December 3, 1963, the day before the second session ended, Archbishop Geraldo Sigaud of Diamantina, Brazil, personally presented to Cardinal Cicognani petitions addressed to Pope Paul and signed by more than 200 Council Fathers from forty-six countries. These called for a special schema in which "the Catholic social doctrine would be set forth with great clarity, and the errors of Marxism, socialism, and communism would be refuted on philosophical, sociological and economic grounds."

There was no reply from the Pope, but eight months later, on August 6, 1964, he published his first encyclical, *Ecclesiam suam*. In it he called for dialogue with atheistic communism, even though—as he said—there were reasons enough which compelled him, his predecessors and everyone with religious values at heart "to condemn the ideological systems which deny God and oppress the Church, systems which are often identified with economic, social and political regimes."

The German-speaking and Scandinavian bishops immediately reacted to the encyclical, declaring in their official remarks on the Church in the modern world schema that it was "probably desirable" to have a "more distinct treatment in the schema of the problem of atheism, and of dialogue with it."

On October 21, 1964, during the third session, the section of the schema dealing with atheism—it carefully avoided the word communism—came up for discussion. Cardinal Suenens, after stating that it did not give lengthy enough treatment to the modern phenomenon of militant atheism in its various forms, called for an investigation on why so many men deny God and attack the faith.

Archbishop Paul Yu Pin of Nanking, China, speaking two days later in the name of 70 Council Fathers, asked for the addition of a new chapter on atheistic communism. The Council must not neglect to discuss it, he said, "because communism is one of the greatest, most evident and most unfortunate of modern phenomena." It had to be treated in order to satisfy the expectations of all peoples, "especially those who groan under the yoke of communism and are forced to endure indescribable sorrows unjustly."

Josef Cardinal Beran, exiled archbishop of Prague, residing in Rome, received a Czechoslovakian newspaper clipping which boasted that communists had succeeded in infiltrating every commission at the Vatican Council.

On April 7, 1965, while the schema was being revised, Pope Paul founded a Secretariat for Non-Believers, with the purpose of fostering dialogue with atheists. Cardinal König of Vienna, who had frequently served in a liaison capacity for the Vatican with the governments of communist countries, was placed in charge.

By September 14, 1965, the opening date of the fourth session, a revision of the atheism section in the schema on the Church in the modern world was in the hands of the Council Fathers, but once again it contained no explicit reference to communism. The silence prompted the circulation of a letter, dated September 29, 1965, signed by 25 bishops, giving ten reasons why Marxist communism should be treated by the Council. A petition in the form of a written intervention requesting such treatment accompanied the letter, which was widely distributed among the Council Fathers.

The letter maintained that eventual silence by the Council on communism, after the latest Popes and the Holy Office had said so much about it, would be "equivalent to disavowing all that has been said and done up till now." Just as Pope Pius XII was at present being publicly reprimanded—but unjustly—for having kept silent on the Jews, the letter warned, so one could well imagine that "tomorrow the Council will be reproved—and justly so—for its silence on communism, which will be taken as a sign of cowardice and conniving." This lengthy letter had been written by Bishop Carli and was distributed by Archbishops Sigaud and Lefebvre, but their names were not included among the 25 signatures. They had purposely withheld them because there was great antagonism against them, both in the liberal camp and in the press.

While making a routine phone call to check out various news sources, I learned from Archbishop Sigaud that 450 Council Fathers had signed this written intervention prepared by the International Group of Fathers. On October 20, 1965, I distributed a news bulletin on this, and three of Rome's largest daily newspapers, *Il Giornale d'Italia, Il Messaggero* and *Il Tempo*, promptly ran front page stories.

The joint commission responsible for the schema on the Church in the modern world distributed its new revision on Saturday, November 13, but again it contained no mention of communism in the text. Furthermore, the interventions signed by the 450 Council Fathers asking for explicit treatment of communism were not referred to in the official report prepared by this commission.

That same day Bishop Carli sent a letter of protest to the Council Presidency, responsible for the enforcement of Council rules, and copies of it to the Cardinal Moderators, General Secretariat and Administrative Tribunal, for their information. He called attention to the fact that "450 Council Fathers," and himself among them, had presented "a certain amendment to the General

Secretariat within the prescribed time," which the commission in making its revision had completely ignored. After quoting several directives from the Rules of Procedure, he stated that they clearly signified that "all amendments must be printed and communicated to the Council Fathers, so that they can decide by vote whether they wish to admit or reject each one."

He also labeled as illegal the action taken by the joint commission, and charged that "this manner of admitting or rejecting amendments of the Council Fathers—and, in our case, even without giving reasons for doing so—turns a commission of no more than 30 persons into a judicial body against which there is no appeal." And although the Council Fathers together with the Supreme Pontiff were in reality the true judges, for all practical purposes they were merely being asked by the commission to state whether or not they were pleased with the decisions taken by the commission. This made it appear, he said, that "the commission members, rather than the Council Fathers, constitute the Council."

As a result of this formal protest, Cardinal Tisserant launched an official investigation.

Since the joint commission had ignored the interventions with the 450 signatures of Council Fathers representing 86 countries, the International Group of Fathers hastily prepared the same amendment in the form of a qualification, since submitting affirmative votes with qualifications would be the last opportunity to amend the text. By letter, dated Saturday, November 13, Council Fathers were invited to sign and submit the qualification during the voting on Monday, November 15. The qualification did not ask for a new condemnation of communism, as the press reported, but only for "a solemn reaffirmation by the Council of the long-standing doctrine of the Church on this matter."

Distribution of the qualification, however, was severely handicapped, since this was the weekend on which 500 Council Fathers journeyed to Florence in chartered buses to participate in the Dante celebration.

On November 15, while the Council Fathers were voting on the atheism section, I distributed to the press a news release explaining that the 450 signed interventions had disappeared and therefore the International Group of Fathers was making a new try at having its voice heard by submitting a qualification, that morning, nearly identical to the intervention.

Immediately after the morning meeting Father Roberto Tucci, S.J., one of the *periti* on the joint commission, gave his usual briefing to the Italian reporters and was asked by them what had happened to the written interventions supported by 450 Council Fathers. "I can confirm the fact that the amendment on communism did not reach either the members of the commission or us *periti* who are part of the commission," he replied. "There is no intrigue here of any sort; perhaps the petition ran into a red light along the way and was stopped." Father Tucci's remark made my story, distributed only an hour earlier, all the more topical, and within 24 hours it appeared on the front pages of *Il Giornale d'Italia, Il Messaggero, Il Tempo, Il Popolo, Il Secolo, Momento-Sera* and *L'Avvenire d'Italia*, and on the inside pages of *Il Giorno, La Stampa, Paese Sera, Corriere della Sera*, and *L'Unità* (communist daily).

On November 16, Mr. Gian Franco Svidercoschi, using the pseudonym "Helveticus," reported in *Il Tempo* that a "prelate" who was an "official" of the joint commission had stated that the communism intervention had arrived "late," and consequently had not been taken into consideration. This conformed to the story given to the press by Father Tucci, and made the International Group of Fathers responsible for the negligence, since it apparently had not transmitted the signed interventions to the General Secretariat on time.

On November 17, Archbishop Sigaud released a statement to the press, stating that he and Archbishop Lefebvre had personally delivered the signed interventions to the General Secretariat at noon on October 9, 1965, within the prescribed time limit. This now shifted the responsibility to the General Secretariat.

On November 18, further details were published in *Il Tempo* by Mr. Svidercoschi, who meanwhile had done some checking. He reported that the General Secretariat had received the interventions within the time limit on Saturday, October 9, had at once telephoned the secretary of the joint commission to inform him that the amendments had arrived, but stated that they would be held over by the General Secretariat until Monday so that the numerous signatures could be checked. This placed responsibility back on the joint commission, and specifically on its secretariat, since—as Mr. Svidercoschi pointed out—the excuse originally given by that secretariat about the interventions having arrived "late" was no longer valid.

Cardinal Tisserant had in the meantime conducted his

own investigation and brought his findings to the attention of Pope Paul.

From four different sources I learned that the person who had withheld the interventions from the members of the joint commission was the commission's secretary, Monsignor Achille Glorieux, of Lille, France, who held nearly half a dozen Vatican positions and had once worked on the staff of *L'Osservatore Romano*. He was secretary likewise of the Commission on the Apostolate of the Laity.

Someone else on the joint commission later admitted that this commission had tabled other interventions as well, but that it had been "stupid" to sidetrack these on communism.

On November 23, at noon, I issued a news release describing Monsignor Glorieux's role in the matter and personally delivered copies of it to the reporters at the Vatican Press Office. As was to be expected, it came to the attention of Vatican authorities.

That afternoon at five o'clock Pope Paul VI received in audience the bishops of Latin America on the occasion of the tenth anniversary of the Episcopal Council of Latin America (CELAM) and delivered an address in which he called attention to "Marxist atheism." He identified it as a dangerous, prevalent and most harmful infiltrating force in the economic and social life of Latin America, and stated that it considered "violent revolution as the only means for solving problems."

On November 24, the morning newspapers ran front page stories on the French prelate who had acted as a "red light" for the interventions on communism, and that same morning the Pope sent the joint commission an order to insert a footnote on the Church's teaching on communism. The commission acceded and cited the encyclicals of Pius XI, Pius XII, John XXIII, and Paul VI; and the words, "just as it has already done," were inserted in the schema as follows: "In her loyal devotion to God and men, the Church cannot cease repudiating, just as it has already done, sorrowfully but as firmly as possible, those poisonous doctrines and actions which contradict reason and the common experience of humanity, and dethrone man from his native excellence." The added words, as the joint commission explicitly stated in its official report to the general assembly, were introduced in order to allude "to the condemnations of communism and Marxism made by the Supreme Pontiffs."

When making his official report to the general assembly in the name of the joint commission, Archbishop Garrone of Toulouse was obliged by Council authorities to make a public admission of negligence for the sake of setting straight the record. He stated that the interventions on communism had "indeed reached the offices of our commission within the proper time, but were not examined when they should have been, because unintentionally they had not been transmitted to the commission members."

However, there was immediately evident a confusion of numbers in the various reports prepared by the joint commission. Archbishop Garrone said that 332 interventions had arrived on time. Another report set the total figure at 334, but stated that only 297 of them had arrived on time. When Archbishop Sigaud went to the Council archivist to check the signatures personally, since he had 435 of the

450 names on file, he was told that the original documents were not yet available and that the published figures were to be considered official. But the joint commission had published conflicting figures, and there was no indication which of these were "official."

Although pleased over the addition of the new words in the body of the text, and over the citation of all the important encyclicals concerning communism in the footnote, Archbishop Sigaud said: "There is a difference between carrying a hat in your pocket, and wearing it on your head."

On December 3, the International Group of Fathers distributed one last letter to the 800 Council Fathers on its mailing list. The letter gave five reasons why the sections of the Church in the modern world schema touching communism, marriage and war were still unsatisfactory, and closed with an appeal for a negative vote on the entire schema, because it was "no longer possible to obtain partial amendments."

The drive, however, drew little response, and only 131 Council Fathers cast negative votes on the atheism section. But the International Group of Fathers remained steadfast, and was largely responsible for the 75 negative votes cast against the Pastoral Constitution on the Church in the Modern World during the final and formal vote of December 7, 1965.

WAR AND NUCLEAR WEAPONS

War and nuclear weapons were treated in Articles 84 and 85 of the revised schema on the Church in the modern world, which was distributed to the Council Fathers on

425

November 12, 1965, late in the fourth session. Archbishop Philip M. Hannan, of New Orleans, Louisiana, was dissatisfied with the two articles and began to prepare amendments. He charged that the section on war was "immature and full of errors," and claimed that, if the text were to be published in its present form, it would become "an object of ridicule in the world's halls of political and military science."

Article 84 was incorrect, he said, when it stated that "any use" of nuclear weapons was "absolutely illicit," since there were several nuclear weapons with a very precise and limited field of destruction. The schema also erred in this article, he said, when it declared that it was "unreasonable to consider war as an apt means of restoring violated rights." Since a military invasion violates the rights of a nation, and since the only means of repelling such an invasion is through the use of arms by war, it therefore followed that war was "an apt and necessary means of restoring violated rights."

Article 85 erred, he said, in that it condemned a nation "for possessing nuclear weapons," and it further erred in stating that "the production and possession of nuclear arms aggravates the causes of war." The causes of war were injustice and unjust aspirations, "not the possession of nuclear arms, which under proper control can prevent injustice and aggression." The same article ignored the fact that "the possession of nuclear arms by some nations had protected extensive areas of the world from possible aggression." Archbishop Hannan had called these items to the attention of the joint commission a year earlier, but his minority opinion had been ignored.

On November 22, 1965, he discussed with Cardinal Shehan, of Baltimore, Maryland, the contents of a letter which he was preparing on Articles 84 and 85, and which he planned to send to all Council Fathers. Cardinal Shehan inquired about the stand of the German hierarchy in the matter, but Archbishop Hannan was not aware of it. In the days that followed, the Archbishop's letter was signed by the following prelates: Cardinals Spellman and Shehan; the archbishops of Washington, D.C., Mexico City, Durban, Hobart, and Parana; the Maronite archbishop of Tyre, Lebanon; and the Franciscan bishop of Tlalnepantla, Mexico.

On December 2, the latest revision of the schema was distributed to the Council Fathers, containing the final qualifications introduced by the joint commission, and the vote was announced for Saturday, two days later. That night, a dozen nuns printed and folded the circular letters and stuffed them into envelopes until 1:00 A.M. There were French, Italian and Spanish translations of the English letter, and the envelopes, already addressed and divided by streets, were individually marked to indicate what language edition was to be inserted. These same nuns had repeatedly assisted with similar drives in the course of the Council.

At 7:30 A.M. on Friday, December 3, a fleet of six cars began delivering copies of the letter to the residences of more than 2000 Council Fathers. The nuns drove one of the cars, and eight other nuns delivered letters on foot to areas where parking space was not available. By 4:30 that afternoon the work was done.

Archbishop Hannan's letter invited the Council Fathers

to cast a negative vote on December 4 on the chapter about war and nuclear weapons, and suggested that the entire schema as well should receive a negative vote, if the "errors" described in his letter were not corrected. He proposed that the document, if rejected, should be transferred to the Synod of Bishops for further study, correction and promulgation.

The Archbishop objected to Article 80 (formerly 84), which stated that "those who possess modern nuclear weapons are provided with a kind of occasion for perpetrating just such abominations" as "the indiscriminate destruction of entire cities or extensive areas along with their population." He also objected to Article 81 (formerly 85), which bluntly stated that, because of the accumulation of nuclear arms, "the causes of war, instead of being eliminated, threaten to become gradually worse."

In his letter he maintained that these sentences ignored the fact that the possession of nuclear arms had preserved freedom for "a very large portion of the world." This defense from aggression, he said, was "not a crime, but a great service." It was as illogical to say that nuclear arms were a cause of war and dissension, he said, "as to say that the law and police force in a city cause the crime and disorder in a city." The letter warned that "the inclusion of these sentences and thoughts in the schema" would certainly hurt "the cause of freedom in the world," and emphasized that they contradicted that part of the address of Pope Paul VI to the United Nations in which he affirmed a nation's right of self-defense. According to Archbishop Hannan, there was "no adequate self-defense for the largest nations in today's world" unless they possessed nuclear weapons.

On Saturday, December 4, the Council Fathers were asked to indicate whether they were pleased with the way in which the joint commission had handled the qualifications on war and nuclear weapons. That same morning word was spread in the Council hall that Cardinal Shehan had signed the letter "without reading it," and that he would not cast a negative vote as requested in the letter. Although the first part of the rumor was false, he actually had changed his mind about how to vote.

Two priests had assisted Archbishop Hannan, and they now suggested that if there were several hundred votes that morning against the chapter on war and nuclear weapons, he would be in an advantageous position and could go directly to the Holy Father, point out the great dissatisfaction among the Council Fathers, and propose how the text might be altered before the overall vote scheduled for Monday morning. But as it happened, the returns on the chapter were not announced until Monday, so this plan fell through.

On December 4, still another rumor began making the rounds. This one claimed that Pope Paul had sent Cardinal Spellman a telegram, asking him to do his best to stop the campaign launched by Archbishop Hannan, and to withdraw his support.

On Sunday, December 5, the joint commission published a letter signed by Bishop Joseph Schröffer, of Eichstätt, Germany, chairman of the subcommission responsible for the chapter on war and nuclear arms, and by Archbishop Garrone, who in the Council hall had read the report on the schema in the name of the joint commission. Their letter stated that the reasons given in "a page signed by Cardinal Spellman and nine other Council Fathers" for casting negative votes against the schema section dealing with war were not valid, because they were based on "an erroneous interpretation of the text."

Archbishop Hannan, taking into account the impression conveyed to the average reader, for whom the pastoral constitution was intended, had stated that in the schema "the possession of nuclear arms is condemned as immoral." The rebuttal of Bishop Schröffer and Archbishop Garrone claimed that "nowhere in Articles 80 and 81 is the possession of nuclear arms condemned as immoral." The words of the text were selected with a purpose, they said, and must be accurately understood. Nor was it denied that freedom could be temporarily preserved through the possession and accumulation of nuclear weapons. It was only denied that the arms race was "a safe way to preserve lasting peace." Nor was it stated that nuclear arms were "causes of war." The letter went on to say that the schema did not contradict "the right, affirmed in the context, of some nation defending itself with violence against unjust aggression."

In addition to the interpretation given by the joint commission in this letter, there was the official comment contained in the reports to the general assembly. These now stated that Article 81 did not intend "to condemn nuclear weapons indiscriminately," and that the text in no way intended to impose "an obligation of unilateral destruction of atomic weapons." These statements, and mention of the right to self-defense, were due to a large extent to the campaign conducted by Archbishop Hannan.

The rumor about the Pope's sending Cardinal Spellman a telegram was still circulating among the Council Fathers on Sunday, so that evening I telephoned Archbishop Hannan to ask if it was true. "I spoke with Cardinal Spellman today," he replied, "and he gave me no indication that he had changed his mind. If he did receive such a telegram, I should think that I would be the first one to learn about it."

Late that Sunday night a Curia cardinal informed some bishops that "over 400 negative votes" had been cast against the chapter on war and nuclear weapons in the voting on Saturday. The same cardinal stated that Cardinal Cicognani was telling members of the Roman Curia to advise as many Council Fathers as possible to vote against the schema on the following day.

The vote on the schema as a whole took place on Monday, December 6. Before the ballot was taken, it was announced that the chapter on war and nuclear weapons had received 483 negative votes on Saturday. Considering themselves beaten, many of those who had voted against the chapter now voted in favor of the schema as a whole, and the text was accepted by a vote of 2,111 to 251.

As the Council Fathers poured out of St. Peter's that morning, I waited at the exit used by the cardinals. After Cardinal Spellman was helped into his car, I went up to his secretary and asked, "Is it true that His Eminence received a telegram from the Pope, asking him to withdraw support from Archbishop Hannan's proposal?" Unhesitatingly he replied, "No, it is not true at all."

When *L'Osservatore Romano* appeared on the newsstand several hours later, it carried word that Pope Paul had already decided that the Pastoral Constitution on the

Church in the Modern World merited his approval, and would be voted on and promulgated at the Public Session on the following day, December 7.

INVITATION TO REDISCOVER GOD

It was Pope Paul VI's special wish that there should be, before the end of the Council, an evening prayer service for promoting Christian unity, attended by the Council Fathers and the observer delegates. The time and place decided upon was Saturday, December 4, 1965, in the basilica of St. Paul Outside-the-Walls. The Pope conducted the service himself; psalms were sung, and there were Scripture readings by a French Catholic, an American Methodist and a Greek Orthodox.

In his address, Pope Paul said, "Your departure saddens us now, and creates a solitude which we did not experience before the Council. We would like to see you with us always." There were more prayers at the tomb of St. Paul, and then Pope Paul held a reception for the observer delegates in the adjacent Benedictine monastery, where his predecessor had made the first announcement of the Council.

Rt. Rev. Dr. John Moorman, leader of the Anglican delegation, addressed the Pope on behalf of the observer delegates and guests, whose number had risen to 103 at the fourth session. "Never once in the four years," he said, "have we felt any resentment at our presence. On the contrary, we have always been led to suppose that our presence has, in more ways than one, contributed to the success of the Council in the great task of reform to which it has set its hand." And he added, "We believe that the days of mutual fear, of rigid exclusiveness and of arrogant self-sufficiency on either side are passing away. The road to unity will indeed be long and difficult; but it may be of comfort to Your Holiness to know that, as a result of our presence here as observers, you will have a company of more than 100 men . . . who, as they go all over the world, will try to carry to the Churches something of the spirit of friendship and tolerance which they have seen in the hall of St. Peter's. Our work as observers is not done. I would like you, dear Holy Father, to think of us as your friends—and indeed as your messengers—as we go our respective ways."

The Pope expressed his joy and consolation at these words. "They give us hope," he said, "that, God willing, we shall meet again. And our meeting will always be in Christ our Lord." As a remembrance of the Council, he gave each observer a tiny bronze bell and a Latin certificate. After being introduced to each of the observers and guests by Cardinal Bea, the Pope returned to the Vatican.

On Monday, December 6, each Council Father received from the Pope a simple gold ring symbolizing the close bonds of charity existing between the Pope and the bishops. Each also received a Latin certificate attesting that he had taken part in the Council.

That same morning the Secretary General read a Bull issued by Pope Paul, proclaiming an extraordinary Jubilee to extend from January 1 to May 29, Pentecost Sunday, 1966. Then the Secretary General expressed his thanks in Latin verse for the cooperation he had received from the Council Fathers. Cardinal Suenens, as Moderator for the day, expressed the Council's thanks to all officials at different levels who had in any way contributed to the organization and conduct of the numerous meetings. When he mentioned Archbishop Felici, the applause was exceptionally prolonged. More than any other official, the Secretary General had won the hearts of the Council Fathers. Despite the weight of administrative work resting on his shoulders, his wit and Latin verse had repeatedly enlivened the meetings of the general assembly, and his witticisms were often repeated by the Council Fathers.

That afternoon, *L'Osservatore Romano* published the long-awaited decree of Pope Paul VI on the reorganization of the Roman Curia. "There is no doubt," read the decree, "that the reorganization must begin with the Congregation of the Holy Office, since the most important business of the Roman Curia is given to it, namely, whatever concerns the doctrine of faith and morals, and other matters intimately connected with this doctrine." The name of the Holy Office was changed to "Sacred Congregation for the Doctrine of the Faith," and numerous other changes were indicated, including the abolition of a special section in the Sacred Congregation responsible for censoring books.

On December 7, at the public session, Pope Paul delivered a long address. He said that "perhaps never before, so much as on this occasion, has the Church felt the need to know, to draw near to, to understand, to penetrate, to serve and to evangelize the society in which it lives. . . . Errors were condemned indeed, because charity demanded this no less than did truth. But for the persons themselves there was only warning, respect and love." The ultimate religious meaning of the Council, he said, might be summed up as "a pressing and friendly invitation to mankind of today to rediscover God in fraternal love."

That morning, on the 544th and last ballot, the Pastoral Constitution on the Church in the Modern World was approved by a vote of 2,309 to 75. It thus became the sixteenth and last Council document to be officially approved and promulgated by the Second Vatican Council. The documents on religious freedom, missionary activity, and the ministry and life of priests were also approved and promulgated that morning.

The closing ceremonies took place on the following day, December 8, 1965, on the expansive front steps of St. Peter's, where special scaffolding and seats had been erected for the occasion.

The three-hour proceedings began with Mass celebrated alone by the Holy Father. Then gifts from him totalling $90,000 were announced for charitable institutions in Palestine, Argentina, India, Pakistan and Cambodia. The Pope also blessed the cornerstone of a church to be erected in Rome as a memorial to the Council, to be called "Mary, Mother of the Church."

Joseph Cardinal Cardijn, founder of the movement of the Young Christian Workers in Belgium in 1925, had proposed earlier in the fourth session that a special paragraph on youth, another on workers and still another on the people of developing nations should be included in the opening pages of the pastoral constitution on the Church in the modern world. Much earlier, on January 4, 1964, Bishop Hengsbach of Essen had stated in *America* that he would consider it extremely important "that the basic results of the Council be summed up in perhaps four or five messages." One of those messages, he said, "might perhaps be addressed to those who rule, who bear the highest responsibility for men's destiny."

The ideas of these two Council Fathers were partially fulfilled in a series of eight special messages read on the closing day of the Council. The first one, read by Pope Paul himself, was directed to the Council Fathers: "The hour of departure and separation has sounded. In a few moments you will leave the Council assembly and go out to meet mankind and bring the good news of the Gospel of Christ and of the renewal of his Church, at which we have been working together for four years." After his message, seven Council Fathers approached the microphone in turn and read messages in French to rulers, intellectuals, laborers, artists, women, youth, and the sick and poor. A representative from each group went up to the papal throne to receive from Pope Paul the text of the message after it was read. The text that had been read for "the poor, the sick and all those who suffer" was handed to a blind man, Mr. Francesco Politi, who mounted the steps with his seeing-eye dog.

Seated at the right hand of the Pope during the ceremony was Cardinal Ottaviani. Early in the Council he had called himself a watchdog who by profession had to guard the truth. His task was greater now, because he had new truths to guard in addition to the old ones. As he looked back over the Council, he could not but remember the abuse that had been heaped upon his head in the Council hall and in the press. But there were also brighter moments, like the day in early October during the fourth session when he was applauded loudly and long for proposing that "from among all nations of the world there be formed one World Republic, in which there would no longer be found that strife which exists among nations. Instead, the whole world would be at peace."

Also seated near the Pope were the four Cardinal Moderators. Each of them had conducted the meetings an average of 34 times. There were those who thought that they had gone too fast, and there were those who thought that they had gone too slow. There were some who had suspected them of partiality, and of using their authority for the promotion of their own views. Being Moderators had not been an easy task. But, except for them, and except for their determination to move ahead, the Second Vatican Council could not have ended on this day.

Almost no one in the vast assembly, after the Pope, had been more influential in the passage of Council legislation than Cardinal Frings. Except for the organization which he had inspired and led, the Council might never have operated efficiently at all. He had leaned heavily upon the theologian Father Rahner; but by the end of the Council, he had come to be more cautious in accepting his proposals. Father Ratzinger, the personal theologian of Cardinal Frings and former student of Father Rahner, had seemed to give an almost unquestioning support to the views of his former teacher during the Council. But as it was drawing to a close, he admitted that he disagreed on various points, and said he would begin to assert himself more after the Council was over.

Finally, the Pope presented Archbishop Felici with the papal brief formally closing the Second Vatican Council. A photographer caught for posterity the radiant smile which covered the features of the Supreme Pontiff at that moment. The tears and heartaches were over. Archbishop Felici went to the microphone a few steps in front and to the left of the Pope, facing the Council Fathers and the crowds in St. Peter's square, and read the official document: "The Second Vatican Ecumenical Council, assembled in the Holy Spirit and under the protection of the Blessed Virgin Mary, whom we have declared Mother of the Church, and of St. Joseph, her glorious spouse, and of the Apostles SS. Peter and Paul, must be numbered without doubt among the greatest events of the Church. . . . We decide moreover that all that has been established by the Council is to be religiously observed by all the faithful, for the glory of God and the dignity of the Church and for the tranquillity and peace of all men."

Later, recalling this moment, Archbishop Felici said that many memories sprang to his mind. There was Pope Paul VI, "in the center of this great assembly, joyful over the happy outcome, decreeing the close of the Council. And there was John XXIII, the originator and first inspirer of this great Council, smilingly giving his blessing from heaven."

Immediately after the reading of the papal brief, Pope Paul VI rose to give his blessing to the Council Fathers and to the crowds. Throwing both arms high in the air, he cried out, "In the name of Our Lord Jesus Christ, go in peace!" The Council was over, and the Council Fathers rose to their feet to clap and cheer.

Then the bells of St. Peter's began to ring.

Epilogue

Upon the fiftieth anniversary of the opening of the Second Vatican Council, and the twentieth anniversary of the publication of *The Catechism of the Catholic Church*, Pope Benedict XVI declared the Year of Faith with his Apostolic Letter *Porta Fidei*. He wrote:

> It seemed to me that timing the launch of the Year of Faith to coincide with the fiftieth anniversary of the opening of the Second Vatican Council would provide a good opportunity to help people understand that the texts bequeathed by the Council Fathers, in the words of Blessed John Paul II, *"have lost nothing of their value or brilliance*. They need to be read correctly, to be widely known and taken to heart as important and normative texts of the Magisterium, within the Church's Tradition. . . . I feel more than ever in duty bound to point to the Council as *the great grace bestowed on the Church in the twentieth century:* there we find a sure compass by which to take our bearings in the century now beginning" (*Porta Fidei*, 5, emphasis in the original).

We affirm, with both pontiffs, that Vatican II was indeed *the great grace of the twentieth century*. But as Benedict XVI noted in this same Letter and elsewhere, the postconciliar period has been filled with "grave difficulties," especially in the Catholic faithful's understanding both of the Council's teaching and of the Faith in general.

Many Catholic readers may remember the immediate aftermath of the Council. It was a time when bishops contradicted bishops, altar railings and tabernacles were ripped from their places, liturgies were treated as a matter of style and taste, and even some of our most respected theologians appeared to be as confused as everyone else. Some saw this as liberation, others as apostasy.

During this time, a soul in search of truth might have encountered a bewildering variety of conflicting "interpretations" of Catholic faith and practice among the clergy, religious brothers and sisters, catechists, and lay leaders he encountered. In the midst of such confusion emerged numerous scandals, the dwindling of many great religious orders, new dissenting sects, and the closing of many long-established parishes.

We should note that such postconciliar turmoil is not unique. The periods immediately following ecumenical councils are often marked by conflict in the Church. After the Arian heresy was condemned at the Council of Nicaea, this heresy continued to spread, and even some bishops and emperors adhered to it. Major schisms followed the Councils of Ephesus and Chalcedon. The controversy of investitures did not disappear for some time after the First Lateran Council, nor did Protestant ideas cease to find their way into the minds of Catholics even after the Council of Trent.

Make no mistake: The upheavals after Vatican II are a grave matter and have caused serious difficulties for many souls. Yet they are also, in a sense, nothing new. Even in the Gospels we find disciples abandoning Our Lord when He defined His teaching.

Christ had disciples who complained, "This saying is

hard, and who can hear it?" Unwilling to accept what He said, they "walked no more with Him" (John 6: 61, 67). In the generations since, the Body of Christ has suffered the same difficulties once endured by its Head.

After the Second Vatican Council closed, the debate began about its proper interpretation (or hermeneutic) and proper implementation. Two opposing views arose. One focused on the text of the Council while keeping in mind the timeless teaching of the Church. The other assumed the text of the Council was a compromise with an antiquated tradition; as a compromise, it did not adequately express the real "spirit of Vatican II."

According to the latter interpretation, Pope Benedict once noted, "it would be necessary not to follow the texts of the Council but its spirit. In this way, obviously, a vast margin was left open for the question on how this spirit should subsequently be defined, and room was consequently made for every whim" (Address to the Roman Curia, December 22, 2005).

Half a century after the Second Vatican Council, the dust is finally beginning to clear. Many of the Catholic faithful are seeing for the first time what the documents of Vatican II actually prescribe—and perhaps more importantly, what they don't. Under the guidance of Pope Benedict XVI, a proper "hermeneutic of reform" became more prominent, which viewed the Council not as a break from the preconciliar Church, but in light of it.

Given that hermeneutic, the Church has experienced a resurgence of her inner vitality. The numbers of young priests and seminarians are growing, and they are responding to their vocations with a strong love of Sacred Tradition. Young women are again taking the habit and filling the choirs of cloistered orders. Active and secular orders and institutes are again beginning to flourish, with enthusiastic participation by the laity.

Many are responding to the call extended to the whole Church to reexamine the truths proclaimed in the Second Vatican Council and *The Catechism of the Catholic Church*. More and more we see souls who are not seeking some radically new "spirit of Vatican II." Nor do they insist on returning to all the particular forms of the preconciliar Church. Instead, they are searching for the eternal unchanging truth found in the Church yesterday, today, and forever.

Appendix

The total cost to the Vatican for the Council and its preparatory work was $7,250,000. Since 2,860 Council Fathers attended all or part of the four sessions, which stretched over 281 days, the average outlay was $2,530 per Council Father, or $9 per day. These costs, however, did not include the expenses borne by the Council Fathers themselves; sixty-seven percent of them paid their own transportation costs, and fifty-three percent paid for their own lodging. Of the total spent by the Vatican, thirty-three percent was used for lodging; thirty percent for transportation; nine percent for furnishing the Council hall; eight percent for the electronic computer, Council Press Office, printing jobs and telephone installations; and twenty percent for other costs.

Sickness, old age, or restrictions imposed by governments prevented 274 Council Fathers from attending. Between the opening and closing dates, 253 Council Fathers died, and 296 new ones were added. Of the 98 cardinals who took part, eleven died before the Council was over; the only cardinal not in attendance was Josef Cardinal Mindszenty of Hungary. The average age of the Council Fathers was sixty. Two thirds belonged to the secular clergy, and the rest were members of religious orders.

The General Secretariat, praised by Pope Paul as a "model" to be imitated in perfecting the services of the Roman Curia, has made use of the most modern techniques to preserve for posterity a complete theological, organizational, and administrative record of the Council. Two hundred large volumes contain alphabetical lists of Council Fathers, indicating how each one voted on all 544 ballots. Through a photocopying process the complete archive has been reproduced a number of times, so that it may be used for study at various locations. It may be a generation or more before the archive will be thrown open to the public.

In addition to having all documents on file, the archive contains a complete magnetic tape recording of all 168 General Congregations, filling 712 reels, each 1,300 feet long, which run for 542 hours. Making transcriptions of these recordings, and translating all Council documents into fourteen languages, were two of the most time-consuming tasks supervised by Monsignor Emilio Governatori, the archivist of Vatican II.

On January 3, 1966, Pope Paul, by an Apostolic Letter, created five Post-Conciliar Commissions. Such commissions had originally been suggested to him by the European and world alliances, because they feared that progressive measures adopted by the Council might be blocked by conservative forces near the Pope once the Council Fathers had all returned home. The task of the new Post-Conciliar Commissions—on Religious, Missions, Christian Education, Apostolate of the Laity, and Bishops and the Government of Dioceses—was to prepare an "Instruction" which would indicate, concretely, how the Council documents were to be implemented. These bodies were to have no legislative authority, but merely interpretive powers, and in preparing their "Instruction" were to adhere closely to the tenor of the solemnly approved and promulgated documents. Upon publication of their norms, the Post-Conciliar Commissions were to be automatically dissolved.

INDEX

Index

Index

Léger, Paul Cardinal, 3, 318; and Blessed Virgin Mary, 226; and collegiality, 75, 119-20; and Divine Office, 51; and Jews, 256; and marriage, 409-10, 413; and religious, 150-51; and religious freedom, 238, 261; and revelation, 58, 262-63; and schools, 343; and seminaries, 338

Legion of Mary, 281

Leiprecht, Bp. Karl, 321, 324

Lenten fast, 53

Leo the Great, St., 229

Leo XIII, 69, 229

Lercaro, Giacomo Cardinal, 63, 186, 315; chosen Moderator, 112, 115; and communications schema, 196; and Jews, 256; and liturgy schema, 205-6

Leven, Bp. Stephen, 185

Lichten, Dr. Joseph, 254

Liénart, Achille Cardinal, 3, 7, 8, 70, 318; to Coordinating Commission, 75; and Jews, 255; and revelation, 64; and Secretariat for Non-Christian Religions, 103-4

Liturgical Commission, 12, 22, 27, 38, 84-89, 200. *See also* Liturgy

Liturgy, 19-29, 37-45, 49-56, 84-89, 200-207

Lourdusamy, Abp. Simon, 386

Luke, Book of, 255

"Lumen gentium," 84

Luther, Martin, 229

Lutheran World Federation, 175, 180

Luxembourg, 49, 214, 400

Lyonnet, Fr. Stanislaus, S.J., 406

Lyons Council, 306

McCann, Abp. Owen, 280

Maccari, Bp. Carlo, 279

Maccarrone, Fr., 350

McDevitt, Bp. Gerald, 304-5

McGrath, Bp. Mark, 312

McManus, Fr. Frederick, 88, 360

McVinney, Bp. Russell, 386

Madagascar, 124, 290, 330

Madrid, 101, 106

Majdanski, Bp. Kazimierz, 412

Marella, Paolo Cardinal, 157, 253, 254

Marists, 326, 331. *See also* specific delegates

Marriage, 146, 202, 310, 404, 408-16; diaconate and, 136*ff*; Indian customs, 40; married couple at Council, 277; of priests, 399-407; sacrament of matrimony, 212, 283

Marsili, Fr. Salvatore, 204

Martin, Abp. Joseph, 183

Marty, Abp. Francois, 402

Mary. *See* Blessed Virgin Mary

Mason, Bp. Edoardo, 161, 162, 386

Mass. *See* Concelebration; Liturgy

Matrimony. *See* Marriage

Matthew, Book of, 119, 348

Maximos IV Saigh. *See* Saigh, Maximos IV

Mayer, Bp. Antonio de Castro, 45-46

"Mediatrix," 127, 128, 131, 225, 226-32

Meglio, Mgr. Giuseppe di, 382

Meinhold (Protestant writer), 129

Mejia, Fr. Jorge, 45-46

Melchite Church, 299, 301. *See also* Saigh, Maximos IV

Ménager, Bp. Jacques, 312

Méndez Arceo, Bp. Sergio, 78, 246, 365

Meouchi, Patriarch Paul, 318

Messaggero, Il, 419, 421

Mexico, 15, 277. *See also* specific delegates

Meyer, Albert Cardinal, 3, 103, 119, 144, 318, 360; and collegiality, 119;

Index

Index

About the Author

The Rev. Ralph Michael Wiltgen, S.V.D., was born in Chicago, Illinois, U.S.A., on December 17, 1921. He joined the Divine Word Missionaries in 1938, was ordained a Roman Catholic priest in 1950, and received his doctorate in Mission Science in Rome in 1953. After serving as national publicity director for his order in the United States and as international publicity director in Rome, Father Wiltgen founded during Vatican II an independent and multilingual Council News Service, which was published in 6 languages and which had over 3,000 subscribers in 108 countries.

Close contacts with the Council Fathers and *periti* (experts) led to his writing *The Rhine Flows into the Tiber* (the original title of *The Inside Story of Vatican II*), which was published in English, French, Dutch, and German.

Among Father Wiltgen's other books are *Gold Coast Mission History 1471-1880*, *The Religious Life Defined*, *The Founding of the Roman Catholic Church in Oceania 1825-1850*, and *The Founding of the Roman Catholic Church in Melanesia and Micronesia*. He died at Techny, Illinois, on December 6, 2002, after a long illness.

Fundamentals of ▶ Catholic Dogma

Dr. Ludwig Ott

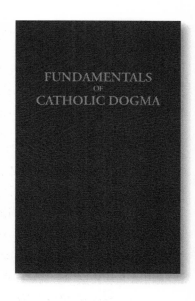

Fundamentals of Catholic Dogma is widely recognized as one of the greatest summaries of Catholic dogma ever published. Since its original publication in German in 1952, it has served as an invaluable reference for students and teachers, clergy and families anyone who needs a clear, concise and systematic presentation of the Catholic faith. This book is a remarkable one-volume encyclopedia of doctrine. It will provide a cornerstone for your personal Catholic library that will help you find the answers to countless questions about the Faith.

978-0-89555-805-3 Hardcover

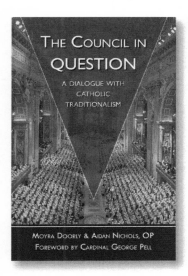

◀ Council in Question

A Dialogue with Catholic Traditionalism

Journalist Moyra Doorly, an SSPX attendee and Dominican Aidan Nichols engage in a vibrant and enlightening discussion on the health and future of the Roman Catholic Church. Doorly takes up the arguments of the Society of Saint Pius X, while Nichols picks up the mantel of the post-Vatican II Church. This fascinating exchange is more than just a dialogue between two factions of the Church, it is a sign and defense of the genuine continuity and development across the millennia in doctrine, liturgy, and church law. A must-read for lovers of Tradition.

978-0-89555-268-6 Paperbound

TANBooks.com • **(800) 437-5876**

Printed in Germany
by Amazon Distribution
GmbH, Leipzig